NICARAGUA BEFORE NOW

HONDURAS

Sandy Bay ● Cayos ●
                      Miskitos

Bilwi (Puerto Cabezas) ●

REGIÓN AUTÓNOMA
ATLÁNTICO NORTE (RAAN)

NUEVA
SEGOVIA

JINOTEGA

NICARAGUA

MADRÍZ

ESTELÍ

MATAGALPA
La Patriota ●   ● Río Blanco
Matagalpa ●
              Matiguás ●

CHINANDEGA

LEÓN

Volcanoes

Chinandega ●
Chichigalpa ●

BOACO

REGIÓN AUTÓNOMA
ATLÁNTICO SUR (RAAS)

MANAGUA

CHONTALES

Managua ★

Bluefields ●   Corn
                             Islands

MASAYA

CARAZO   GRANADA

RIVAS

PACIFIC
OCEAN

Lago de
Nicaragua

RÍO
SAN JUAN

CARIBBEAN
SEA

Río San Juan

COSTA RICA

0 10 20 30 40 miles

Map by Gerry Krieg

Nicaragua Before Now

*Factory Work, Farming, and Fishing in a
Low-wage Global Economy*

Photographs and Interviews by
Nell Farrell

UNIVERSITY OF NEW MEXICO PRESS   ALBUQUERQUE

© 2010 by the University of New Mexico Press

All rights reserved. Published 2010

Printed in the United States of America

15   14   13   12   11   10   1   2   3   4   5   6

Library of Congress Cataloging-in-Publication Data

Farrell, Nell, 1974–

Nicaragua before now : factory work, farming, and fishing in a

low-wage global economy /photographs and interviews by Nell Farrell.

p. cm.

Includes bibliographical references.

ISBN 978-0-8263-4608-7 (pbk. : alk. paper)

1. Nicaragua—Economic conditions—1979–

2. Industries—Nicaragua.

3. Nicaragua—Description and travel.

I. Title.

HC146.F37 2010

331.097285—dc22

2010004930

Book design and type composition by Melissa Tandysh

Composed in 10.5/14 Dante MT Std

Display type is Bernhard Modern Std

For Patrick

Photographs by themselves certainly cannot tell "the whole truth"—they are always only instants. What they do most persistently is to register the relation of photographer to subject—the distance from one to another—and this understanding is a profoundly important political process.

—David Levi Strauss

CONTENTS

ACKNOWLEDGMENTS

THE STORIES AND PHOTOGRAPHS COLLECTED IN THIS BOOK CREATE A portrait of young wageworkers in a developing country at the inception of our globalized twenty-first century. As a social history, the relevance of the case studies extends beyond Central America and beyond Latin America, but they take place in Nicaragua.

This work was only possible because of the incredible generosity and openness of the people portrayed, as well as countless others who guided me through doing research in a foreign country, among them David Dye, Margarita Montealegre, and Gustavo Wilson.

Stateside I am indebted to my Latin American Studies thesis committee at the University of New Mexico: Miguel Gandert, Holly Barnet-Sanchez, Bill Stanley, and Laura Andre. Miguel has been a wise and caring mentor for many years now. Bill Stanley was a dedicated and invaluable resource and counsel. A grant from the Office of Graduate Studies at UNM helped offset travel costs. Jack Spence at the University of Massachusetts, Boston went above and beyond to share his contacts and expertise as a colleague and a reader. New Mexico author V. B. Price opened the door to publication. My parents, Thomas and Anne Farrell, provided unending encouragement and support. And my husband, Patrick Hubenthal—who was in Nicaragua with me—has been editor and copilot from beginning to end.

In numerous instances, I present the facts as relayed to me by the people telling their stories, which may contradict each other or other sources.

The photographs in this book were shot in color and can be viewed in their intended format at www.nellfarrell.com.

On the San Rafael finca *in Matiguás, Pablo Damian herds his cows toward the corral for milking.*

Overview

I WAS LOOKING FOR GLOBALIZATION, FOR EFFECTS OF THE TRANSNATIONAL
on the local, for traces of economic policy in the lives of individuals. The
Central American Free Trade Agreement (CAFTA) had recently passed in
the U.S. Congress and was being debated in Nicaragua in the fall of 2005,
when I spent three months there photographing and informally inter-
viewing people who would be affected by the agreement, whose lives in
many cases were already influenced by the global wage economy. In the
relatively unregulated environment depicted, people are highly vulnerable to change: industries viable now, later may not be; some will expand,
some will become unprofitable. Without intermediary safety nets, the
global framework acts directly upon individuals. At the same time, the
accounts of these individuals are illustrative beyond their personal experience, beyond the industries in which they work.

I focused on the twenty-something generation, who represent the
median age group in Nicaragua.[1] I first visited the turbid capital city of
Managua, where I spent time with young women who work in the *maquila*
industry, the factories in the free trade zone. Then into the interior, to the
state of Matagalpa, where I lived with families on dairy farms, their livelihoods as long established as they are precarious. Third, to the blisteringly
hot sugarcane fields of Chinandega, where I witnessed the exertion and
the susceptibility of the sugarcane cutters. And lastly, the Miskito Coast,
where indigenous lobster divers become paralyzed by the weight of the
Caribbean.

CAFTA

On October 10, 2005, the Nicaraguan Asamblea Nacional, or Congress,
approved the Central American Free Trade Agreement (officially DR-CAFTA,
between the Dominican Republic, Guatemala, El Salvador, Honduras,
Nicaragua, Costa Rica, and the United States). Every day for months prior

Buses stop outside of the Zona Franca las Mercedes in Managua as workers enter. Behind them an FSLN campaign banner proclaims 'Forward to the golden dawn of the people! No to the Free Trade Agreement!'

to and following that, Nicaraguan newspapers would carry multiple stories not only explaining and opining on the economic pros and cons, but reporting on the politics involved in the passage of the treaty. Sandinista party representatives were accused of not giving audience to pro-CAFTA citizens; protests and progress in neighboring Costa Rica regarding prospective approval of the agreement were monitored (it passed in October 2007); and photographs were published of near blows in the Asamblea over whether to ratify CAFTA.[2] I read many veiled threats by government officials and businesspeople, in quotes about companies they said would abandon or reject

Nicaragua if CAFTA were not passed, taking thousands of jobs, or potential jobs, with them. Every citizen could offer an opinion. Even though some of those were based on hearsay, as I talked with factory management, peasants, and taxi drivers, what emerged was a complex picture; the search cannot be to find out if free trade is bad or good, but rather to try to understand the coexistence of its effects, both negative and positive. Trade liberalization involves adjustment, and so CAFTA will bring changes deep and wide; this volume is a presentation of one person's exploration of the initial phase of that process.

The *Economist* describes CAFTA as "a modest agreement between a whale . . . and six minnows."[3] Those six "minnow" countries' *combined* output is "around US$85 billion, about the size of the economy of Nevada."[4] In order for CAFTA to get through the U.S. Senate (which it did on June 30, 2005, with a contentious fifty-four to forty-five votes), it had to mollify the U.S. sugar industry, which was adamantly opposed, afraid that the importation of Central American sugar would be the beginning of the end of protection for their industry. The Bush administration countered that the imports would not surpass one hundred thousand metric tons per year, while sugar production in this country per year is 7.8 million metric tons. Thus, protected industries may see shifts, but since 80 percent of imports from Central America already enter this country tariff-free, they will be minor.[5] Meanwhile, Nicaraguan sugar producers look forward to this increase in access to the U.S. market. The *Economist* adds that tariffs on imports into Central America were lowered from 45 to 7 percent, as long ago as 1985.[6]

Regardless of these numbers, there are those who predict that CAFTA will cause the dumping of U.S. goods in the Nicaraguan market. To show that competition in the "open" market does not take place on a level playing field,[7] they compare the subsidies insisted upon by U.S. agriculture to the U.S. prohibition of Nicaragua to enact economic safeguards for its own farmers. In the Central American press and popular culture, this played out in a number of ways. Daniel Ortega called the PLC (Arnoldo Alemán and Enrique Bolaños' party)[8] a dog obeying its master, the United States. The newspapers alleged that in exchange for a 'package'* of favors, the FSLN (Ortega's party) had allowed the PLC to 'calm the U.S.' by passing CAFTA. And in addition to "no al TLC" (no to the Free Trade Agreement), in Costa Rica protesters also shouted, "fuera nuevos filibusteros" (out with the new filibusters) and "no queremos ser otra colonia norteamericana" (we don't

---

* Single quotation marks are used to indicate that the original quote is in Spanish and the English translation presented is my own.

Cutting sugarcane in Chinandega.

want to be another North American colony).[9] Though most U.S. citizens do not know what CAFTA is (and indeed it will have little effect on our economy), it will probably have deep impact on the lives of Central Americans.

In the discussion regarding what tariffs for which agricultural products, how long before they are implemented, and what the outcome of competition between local and imported crops may be, one author believes it comes down to this: "Nicaragua's only hope under CAFTA may be to dramatically increase manufacturing employment," and if Mexico's ability to create jobs under NAFTA is an indication, it won't be fast enough.[10] In a paid newspaper supplement, the Nicaraguan government touts the benefits that the textile sector will experience immediately under CAFTA. It quotes the president of the Nicaraguan Association of the Manufacturing and Textile Industry, who estimates that the investments CAFTA will attract will create fifteen thousand direct jobs in this sector and fifty thousand indirect jobs[11] (mostly services such as construction, transportation, food stands, garbage collection, etc.). Another part of the picture is made evident in a newspaper article that reports a visit by the Taiwanese president to Guatemala. Though Guatemalan businesspeople responded to the president's promises with hope for increased exports to Taiwan, the underlying theme of the meetings was Taiwan's desire to establish more factories in Guatemala, to produce goods to be exported to the United States under CAFTA.[12] With the lowest wages in the region,[13] Nicaragua can hope to attract manufacturers—for example, of American and Japanese car parts—that currently have plants in Mexico,[14] although this "race to the bottom" means those same plants will likely pick up and move across the ocean when lower wages are found elsewhere. William Robinson explains, "The total mobility achieved by capital has allowed it to search out around the world the most favorable conditions for different phases of globalized production," whether regarding labor, laws, or social milieu.[15]

Nicaraguans hope that CAFTA will bring more U.S. investment to their country, and therefore jobs. The Ministry of Promotion (Fomento) predicted that in its first year of implementation, US$500 million would be invested in nineteen companies, creating nineteen thousand jobs.[16] Laura Carlson, director of the Americas Program of the International Relations Center (IRC) in Mexico City, worries not if, but how this change will occur, and outlines three problem areas that CAFTA could exacerbate.[17] First, many fear that environmental laws and labor rights will not be respected in those countries to which U.S. jobs are moving, therefore free trade agreements "create a downward pressure on workers' quality of life in all countries involved." Second, free trade allows the United States to import more than it exports, creating a trade deficit. And third, free trade tends to benefit those who already have resources, as well as shifting wealth and power from public to private hands. When this occurs in services such as education, health care, and ownership of natural resources, lack of access can be devastating not only to individuals, but to societies. While the elite benefit, the mass of the population remains in poverty, which means hunger, migration, and instability.[18] But "the [Bush] Administration continues to frame the issue of free trade and democracy as two sides of the same coin, rather than acknowledging that one is an economic platform that a well-functioning democracy may choose not to pursue."[19]

A nation does not have to choose neoliberalism in order to be democratic, but economic viability is indeed a prerequisite for a peacefully governed society. The citizenry of most Central American countries is divided on whether or not neoliberalism is the best route, but their leaders continue to move in that direction. In an article discussing CAFTA, the *Washington Post* reports, "What Central American leaders say they get out of it [CAFTA] is an anchor in the democratic community of nations. 'It consolidates our governments and creates more confidence in our way of life,' Honduran President Ricardo Maduro said after leaving the White House meeting with Bush."[20]

According to some analysts, though, laissez-faire is often "chosen" under pressure from external sources. Discussing the postwar early 1990s in Nicaragua, Robinson states, "World Bank and IMF representatives, together with AID [U.S. Agency for International Development] officials, designed a comprehensive neoliberal structural adjustment program and made all credits, disbursements, and debt restructuring contingent on compliance with this program."[21] This means that in exchange for financial help, Nicaragua complies with what those agencies deem is the best way for it to run its government and economy.[22] The result is massive debt, often followed by the inability to pay it off, and thus further indentureship to global institutions.[23] "By 1992, Nicaragua's foreign debt stood at nearly $11 billion, one of the highest per-capita debts in the world."[24] Nearly half of the foreign aid received went to servicing that debt.[25]

From a Latin American point of view, there are other considerations surrounding CAFTA. "After twenty-five years of following free trade doctrine (opening markets, privatizing basic services, deregulating industry, lowering tariffs, orienting their production for export, and consecrating intellectual property), Latin Americans have achieved the lowest rate of economic growth in their history."[26] The most specific point of comparison for CAFTA is NAFTA, the North American Free Trade Agreement, between the United States, Canada, and Mexico. According to Global Exchange, NAFTA not only cost the United States one million jobs and thirty-eight thousand family farms,[27] but in Mexico it caused 1.5 million farmers to abandon their land.[28] Global Exchange argues that the free trade model favors export-oriented agribusiness; small U.S. farmers can't compete with those corporations, and neither can Mexican farmers.[29] At least four hundred thousand people (or 30 percent of the Nicaraguan workforce) are directly employed in agriculture, with at least another six hundred thousand dependent upon it.[30]

Sabemos que ese tratado es para terminar de encerrarnos cuando nos echan a competir con productores subsidiados de Estados Unidos, mientras nosotros no tenemos caminos, ni financiamento, problemas de propiedades, un medio ambiente destruido, falta de agua, hambre y pobreza.

> —Ariel Bucardo, president of the National Farm
> and Cattle Union (UNAG in its Spanish initials)[31]

Si Nicaragua entra a este acuerdo de libertad comerical en las condiciones actuales en que se encuentra su economía local y la posición del Gobierno, lo que espera a los productos nacionales es ser fácilmente desplazados por otros productos del área y condenarnos al consumo de productos extranjeros que se ofertan a menor precio, como consequencia el exterminio del capital de los productores locales.

> —Ricardo Sánchez Calero, *La Prensa* columnist[32]

The U.S. government and Latin American producers are not the only players in the game. The above quotes refer to a third party: the Nicaraguan government. Many people I talked to were wary of free trade because domestic laws, infrastructure, and financing (or lack thereof) handicap their ability to compete.

The *Economist* concedes that, under CAFTA, some Nicaraguan products currently protected by tariffs will lose out to cheaper foreign imports, but notes that the treaty grants many sensitive crops years to "phase out protection."[33] Dairy products, for example, are given twenty years. "This should give farmers plenty of time to adjust, even if it deprives the poor of cheaper milk in the meantime," claims the *Economist*.[34]

But in an op-ed piece entitled "CAFTA Will Be Like a Brand-Name Hurricane Mitch," the president of FENACOOP (Nicaragua's National Federation of Agricultural and Agroindustrial Cooperatives),[35] Sinforiano Cáceres, calls the Central American countries to task for having negotiated with the United States as separate entities.[36] He predicts an effect that he calls triangulation. As an example, U.S. milk receives a 65 percent import tax in Nicaragua, while in Honduras the duty is only 20 percent. Because products can move freely between Central American countries, the United States will export milk to Honduras to be sold in Nicaragua. Cáceres contends that additionally, under CAFTA, dairy will have to compete against U.S. equivalents (unlike peanuts, for example, which do not have a comparable industry in the United States), most specifically powdered milk, which sells at half the price of local liquid milk. He predicts that Parmalat, the largest processor and marketer of milk in Nicaragua, will start making its cheeses from U.S. powdered milk.[37] For a society, the question that emerges from this debate is whether the priority is for the poor to have access to cheap milk, or whether to protect its producers. Those against CAFTA privilege the latter, while those who believe it will create jobs argue that the small agricultural producer's way of life is no longer viable anyway.[38]

A clause of CAFTA allows corporations to sue governments if they do anything that inhibits profits, such as upholding health and environmental safety laws.[39] Allowing the rights of corporations to trump the rights of the people is what gives "free trade" and "globalization" a bad name, when those phenomena are not inherently negative. Cáceres concludes, "Accepting the government's propaganda, we must assume that CAFTA is an instrument to promote development. But without a development strategy, the instrument replaces the strategy."[40] A country becomes dependent on imported—if possibly cheaper—food instead of ensuring self-reliance. Employment is primarily in export industries. The archbishop of Tegucigalpa, Honduras, stated his worries thus: "Para mí una de las grandes interrogantes frente a estos tratados es si son verdaderamente para que la humanidad progrese o para que progrese el mercado."[41] (For me one of the great questions in the face of these treaties is if they are truly for the progress of humanity or for the progress of the market.) I would add that many who promote the market do so with the belief that it will create progress for humanity.[42] But while that belief may be sincere, it is often insensitive to the lived reality of the majority of people, who must wait for the fruition of a macroeconomic plan before their quality of life potentially nears that of the plan's authors.

Background

An oft-repeated statistic about Nicaragua is this: It is the second poorest country in the Western Hemisphere (after Haiti). Thereby it is also the poorest Spanish-speaking country in the world. In 2001, the Nicaraguan Statistics and Census Bureau (INEC) published their finding that "relative poverty," defined as basic needs being unsatisfied, was at 75 percent.[43] Half of the workforce is underemployed. Per capita GDP is US$750 per year.[44] Nicaragua has never been densely populated,[45] nor has it ever been rich in mineral deposits, and so since colonial times the export of a few agricultural products—controlled by a small number of wealthy families, while the peasant majority tilled precolonial food crops—has molded its culture.

Lake Nicaragua—the second largest in Latin America—has also had great influence on the country's history. With a river connecting it to the Caribbean and a relatively narrow strip of land between it and the Pacific, the potential for digging a canal "made Nicaragua the object of frequent foreign intrigue and intervention,"[46] culminating in the 1916

Cayos Miskitos. Lobster diver dwelling.

Bryan-Chamorro Treaty, which ceded exclusive digging rights in perpetuity to the United States.[47] The waterway never came to be—as the United States already controlled the Panama Canal and in Nicaragua only sought to eliminate potential competition—but because of the possibility, as well as other investments and general interest in establishing democracy and maintaining stability, the United States was directly involved in the shaping of twentieth-century Nicaragua. Thomas Walker describes the influence as proceeding "first by direct armed intervention (from 1912 to 1925 and from 1926 to 1933), later through the client dictatorships of the Somoza family (from 1936 to 1979), and finally through subservient conservative democracies (from 1990 to the present)."[48]

Like Nicaragua, many Latin America countries have seen coups d'état, and many have seen dictators, but it is one of only a few in which a leftist revolution overthrew a dictatorial regime and went on to establish a government, which has earned it much attention from scholars and idealists in recent decades.[49] Thomas Walker's understanding of the revolution's causality can be summarized as follows: Nicaragua is one of the rare Latin American countries to have had a dynastic dictatorship; three members of the Somoza family held power.[50] During that period, the elites of Central America made their money from coffee while the majority of people were plantation laborers or subsistence farmers. In the 1960s and 1970s—in a dynamic that continues to this day—the export crops of cotton, sugar, and beef expanded, pushing small farmers off their land without creating sufficient jobs to absorb them. This was a significant factor in the buildup to the armed conflicts that occurred across the region in the 1980s.[51] For Nicaraguans, the turning point came in the aftermath of the 1972 earthquake that destroyed the capital city and killed over ten thousand people. International aid poured in yet the people saw little of it; Anastasio Somoza not only used the emergency as an excuse to grab more power, but he and his National Guard also rather openly embezzled much of the aid money. The FSLN (Sandinista National Liberation Front) began to form in earnest then, practicing guerilla tactics as well as attracting elites into their ranks. Somoza's repressive measures worsened in response. The Catholic Church, the United States, and Amnesty International all turned against him. Finally in 1979 he was overthrown in a revolution that took the lives of fifty thousand Nicaraguans in its last eighteen months and resulted in a Sandinista victory and government.[52]

In *A Brief History of Central America*, Hector Pérez-Brignoli discusses the causes and effects of the above story.[53] He identifies three principal elements of the Sandinista ideology: nationalism and anti-imperialism, represented by the image of Sandino (who fought against U.S. invasion in the early 1900s); Third World socialism, after the Cuban Revolution; and "People's Church" Christianity, otherwise known as liberation theology. At the outset, their priorities were to create "new forms of ownership . . . an alternative to the market economy model" and to grow the capacity to provide basic commodities domestically. Daniel Ortega, the movement's leader, became president and stayed in power for the duration of the 1980s.

Once again, for the sake of "stability in the region," the United States intervened. The infamous Iran-Contra Affair of the mid-1980s—in which U.S. president Ronald Reagan orchestrated the illegal sale of arms to Iran to help fund the anti-Sandinista militants, known as *contras*—was the quintessence of U.S. involvement. By the late 1980s, U.S.-trained and funded troops numbered twenty thousand, fighting in a struggle in which thirty-one thousand more people died.[54] Thus, war and other internal problems (economic collapse born of missteps in governance and antagonism from big business and the Church, for example) resulted in increased heavy-handedness by the Sandinista regime and its eventual electoral defeat. In 1990, a populace exhausted by war and death and deprivation voted out the Sandinistas.

Theories vary as to why the people voted for Violeta Chamorro and a neoliberal economy. Under the Sandinistas the economy was ailing, whether due to the ongoing war against the *contras* or to incompetence and insolvency on the part of the Sandinistas. In order to receive U.S. and World Bank aid, Nicaragua would have to adhere to the neoliberal model. Others point to Chamorro's personal history: Her husband was assassi-nated by Somoza and she had sons on either side of the Sandinista / anti-Sandinista struggle; she became a mother figure for Nicaragua.[55] Some say Miami-based elites must have funded the electoral opposition, because in actuality there was little unity among them, and although the Sandinistas were voted out, the *contras* never became a cohesive political force.[56] In the changeover of power, many upper-level Sandinistas aligned themselves with the incoming party; *la piñata* is the popular term used to describe the way this group sacked property and money before turning over the government. The infamy of this behavior still resonates in Nicaraguan politics, and along with the "Pact" discussed below, compromised the legitimacy of the FSLN.[57]

One of Chamorro's first goals was to meet International Monetary Fund (IMF) "standards and receive Economic Structural Adjustment Funds . . . by eliminating remaining consumer subsidies and privatizing 80 per-cent of state-owned industrial and agricultural enterprises."[58] Emphasis was on attracting foreign investment, as it still is today in the business community, and government funds were diverted away from rural credit and the public sector in general. This had the effect of destroying the live-lihoods of many precarious small farmers; many who had received plots under Sandinista land reform had to sell to large landowners (who often produce for export). Previous to this, "peasant producers accounted for nearly 100 percent of domestic food production," and so "per capita food consumption fell by 31 percent between 1990 and 1992."[59] One way in which these programs are presented to the public is in terms of *not* being Sandinista. In my travels I found the same to be true with CAFTA; national politics play out according to a polarized dynamic. Observer David Dye shows that the alternation of power in Nicaragua is not a healthy debate on the direction of the country within a democratic system, but rather a grappling over what kind of system to have at all, between those groups desirous of authoritarian power:

> The end of the Nicaraguan revolution came shortly after the fall of the Berlin wall and coincided in time—the year 1990—with the upswing of the modern era of globalization. From that moment onward, the country has tried to come to grips with the challenges that the globalization process poses. It does so, however, dangerously lacking a true national state capable of managing both the "neo-liberal" economic policies and the modern liberal democracy demanded by the international system.[60]

Chamorro was succeeded by the conservative Arnoldo Alemán (1997–2002), and ever since then politics in Nicaragua have revolved around him and Ortega. Enrique Bolaños, president from 2002 to 2007, was Alemán's vice president and chosen successor. Instead of allowing Alemán to retain control as he expected, Bolaños made much of ending corruption in the government. Alemán was tried for embezzling US$100 million, convicted, and placed under house arrest. "His hacienda became almost another branch of the government," writes Jack Spence of Hemisphere Initiatives.[61] Alemán's comfort in confinement is determined by Ortega's pleasure; he is shifted from house to hospital to jail with the political winds. These two previous enemies have created what is referred to as "the Pact" in order to mete out power to their respective parties. David Dye blames this political bargaining for the disenchantment of the people, who express belief in and desire for democracy and follow the news avidly, but are cynical about change for the better. "People once famous for their political combativity, Nicaraguans today are inordinately difficult to mobilize for purposes of political protest."[62]

Since his deposal in 1990, Daniel Ortega has run in every presidential election; the FSLN always winning around 40 percent of the vote.[63] In 2006 this was also the case, but because of a change in electoral law—negotiated by his own party—Ortega was able to claim a victory.[64] Before his win, fear of military or economic interference by the United States were he to be elected was considered the reason that the FSLN could never garner the majority. After his win, the public is seen to have voted its conscience in the face of U.S. threats. "[B]eneath the tides of globalization and free trade, an undercurrent draws Latin America back to the language of class war," notes the *Observer* of London;[65] Ortega is grouped with leftward leaders of Latin America such as Hugo Chávez and Evo Morales, but the

Economist dubs his first ten months in office "opportunist and erratic."[66] The Nicaraguan ambassador to the United States argues that Ortega is working with the IMF for stability and is a supporter of CAFTA for the expanded markets it could provide, while his domestic policy focuses on the immediate alleviation of poverty.[67]

In the previous quote, David Dye places current Nicaraguan politics into the context of "the upswing of the modern era of globalization," which many blame for the country's economic and societal ills as well. In a 2003 paper on family life in the region prepared for the United Nations, Godfrey St. Bernard provides a working definition: "Globalization has the effect of expanding the extent of openness that is characteristic of a given nation or territory."[68] He identifies tourism, electronic media (read: TV), and "agreements arising out of regional integration initiatives" (CAFTA, for example) as areas where globalization is manifested. He understands emigration to be one product of this openness, specifically economic openness. Imported goods drive down the prices farmers can get, ultimately pressuring people to seek a living elsewhere. Six million legal immigrants enter the United States each year; 37 percent of them come from Latin America; Nicaragua is among the top six countries in that group (Mexico represents the majority), with a "net out-migration" of twelve thousand people per year, both to Costa Rica and the United States.[69]

These are all effects of globalization, but it has deeper implications for our identities and for the definitions of our institutions. William Robinson shows that "[t]he increasing dissolution of the factor of space in production and the separation of the logic of production from that of geography is without historical precedent."[70] John Rapley explains the ramifications of this: With neoliberalism (while theoretically not equivalent to globalization, in this discussion the two are inextricable), ownership and distribution rights shift to the private sector. Efficiency becomes the goal even for "products" like health and well-being; and the global economy is seen to be the most efficient. One factor in this is that the domestic market is quickly saturated in poor countries, where the population has little capacity to consume. These "neoliberal policies have had the effect of raising aggregate income but skewing its distribution,"[71] and "the result has been a shift in the balance of class power and a concentration of wealth on a global scale."[72]

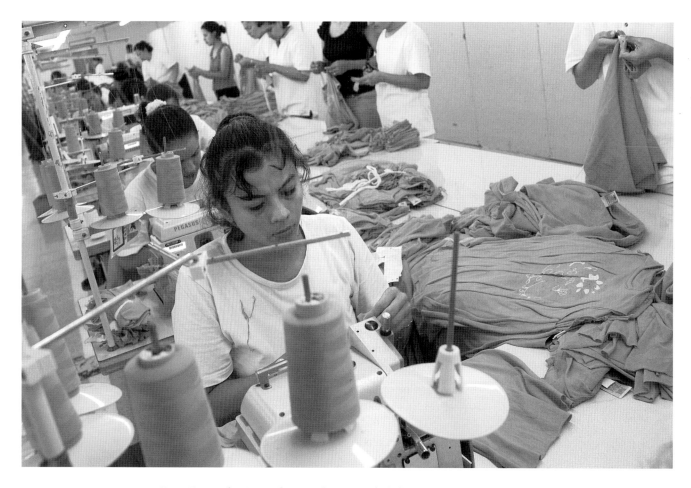

Zona Franca las Mercedes. Inside a *maquila* belonging to Istmo Textil, a Korean
company that has been in Nicaragua for eight years. This plant has over 900 employees.

ONE

Maquilas

Introduction

IN MY MIND, *MAQUILAS* ARE IN JUAREZ, WHERE WOMEN ARE DYING SORDID deaths.[1] But Managua is not Juarez, and while I was warned time and again that it was dangerous to be there, and saw for myself the dynamics of exploitation, what I found upon entering that world were nuances. *Maquilas* account for over a quarter of jobs in Nicaragua.[2] At a three-day workshop at the María Elena Cuadra Women's Movement (MEC),[3] a unionlike organization for *maquila* workers, we went around the room saying our names and what we liked. Second only to 'I like music' was the response 'I like to work.' Some women I spoke with enjoyed the atmosphere of the job (the camaraderie, the radio playing), others enjoyed the satisfaction of the work itself, of moving quickly and precisely to produce large quantities. But more commonly, they were glad for the job, and glad for the pay. They still may have wanted to get out, and almost always hoped that their daughters wouldn't follow in their stead. They felt the repercussions on their health, or knew that the jobs were dead ends. But no one said they wished the *maquilas* didn't exist, and many expressed gratitude for the opportunity they afforded.

It was through MEC that I met the people I would photograph for this segment of my project. Although thousands of women are trained in MEC programs, those depicted here are not representative of all workers. Some had collaborated with foreign researchers before. At least two were inspectors on the job, although only 6 percent of *maquila* workers have this position, and all of them were high school graduates, representing just 19 percent of *maquila* workers.[4] They did not all live in the same barrio nor work in the same *maquila*. By chance, four of the six women depicted

All of the photographs in this chapter were made in Managua.

15

do not have children.[5] Perhaps it is in part because of these particular exceptions that we were able to communicate on such a personal level.

Maquilas exist within *zonas francas* (free trade zones)[6] and are overseen by the Corporación Zona Franca (CZF), a government entity. The stated goal of the *zonas francas* is to promote foreign investment and generate employment.[7] I visited the Zona Franca Las Mercedes, in Managua. It is government owned (the majority are privately owned, which is the goal) and comprises fifteen different companies, employing thirty-two thousand people in all. The vast majority of *maquilas* in Nicaragua produce clothing (which is true at Las Mercedes as well). Seventy-nine percent of the capital in the *zonas francas* comes from Asia;[8] most of the corporations are Korean, with the United States and Taiwan tying at second. Ninety-nine percent of their product is sold in the United States.[9] The labor consultant at the CZF, Emilio Noguera, explained the workings of Las Mercedes and toured me around. The first plant we entered was brand new: a small, sterile medical parts operation. This would be in contrast to what I did not see; those that are located in the old Sandinista jails (the principal use for this site during their governance), where roofs are lower and ventilation worse. The director of the CZF, Ramón Lacayo, remarked that they are transforming these, one by one, into *naves de iluminación*. Sr. Lacayo also said that with CAFTA, they hope to grow 20 to 25 percent each year for at least five years.

According to the CZF, on the eve of the Sandinista revolution three thousand workers were employed by eight companies in Las Mercedes. Most of those companies fled in 1979, due to the prospect of nationalization by the incoming socialist government. In 1990, when Daniel Ortega lost the presidential election, there were nine hundred factory jobs in five state-owned companies.[10] Then in 1991, during the presidency of Violeta Chamorro, a governmental decree reinitiated the program with the creation of *zonas francas industriales de exportación*, offering fiscal benefits (tax breaks) to companies interested in doing business in Nicaragua.[11] By 1996, ten thousand people were employed, and by 2004, sixty-six thousand. The CZF estimates that for each direct (or factory) job, three indirect jobs are created, and that five people benefit from every salary.

The average wage among the women that I photographed was US$100 per month, about fifty cents an hour.[12] Most of them affirmed that pay depends on production, and that overtime is usually an option. Their jobs varied from five to seven days a week, with a nine-hour workday on weekdays the minimum. The cost to cover basic household needs for a family of six in Managua has risen quickly in the last few years, to reach the equivalent of US$160 per month.[13] Thus, though a *maquila* job does not cover living expenses, it is usually higher than the average monthly salary in Nicaragua, which *La Prensa* reports fluctuates between US$45 and US$108 per month.[14] It is in part for this that the CZF can state in their publicity, 'Our country has the lowest rating in the region of absenteeism and turnover in personnel.'[15]

Anthropologist Jon Ander Bilbao argues that *maquilas* are an aspirin that alleviates societal 'pain,' but not the ills that cause it.[16] As the foreign-owned corporations are not taxed, the only profits to stay in Nicaragua are workers' wages. And *maquilas* are not reliable. Thousands of jobs can be lost if a market disappears, as happened when 9/11 slowed U.S. consumption in 2001. If workers are not pliable enough, a factory will close its doors from one day to the next to seek a more 'hospitable' environment.[17]

UNIVERSIDAD CENTROAMERICANA

Every Saturday at 8:00 a.m., a classroom at the private Universidad Centroamericana (UCA) fills up with women who are otherwise not university students, who are forgoing pay and risking the ire of their supervisors to be here. The Economics and Gender Studies departments, at the instigation of MEC, are co-creators of this semester-long training for community leaders; funding from Oxfam Canada stipulated that women from other organizations be drawn in, therefore representatives from rural farming cooperatives—who get up at 4:00 a.m. to travel to the city—are present in addition to *maquila* workers. All of those chosen to participate graduated from high school, though for most, attending the university was a distant dream. The aim is to teach the women about the mechanisms of oppression (race, class, and gender) and help them to find power within the system. The professor does not shy from theory and abstract concepts, though she always relates them back to students' lived experience. The women learn that they are generating wealth and making a contribution, on a familial level and in the *maquila*. The objectives of the program are thus twofold; to raise women's self-esteem and help them make more informed decisions in their own lives, as well as give them the tools to represent their own interests in larger societal debates as they take place in their communities.

Class begins with the question 'What is a closed versus open economy?' Like when the United States embargoed Nicaragua, says one student. Every so often it gets a little rowdy, and much of the time the "Profe" is speaking over other voices. But the women in this class are used to long hours of intense concentration from their jobs; the professor keeps lecturing and the students keep asking questions, doing sample problems, and taking notes. The professor makes no bones about Nicaragua's situation:

We import three times what we export. We are underdeveloped. She explains the difference between growth (production going up from year to year) and development (people living with more dignity) and the students exclaim that although there is growth, their lives remain the same.[18] The professor mentions a study showing that *maquila* workers are actually worse off over time, due in large part to familial disintegration provoked by long work hours. A woman contributes that hers is one such family; the professor smiles her perpetual smile, gives a sympathetic glance, and says, 'Yes, there are cases.'

The course coordinator relates how it was a revelation for the students to learn that society's idea of women is constructed and therefore can be deconstructed. Nonetheless, the professor is wearing a skintight, fire-engine-red miniskirt dress and stiletto heels. The students' attire ranges from a fancy black dress with net sleeves to a second-hand "City of Edgewood 5K Independence Day Race" T-shirt and sweatpants. During break, some of the older women begin to talk about their lives, such rich stories that I forget momentarily that my project focuses on twenty-somethings. At lunch, sitting with the younger women in the cafeteria, I find that although their lives are less complicated, especially those without children who live with their parents, their stories are still evocative.

Virginia is nineteen, Darling twenty-two, and Dora twenty-five. Later when I look at my photos of them sitting around the table, I'm saddened by how Dora looks not three years older than Darling, but ten. Darling, whose round face and big eyes fit her name, may dress fetchingly, but as with the economics professor in her heels, the "feminine" trappings do not indicate any "feminine" passivity. Darling did not hesitate when I asked her reason for taking this class: to get out of the *maquila*. She comments that the class is clarifying ideas that she half knew, that she had had in her head but hadn't articulated.

They describe their jobs to me. Darling is a shirt inspector at the Santa María *maquila*. The rest of the girls are *operarias* (sewing machine operators). Dora works at Hanes and is paid by the piece. The complexity of the pattern she is assigned as well as its retail price dictate her wage; which design she gets is a matter of luck. Hanes runs night and day. Dora works days, seven full shifts a week. Base pay is C$250 (US$15) per week.[19] They explain how they are given a *meta*, a minimum number to reach each day. Another woman joins us, Dagnara, who elucidates that she is expected to complete two articles every minute. She says that the company she works for used to pay workers generously who exceeded their *meta*, before realizing that lower production and higher turnover generated a better profit margin than incentives. Management can raise the daily *meta* at will,

Dagnara adds, and as long as the company meets legal minimum wage, the government cannot or will not defend the workers.

Dagnara and Dora are both sitting with their hands resting on the table, and Dagnara calls my attention to their matching scars. Dora's looks like a suicide attempt, Dagnara's is on the back of her hand: ganglion cysts that grow on the joints and tendons of the hand. Although the lumps are benign, they can be painful and, in Nicaragua at least, surgery is the solution. Dagnara complains that it's classified as a common ailment; not recognized by the government as work related. She is the only one in this group with a child, and she is much angrier than the other women about her working conditions. She says she doesn't have a problem with the *zona franca* itself, but it makes her angry that with CAFTA, [then] President Bolaños doesn't negotiate for better protection on behalf of Nicaraguan workers. She reasons that the country is so bad off, he must be obliged to take whatever he can get. Darling adds that whether or not CAFTA passes, their situation will probably remain much the same; if wages go up, so will living expenses. Dora simply states, 'CAFTA is not desirable for us.' Would most workers agree? They shake their heads in the negative; it's mixed. They specify that younger workers are more likely to be in favor, and those with more experience against. None of them have ever held another job, and as much as they'd like to, none would quit unless they found another equally stable source of income; leaving for anything temporary isn't worth it. All of the girls laugh easily and I wonder if in twenty years their eyes will continue to belie with amusement the sadness in their words.

PARQUE INDUSTRIAL LAS MERCEDES[20]

Emilio Noguera Cáceres looks like a shark; his hair is greased back, he wears a pink button-down shirt, and he talks fast. He has spent his career defending workers from within the system. 'When the workers are in the right, I stand up for them. When the company is, I say that too.' He tells me he was fired from the Department of Labor for not playing politics. He acknowledges up front the problems with the *maquilas*: yes, the pay is low, yes, the work is terrible, but 'any job is better than no job.' I try to maintain my guard, assuming that these guys know exactly what I want to hear, but Emilio has a modest desk in a cubicle, just like the administrative assistants that surround him in their matching outfits, a different color for each day of the week. Granted, he also gets into his smooth silver car, slides on his dark glasses, puts our lunch on the company tab and talks on his cell phone incessantly. So when he identifies himself with Nicaragua's masses, 'we the poor,' I don't buy it. But Emilio certainly seems to believe passionately that the rule of law should reign, bringing justice equally to all.

The entrance to the Zona Franca las Mercedes during the morning rush.

Emilio cruises the streets of the *zona franca* at lunchtime (they are public, though one must pass through a guard station to enter Las Mercedes). Workers are everywhere, clustered with friends. A young girl inside a yard—private property, rented out to corporations by the government—leans against a chain-link fence and talks to a boy on the outside. Emilio clarifies further, 'The CZF is a state-owned public enterprise that administers the installations.'[21] We pass two different groups of men playing baseball. In the center of the *zona* is a public park; green leaves and green grass are punctuated only by bright red Coca Cola benches and one food stand. Emilio takes me by the side yard of one *maquila* where three perfectly aligned rows of trees have been planted. Some companies are good, he says, indicating this one, some are average, some are bad, just like workers.

We tour Hansae, a Korean clothing company that has been in Nicaragua for seven years, with two plants in Las Mercedes and five more in other *zonas*. They sell to Wal-Mart and Kmart. The workers have the option of belonging to the Sandinista union or one from the Center for Nicaraguan Workers.[22] When I get out of the car with my camera, the manager immediately stops me. I can go in, but for pictures, I will need special permission. My first impressions are sensual. It is hot; not brutally so, as the ceilings are high and there are fans, but no A/C. The radio is blaring, which could either be irritating or entertaining, depending on your mood. There are mountains of brilliant color; I wonder if the workers get sick of a certain one or if they stop seeing them.

I had expected to see men in the cutting area, using the saws, and packing boxes, but it was a visual shock to see young guys with tattoos furiously working the sewing machines. A number of them had bandanas over their noses and mouths, a few had actual dust masks. They were racing to the urgent whir of their machines, and the inspectors were keeping pace. Some of the other positions were proceeding at a more comfortable rhythm. I was not allowed to take notes, but these are the basic steps I observed: first they unfurl vast sheets of fabric into stacks inches thick; they cut out pieces of the pattern with a jigsaw; then the parts are sewn together, the label pressed in, each article inspected, ironed, and run through a metal detector, in case any pins were forgotten; then they fold each piece and slide it into an individual plastic bag, and then a large box. They turn out a minimum of twenty thousand articles daily (there are eight lines of workers, and each line is expected to aim for three thousand a day). At the end of the tour, they give me one of the cotton T-shirts that I've just seen made, with decorative studs, destined for Wal-Mart.

Emilio's phone rings. It is Nicaragua's secretary of labor regarding the United States' plan to list Nicaragua on an annual Department of State human rights violations report because of a Las Mercedes *maquila*. Emilio wants the secretary to come inspect, hoping to avoid the extreme measure that the government now proposes of closing down the plant (after it ignored previous complaints about the company, he adds, because of political connections); he advocates a fine or warning. The CZF does not have the power to sanction companies, but Emilio says CAFTA will force Nicaragua to comply with international law. He is not the first to assert that Central America has 'excellent laws,' but that the governments do not apply them. He lists the companies—Gap, Timberline—who will shun Nicaragua in fear of boycotts if they hear that human rights are violated. He worries that instead of pinning the issue on the individual companies where they originate, investors will associate the entire country with human rights problems.

Emilio blames the low salaries paid in the *maquilas* on the fact that Nicaragua is still a country emerging from war: We had an armed conflict during the 1970s and 1980s that left the country in ashes and with no infrastructure. People have to relearn how to solve problems; they had become accustomed to digging in their heels and yelling their demands, and if they didn't get what they wanted, taking up arms. Businessmen are afraid to invest, worried that the Sandinistas may come back and nationalize everything. He hopes that wages will rise when an increase in investment brings more companies that have to compete for employees. But when jobs are scarce, people cling to what they have, regardless of inferior conditions. And if the transnational corporations are forced to pay taxes, they won't come to Nicaragua. Nicaragua is the least industrialized country in the region and is therefore granted preferential treatment under CAFTA. For a specified period, it is permitted to import fabric from a third country and still label its clothing 'Made in Nicaragua,' thereby avoiding quotas. Eventually they will be required to establish the entire chain of production (from growing their own cotton to making their own buttons), thereby also obtaining more exportable materials. His vision is that the *maquilas* be only a step on the path to development, 'We do not want the *maquilas* to represent hope.'

People imagine the *maquilas* to look like the photographs they've seen of child labor or dank factories in the Great Depression in the United States, but it's not like that, Emilio protests. He lists the workers' rights: an eight-hour workday, six days a week (or nine hours and forty minutes Monday through Friday), for a total of a forty-eight-hour workweek. Extra hours cannot be obligatory and must be paid double. Companies must hire a night shift if they need more hours. He informs me that the minimum wage is C$1,300 (US$76) a month, but the average is C$2,500 (US$147). He suggests that when workers say they earn less, I should ask how many days they actually worked. With regard to working conditions, official inspections should take place every six months, but Emilio concedes that this does not happen. Regarding work-related illnesses, he agrees that respiratory problems are the most serious. He did not know what I was referring to when I asked about the ganglion cysts.

As I wait for my ride home at the end of the workday, cars come zooming back into the parking lot and CZF employees pile out. They have all been going to the Asamblea building for weeks now, trying to get CAFTA approved. Today they succeeded. Young men race into the building, one raises his fist triumphantly, 'We got CAFTA!'

Dora Emilia Narvaez (twenty-five)
Darling Ampie (twenty-two)
MONDAY, SEPTEMBER 26

I wait for Dora and Darling on the university steps the Monday after the UCA class. They have late homework to turn in; giggling nervously, they interrupt the professor while he teaches a class. This was the easiest place we could figure to meet; from here they will show me the route to their house. I usually travel by taxi, for the equivalent of about two dollars a trip, but the public bus costs C$2.5 (US$0.15), so we ride first to my rented room and then on to their place so that I will know how to get there.

The bus from UCA is nearly empty when we board; it remains parked for some time and passengers begin to whistle and call out. Darling is amused by their stress. The buses here are old school buses from the United States, decked out with macho cartoon decals, plastic ribbons wrapped around every possible surface, "Jesucristo" placards, and a glittery gearshift. But this one has broken down. We pile off and everyone runs to get a seat on a different one. As always, it's standing room only. More specifically, it's body-to-body. All of the sexuality that is present at the university, indeed in any street, melts away; bodies must become neutral. Even though we are two-deep in the narrow aisle, more passengers squeeze between. There is no aggression, even though they push through determinedly. Impatience and claustrophobia will do you no good. Loud rap music, kids smoking in the back, someone's elbow dangerously close to your face, take a deep breath. It's a combination of a carnival ride and an undignified and dangerous travail. Sometimes you can only laugh along with the person you're body slamming as the bus lurches, jerks, and swerves all at once.

Dora and Darling take it all in stride. When I describe what's on the corner of the street I live on, they know immediately where it is. Maybe

Darling's ride to the zona franca.

because this is a rare day off, an out-of-the-ordinary outing, when we miss our connection they are not annoyed. Instead Darling buys us each a bag of spicy chips and we pass the time. We finally arrive in Reparto Schick (a *reparto* is a housing development or barrio), immediately stepping off the paved street onto a mud lane. Dora's address in the Nicaraguan fashion is 'from where the statue used to be, one block toward the lake (north), one block up (east, where the sun rises) and another half block toward the lake.' Later I pass the median where a pedestal stands, with no bust of the former Nicaraguan president René Schick. From their trendy and crisp manner of dress, I had imagined their houses to be trim and colorful; instead my first impressions are of the dirt floors and walls constructed of cement block and wooden planks.

Tortillas are piling up on a table; Dora's mom sells food out a hatch in the semi-indoor kitchen. Two other young women chat while they help out. One is a friend, who sells squares of cake from a plastic bin. She leaves to continue vending soon after we arrive. She used to work in the *zona*, Dora remarks. The other is Dora's younger sister, Skarleth. Dora's mom, Rosa Emilia, immediately serves me a plate of fresh tortillas and smoked cheese. Then a plate of rice and, from a gigantic pot, beans. Dora moves about determinedly, doing chores, avoiding the camera.

Dora confides to me that she has asthma. One of her mother's best friends emigrated to Florida and supplies Dora with inhalers and other medications; something not within reach of poor people here, Dora declares. Her mom wishes she wouldn't work in the *maquilas* because it worsens her condition, but she feels that she must make the money. Her cousin Jamileth stops by. She works in a *maquila* too. Dora explains how one works on and off in the *zona*, resigning for mistreatment, for sickness, for exhaustion. Rosa Emilia worked in one; she quit after two hours, they relate laughing. Before I leave, Dora takes me down the street to introduce me to other family members, whom she presents as too old to work in the *zona* (they are in their forties). Rosa Emilia offers me another plate of food to take home, and they present me with two washcloths; they sew colored lace around the edges and sell these. Nicaraguans carry them, I've noticed, to mop up the sweat as they go about their day in the urban, tropical heat. They refuse payment but suggest that after I'm famous, I can be the godmother to an orphaned neighbor girl who they help maintain.

Dora walks me a few houses further down the street to leave me at Darling's. There they offer me Coke from a bottle drawn out of a cooler while we watch the news—a tornado had struck Darling's dad's hometown—and we compare notes on who felt yesterday's earthquake. Her mom is in the backyard cooking. She cooks all day, and in the evening the whole family—Darling, her parents, her sister with her three kids, and her sister-in-law with her daughter (Darling's brothers are already there)—drives over to where her dad has his auto body shop and where they set up their *fritanga* (a table set up on the street at dinnertime, usually in front of one's house, where home-cooked food is sold). It is better for them to sell in this neighborhood of upright houses and paved streets. Darling mentions offhandedly that on weekdays she goes straight from work to join her family at the shop, where they sell until they are sold out, around ten or eleven at night. In addition, she helps her mom before work, making salad and packing food to sell in the mornings to school kids. Darling gets up at 4:30 a.m., as it takes her an hour by bus to get to work. She is endlessly cheerful and helpful; full of energy to interact with her nieces and nephews. When I comment that their days are long, that they work so hard, they nod in agreement but don't dwell on it.

When her dad arrives, they load up all of the different dishes her mom has prepared and try to figure out what they are forgetting. Every day they forget something, Darling laughs, as they always laugh in this family. Eventually we pile into the low-slung seats of the car, four adults in back and her parents in front. Everyone but the driver and me has a kid on her lap. As we chug down the street in this metal shell, I have the sensation of being in a boat. The women ask numerous times if he got gas, but he avoids the question. He is clearly a much-adored father; mild-mannered and loving with his grandchildren. Still, we run out of gas in the middle of the first busy intersection. Sisters pile out to push, and as it's downhill, we make it to the shop anyway. As soon as we arrive and they set up the table, they set about feeding me. Disappointingly, I am served on a Styrofoam plate with a metal spoon and plastic cup of Coke, while the family eats off of banana leaves and pour their Coke into little plastic bags, which they bite a hole in to sip from. When they take my empty plate and stuff it down the street drain, they joke, 'This is our trashcan.'

While we wait for customers, I ask how they got involved with MEC. A neighbor invited Darling's mom, and soon thereafter they received scholarships to learn a trade. Many of the courses were in skills in which women are traditionally underrepresented; Darling learned refrigeration. She has not been able to make a living from these skills, though, which she blames on both the high competition in Managua and on discrimination. She explains that not only wouldn't customers trust a woman to fix their A/C, but a bank wouldn't loan her the capital necessary to start up that kind of business. Darling has also trained as a secretary, as well as studying natural medicine for a year. Still, she can't find a job anywhere besides the *maquila*, and has been working there for two years now. I ask about the training required for that job, and they reply that only if you apply very young will they teach you how to use the machines; somehow most people already have experience. Juana, Darling's mother, tells her story next. For five years she worked in the *maquilas*, but quit as it was damaging her lungs. She still works every day, she iterates, but for herself; two months ago they started the *fritanga*. Before, she had time to volunteer as a *promotora* for MEC, going from house to house and inviting neighborhood women to classes and events. "Se despiertan a ellas" (It wakes them up), regarding their rights at work or abuse from husbands or sons, she explains.

When I bring up CAFTA, they laugh as they recall a recent interchange with a grocer about imported onions and bananas: bananas are produced here and exported, leaving them to buy the expensive Guatemalan ones, says Juana. She worries that people like her will be hurt by CAFTA if big chains come into the neighborhood and squeeze her out.

FRIDAY, SEPTEMBER 30

At Dora's the electricity has been shut off since Tuesday for overdue payment. Agustín is turning tortillas, as he was last time I visited. I ask what he does and he assumes I mean around the house; he helps with the tortillas and washes his own clothes. He doesn't have a job and he left school this year as his aunt, Dora's mom, no longer had the money to send him. After Rosa Emilia serves me breakfast—I have to remember never to eat before coming over—Dora takes me into her room. Her mother built it for her, separate from the rest of the house, which her ex–stepdad constructed. The house consists of the entryway where Agustín sets up his bed, Dora's mom's bedroom, and a long hallway to the three-sided kitchen and the back patio with the bathroom and sink. Crossing this small patio, we enter Dora's room, with a double bed where she and Skarleth sleep. There is also a TV, a wardrobe, and stacked plastic bins full of the family's personal belongings. It is extremely neat and spare. When I comment on this, Dora says they would display more if they had shelves.

Indeed, inside the door of the wardrobe there is an arrangement of medicines, perfumes, and figurines that Dora proudly picks up one by one to show me. There is a doll that she received for her *quinceaños* (fifteenth birthday, celebrated like a coming-out party). Dora displays wonder that she has kept it for eleven years, as if life feels tenuous to her. I admire a black fan and she thrusts it at me, it is mine to keep. Her inhaler and liquid oxygen demand as much description as the sentimental items. She reaches under her pillow and pulls out another inhaler. On bad days, she might have to use three of the oxygen tabs, at C$50 each (US$2.94) she exclaims. Again, it is her mother's friend in the United States who provides them. 'The *maquila* has done me a lot of damage.' Dora has been in and out of the *zona* since she was eighteen. As of her next birthday, when she turns twenty-six, she will be less desirable, for which I am glad.

We sit on her bed with a stack of photo albums. She dutifully opens her sister's first, then shows me hers. Dora's *quinceaños* was a spectacle to behold; long lines of attendants and *jardineros*, the child attendants, and Dora's traditional pink dress with exaggerated puffed sleeves. Dora emphasizes how hard her mom worked to make it possible and doesn't seem at all fazed by the fact that it ended early due to an argument or that her pile of presents was stolen during the same party. We flip through the rest of the pages, one snapshot after another of other people's *quinceaños* that she has attended or taken part in. Skarleth joins us to present me with

The girls have me take a picture of Dora's cousin, Agustín, tending tortillas on the fire; it's rare to see a man doing this they tell me.

a ceramic vase with two swans, a white flowered mug, and another washcloth that she has edged with ribbon. She and I have barely ever conversed, and Dora says later how surprised she was by this gesture, that Skarleth is rarely sentimental or expressive.

When there are no neighbors calling at the window, Dora's mom goes for her sewing. Indeed, later in the day a woman stops by to order a white towel with blue trim. Rosa Emilia says that most Nicaraguans don't like to work; she is not the first person to make this comment to me. The conversation turns to religion and after I state my beliefs she brings out her Bible and has me read the first few sentences of Genesis. Rosa Emilia goes to church four times a week for two hours. I wonder how this could fit into Dora's schedule, and she admits that she goes when she's invited, but otherwise does not attend.

Darling is the one to reveal that Dora has a boyfriend, that they've been together six years, that Dora is a 'free thinker' and does not want to get married. Dora confirms this, saying that she does not want kids. Darling, pretty and girlish, surprises me by saying she has never had a boyfriend, though she'd like to. She used to go out with her friends more, before everyone's working life took over, although, Darling observes, even when you get home tired, if you go out dancing it gives you energy. We are gathered out back of Darling's house now—at 2:00 p.m., when the *telenovelas* (soap operas) are over, she and her mom begin preparing the *fritanga*— and Dora keeps everyone laughing with her sharp tongue. Darling's sister is there and different neighbors drop by. Dora is cutting out economics articles from a stack of old newspapers for tomorrow's UCA class. Darling, as usual, is giving directions to everyone else, though instead of seeming bossy it highlights how intimately their fates are intertwined. Much laughter and gossip and advice ensue. I am again struck by the relaxed atmosphere. This includes throwing tin cans out the kitchen window instead of into the trash. Darling's sister—who later cleans the whole house without a word—cuts a label off a shirt and drops it on the floor. Dishes are washed until they look clean, not until they are sanitized. As her mom cooks and neighbors yell messages and a fight breaks out down the street among the glue-sniffing kids, Darling bathes with water from a bucket in an outdoor stall, a sheet pulled between her and the fray. A neighbor woman pats out a tortilla; there's no need to ask if they can use the help.

The conversation turns to who has recently left to attempt entering the United States as a *mojado*, who has already arrived, and who is trying to obtain a visa to visit her dying mother (the U.S. embassy refused her twice at the expense of US$100 a try, the moral of the story being that it's better to go illegally). Then Darling brings out some clothes and tries to sell them to the other women. Earlier Dora had explained that she and her sister put on raffles for a cash prize; now Darling reveals her side project of buying clothes on layaway and reselling them to friends. She says she never loses, because if something doesn't sell, she gets to keep it, and she and her mom seem to have fun picking stuff out together. Juana calls out to a neighbor kid to take one of her skirts to his mom so that she can put in a zipper; this is the division of labor.

Darling brings out her photo albums and dumps them in my lap. As I flip through, two images catch my attention. One is of a group standing around a grey and skinny male cadaver. At first I am shocked by the morbidity, but then I remember her saying that she studied natural medicine.

She says her friends think it's sick too, but that when you are there, it becomes normal. Only eating lunch was disgusting, as there was no cafeteria and so she ate quickly and with a cloth over her food. The other snapshot that holds my gaze is a portrait of the family nineteen years ago. Darling's dad looks like a classic Sandinista; it's 1985 and he sports a beret and beard like all the revolutionaries. But Juana chimes in to explain that he hid out so as not to have to join the army.

THURSDAY TO FRIDAY, OCTOBER 6 & 7 (DARLING)

Darling and I had agreed that I would meet them at the *fritanga* and then sleep over in order to accompany her on her early morning ride to work. In a city with virtually no street names or numbers, a city that I hardly ever dare to venture out in at night, one really must know where one is going; they hadn't known the exact description of the corner where they sell, so I am lucky to spot the table set up under a streetlight a block from where my taxi searches. They say they thought I wasn't coming—it had gotten so late—but we stay for another hour until they decide to pack up. Sales are slow, and I wonder how these few cordobas could be worth the amount of labor required to produce the spread. Juana addresses all of the customers as "amor," and Darling calls out, 'What will you have?' But mostly they and Rosita, the sister-in-law, and her daughter perch on child-sized chairs on the sidewalk and tell stories.

We talk about Hurricane Stan and the dramatic images they'd seen on the news, until the man who lives behind the sidewalk where we sit emerges to join the conversation. As I try to balance my dinner of *maduro con queso* (softened plantain with cheese) while clutching the Glu Glu that Darling had insisted I try (grape syrup drink in a little plastic bag, with an unfortunate name to my English-speaking ears, given the kids that sniff glue on Managua's streets), along with a piece of gum that she also bought me, the neighbor describes how his dog was bleeding from her mouth and the procedures that they'd undergone at the vet. The neighbor is pleasant and well spoken, but he never stops to take a breath. So when he asks if I believe in God, I only get a few words in before he begins to elaborate on his Gnosticism and spirituality, and eventually his astral, out-of-body experiences. Darling grew up going to the Seventh-day Adventist Church, but now it's only her father who attends. Someone from the family always accompanies him, but when she goes, she gets antsy. 'Why do you come if you're only praying to leave?' her father asks her. In their faith one does not work or study on Saturday, and so for Darling the break came when she wanted to study natural medicine, which required her to take classes on both weekend days.

Darling on her way to work.

Darling's eyes are heavy-lidded as she tries to absorb the neighbor's soliloquy on Jesus Christ. Juana is sleeping on her feet. Darling tells me how at her old job she would go into the bathroom at exactly one o'clock—knowing that at that hour it had just been scrubbed—and sit down to sleep for half an hour, until the loudspeaker called 'Darling Ampie to her place.' She doesn't do it at the company she works for now; the bathrooms aren't so clean. The family decides to pack up for the evening; it takes no time to load the food through the non-existent back window of the car. Juana conscientiously sweeps the cabbage shavings and loose papers from the sidewalk and into the curbside drain. The table and chairs are carried back into the garage and we get in the car, swaying home on a wish and a prayer. We are four now instead of the ten that were along last time I rode in this car.

I wonder if it's hard to be the youngest sibling of a large family. But Darling seems enchanted by her parents, and vice versa. They keep up a running commentary peppered with affectionate phrases and much patience. Her father is older than her mother, who has mentioned how he used to drink and run around until he became an *evangelista* fifteen years ago. Now he's a quiet man and a good husband.

We arrive home and sit down to watch TV, but are too tired. A cockroach bigger than my palm crawls up the wall and Juana sprays some poison on it. Then she goes to bed. Darling and I do the same. Her dad tries to stay up with the TV loud as we fall asleep, but soon he too retires, and finally the lights go out. Darling's parents sleep behind a curtain on the other side of the wall. Whenever anyone gets up to go to the bathroom, the overhead lights blare. Every wheeze and creak can be heard, although the house is not cramped; Darling has her own room and her own bed. When all four siblings lived at home, what is now the living room was the whole house; four years ago they rebuilt with cement block and enlarged.

Although Darling is twenty-two and wears platform shoes and hip-hugger jeans and eyeliner and carries a fashionable mini-purse, her bedroom does not reflect this. Two shovels lean against a wall and a rusty handsaw hangs above a rickety bed. On a shelf consisting of a board balanced on bricks lie her photo album and a Bible. Her clothes are stored in a pile. Her shoes perch with the heels hooked over a ledge (including the silver-strapped, super-high platforms that she wears to the market; they keep her up out of the muck), and four bottles of cheap perfume balance on another. Eight different Tweety placards and one poster-sized portrait of her as a *quinceañera* hang on the walls, which meet the floor in a seeping moisture stain. I dream we are to wake up at midnight, then I dream we oversleep and get up at 9:00 a.m. Finally in the predawn, Juana turns on the light and I think the family must be rising. But she turns it back off and returns to bed. Soon after, Darling wakes and the light is back on. She hurries to bathe, dress, and brush her teeth. A bus driver whose route is the *zona franca* lives in the house facing theirs.

The first two passengers after us are sisters who apply their makeup as the bus lurches. As many men board as women, until it is packed. Half of the people get off at the entrance to the first industrial park and the rest wait for the Zona Franca Las Mercedes, where Darling works. Even though I'd had it described to me, I am not prepared for just how many workers are streaming off buses, crisscrossing the highway, jamming through the chain-link chute to get to the front gate and clock in on time. Along the fence, vendors are lined up hawking coffee (in small plastic bags

Darling on the bus to work.

tied and perched atop Styrofoam cups), cake, juice, and other breakfast items. There are also recruiters from a hospital, from the military; this is a good opportunity to pitch to an audience of thousands. I follow Darling to the guard station at the entrance to the *zona* and do not try to go any further. I already feel I am trespassing, although no one seems to care.

SUNDAY, OCTOBER 16 (DORA)

As usual, the taxi driver warns me that Reparto Schick is dangerous, that he wouldn't venture any deeper into the barrio, and never after 9:00 p.m. He gives the reason: gangs. The one that seems to strike fear into everyone is called Comemuertos (eaters of the dead) and he explains that they are *desalmado* (without souls), which I at first hear as *desarmado* (unarmed).

Above: Dora making tortillas at her mother's kitchen table. Below: Plastic bags cut round serve to separate uncooked tortillas and can be reused.

It's Sunday morning. Dora and her mom are *palmeando*, making tortillas. Usually on Sundays Rosa Emilia goes to church and Dora goes visiting, but this week they are especially broke (payday fell on a Saturday, so she must go back tomorrow for her check), and thankful to have this fallback. Rosa Emilia is turning the tortillas on the fire with a wet knife, filling a plastic tub with them, to be bought still steaming in ones and twos by neighbors, who hand in their own little scratched-up plastic tubs and ask for five cents' worth of beans too. They also sell *cuajaditos*; little round, smoked cheeses that cost one cordoba. I ask if selling food provides a living; we earn enough to be able to eat, Dora indicates.

In Nicaraguan society, many of Dora's traits might be considered masculine. In addition to having no aspirations of motherhood, she is forthright and independent, and physically she is not delicate. It is unexpected then to come upon the domestic vision of her seated at the kitchen table, working the *masa* (dough). But she plans that by the end of this month, that's all she'll be doing. She's not going back to the *maquilas*. She returned to work last week, after taking leave for the surgery on her hand, and was ill the whole time. She notes that exactly one year before she got the ganglion cyst, this August, she had been hospitalized when the glands in her throat swelled up and she couldn't swallow. When her mom gave her orange juice, it came out her nose. She is fearful that this time she will need surgery that could leave her mute.

I follow Dora out to the patio where she washes and cuts vegetables for her mom. Dora hates vegetables, but her mom mixes spinach in with scrambled eggs, adds celery to rice, and likes to point out to me how unusual this is in Nicaragua. Dora gets water from a huge metal barrel coated on the inside with cement. There's a plastic bag floating in it. The sink does have running water, but they fill the barrel because the service is not reliable. They toss a bag of chlorine in, what I had thought was trash, plus empty and scrub the construction barrel–sized container daily. As she washes, she talks: Her sister Skarleth went to live with her husband—her boyfriend actually—and his family. Rosa Emilia made her leave, for staying out too late with him one too many times. Today, however, she comes over and visits, hangs out her laundry, shares the news that her ID card has turned up after being stolen. (This morning, on the radio, I heard about a taxi driver taking his fare off route and robbing him. Dora and her mom mentioned earlier that someone took four chickens from their yard.) Dora is now talking under her breath and I hardly understand, she's running her words together. She doesn't know how her sister can be so arrogant.

She takes me into her room and plants me in front of the television, a present from her boyfriend, along with a DVD player. They're fighting right now, and she told him to take it back but he said keep it. She goes out to clean the bathroom. I try to be interested in TV, but it's mostly static. Then Dora leaves me in the kitchen to eat spinach with her mom, disappearing again. Rosa Emilia pulls the condiments out of the broken microwave, where she stores them, and says they will send the gas stove out to be fixed and expand the kitchen by the time I visit next, in however many years. She talks about her trip to Guatemala to visit one of her best friends who moved there. She worked extra to save up, bought dry beans and rice to take with her, and stayed for a month. She disappears into her bedroom and brings me a stack of Guatemalan newspapers to peruse.

SUNDAY, DECEMBER 11

I pass through Managua on my way back to the United States, and visit Dora and Darling to say goodbye. Darling's family has changed the living room around again, like they always do. But this time they painted it pink. They are cooking inside now, over gas; firewood was too expensive, too scarce, they explain. The somewhat forced happy atmosphere is the same, with everyone laughing at the kids' antics and the TV loud enough to make sustained conversation impossible. At Dora's, she and her mom show me the embroidered towels they've been working on, far more

Dora sweeping the entryway of her mom's house.

sophisticated than the ones I'd seen previously, with lettering and designs in shiny thread. Dora confides that she wants to attend law school and that her mom's friend in the States may support her while she studies. She is afraid she'll get too frustrated and not have the attention span to finish, but I think the idea fits Dora perfectly.

Teresa Ruth Olivares Mejia (twenty-seven)

Teresa is exemplary of what well-meaning proponents of the *zona franca* hope for, that a job provides you the extra income to pay for school, which in turn allows you to find better employment. Many workers though are too tired for more than their job, or they have to work weekend days when they could be in school. Teresa takes three classes on Sunday, in addition to the Saturday class at UCA. She says sometimes she feels like her head will explode from so much studying. She emphasizes that most of the women she works with are not well educated, that indeed you do not need to know how to read in order to be hired. One observer noted that the *maquilas* are plundering Nicaragua's principal resource: its human resource.[23] This creates the circular effect of an uneducated population and jobs that require no education.[24]

Since she was little, Teresa—Teresita, if you're talking to her mom—has been acutely aware of the family's economic situation, and so she is the only one of her mother's nine children who doesn't have kids of her own. She is also the only one in college. One sister completed two years at the university, but then got pregnant and quit. When I visited Teresa's house she proudly read me a report she had done for class, meaningful to her because she had analyzed a company that she had once worked for, using experiential knowledge instead of secondary sources. I was struck by the potential. How many *maquila* workers have the skills to communicate in writing the reality that only they know? The high esteem in which she holds this company (it is the only one in Central America to handle the thick, slippery fabric of winter coats), her respect for the *chinos* (Chinese) who run many of the *maquilas*, her appreciation of the same products that have made her sick, and her desire to study and make a career of the industry where she has spent the better part of her adult life on a factory floor, show me how the *maquilas* not only alter the workers' lived reality, but their vision of reality.

The Universidad de las Américas (ULAN) is one of many small universities in Managua. It is only eight years old, and the buildings are unfinished. A single horseshoe of classrooms and a parking lot, it is a far cry from UCA, which is a private, quiet, green oasis in this metropolis. Between classes we sit at an outdoor snack bar that juts into the parking lot. ULAN

Teresa and Coki the dog.

is a school for management, marketing, tourism, accounting; these are the popular majors in Nicaragua. Teresa is studying banking and finance. Why did she choose this? If you are in charge of a large company's finances, how can they not pay you well? she responds. Despite having fallen behind in credit hours the numerous times that she couldn't make her tuition payments, Teresa will finally be eligible for her bachelor's degree after these three classes and one more seminar. That seminar and the degree, however, will cost her another US$500. Given Teresa's salary, it would be nearly impossible for her to save up this quantity.

Those pants that are made from extremely thick material, so thick that it made her hands swell up just to handle it, with fabric that exhales chemicals and an excess of *peluza* (lint) and only men are hired to sew the inseam because it's so stiff to fold; those are the jeans I wear every day. Petite Teresa got on the line with the men and impressed the manager, who said it must be because she's left-handed that she's so smart. She goes on to describe the other garments made of the same material; the kids' shorts, "una preciosidad" (embroidered by the women; sewing machines are programmed with the designs, then washed with chlorine). She lasted one year on that line, and when she wasn't ill, she could go as fast as the men. But by the end of that time she was spending two or three days of each pay period out sick, so it wasn't worth it, though she could earn up to C$4,000 (US$235) per month along with the men. Other jobs, no matter how many articles you turn out, don't earn you much; the brands that hire companies in Nicaragua do not produce high-end clothing.

Teresa has worked "de toditas las maquinas"; every last one of the machines that there is to work in the *zona franca*. She has worked at five different companies and never been fired, and she has never quit for more than a month at a time. Her last position was in serigraphy, and after just three months her skin reacted; the work is too dirty, she states. Her longest stint was for three and a half years; she can't believe it looking back, but at that job she earned up to C$1,600 per month (US$94) working until

Loniel and Teresa.

8:00 p.m. every night and on Saturday and Sunday. At her next job, she earned half that. Now Teresa has her hopes pinned on an uncle who has a government job and might be able to find something for her, something secretarial (she has no experience in an office, but is confident that she can learn fast), something that pays a better starting salary. Unless you have contacts, even if there's a vacancy you won't get hired for a job like that, she explains.

It has happened repeatedly that after describing their daily work schedule to me, women reveal that right now, however, they are not working. Teresa has not worked in the *zona* for five months, in fact the doctor told her she can't go back because of the cough she's developed, which is why I can visit her at her house on a Wednesday morning. Teresa has spent the last decade of her life in the *maquilas*; she started working there when she was sixteen. They say that you can work five years and keep your health; Teresa half jokes that after that point you'll spend most of your time in the doctor's office anyway. She has headaches and back pain, but most serious is the respiratory problem developed from an allergy to *peluza*. She recounts the story of a friend at work whose lungs filled with water and she died.

I imagine the kind of regret that has no remedy. Five years of work in return for a healthy life. But when I try to ascertain if she laments her decisions, Teresa answers obliquely that if she hadn't worked in the *maquilas* she wouldn't have had the means to get educated. 'I earn little and am repressed, but everything depends on sacrifice.' If you dream, you can reach your goal, she professes, which would sound hollow coming from someone who wasn't living by it to beat incredible odds. Teresa worked those ten years in order to be able to study. She is thankful that there was work to be had and she is determined not to spend her whole life in a *maquila*.

Discussing the cost of tuition, Teresa reveals that after sewing all day at the *maquila*, she earns extra money as a seamstress. I had noticed her elegant wardrobe, her outfits cut perfectly to her lithe figure, but I thought perhaps it was her form that was striking. When I visit Teresa at home, she shows me her photo album. Family weddings, communions, and above all *quinceaños*; Teresa has costumed them all, along with all of their attendants. She will also sell you three little girl's dresses for C$180 (US$11). You bring her an idea or a picture and she creates a dress. On payday at the *maquila* she can sell up to six dresses if she has them ready. With pleasure at the scandal of it, she describes one woman who came to her with the idea of a dress cut down to here and up to here with connecting strips of fabric in the deep V's. Sometimes she wonders if she shouldn't learn another specialty in tailoring, but she shakes her head; she's invested too much in her education to become distracted now.

Flor talks to her granddaughter, Loniel,
as she eats lunch sitting at Teresa's sewing table.

Teresa lives 8 miles outside of Managua; the noise and crowds of the city disperse, along the road it is flat and green. When I get off the bus, I am on a paved road but not yet to the town of Tipitapa. My directions are: fourth house, pink, arches, no bars. I find it easily, but the house is shut up; the simple, sturdy shutters closed. Teresa's porch is bare except for sandbags at one end, to stop floodwater from the street, I assume. But a pink house with arches will be inviting regardless. I knock and no one comes. I knock again and Teresa opens the door—hands wet, she's washing dishes she says, and sits me in front of the TV where her brother is watching a nature show. It is not quite 9:00 a.m.

Above: The side yard of Teresa's home. Below: Teresa and Loniel.

Theirs is a well-constructed home; it is unusual to be in a house where the walls are block instead of scrap. The walls don't meet the roof, purposeful in this tropical clime. Teresa's family has lived here for twenty-two years; recently, the four siblings who work in the *zona* paid to have the house rebuilt. In the living room there are two beds; Teresa's twelve-year-old nephew, Francisco, sleeps under the pink mosquito netting (his mom works in the *zona* and he doesn't like to be alone the long hours).

Three-year-old Loniel's father left in February for his home country. He and her mother, Teresa's sister, met in the *maquila*, where he was a boss and she a worker. Previously, I'd only heard negative stories about the *chinos*, but Teresa has another point of view; they did used to treat the workers badly, even hitting them, but not anymore. Now there are laws in place. She absolves them regardless, as they were sent here by their companies. She recounts how at first the workers had to teach their bosses Spanish. She herself went over the parts of a sewing machine word by word with a supervisor, the *china* taking notes and studying in the evenings at home. 'They are very intelligent,' Teresa concludes admiringly.

Behind the house is a refurbished chicken coop the family planned to rent out to a *zona franca* worker, but now it is where Joel sleeps. Joel is Teresa's younger brother, also in his twenties. He is mute and partially deaf. (Silently he watches; coming in at one point from outside to turn on the kitchen light as I struggle to photograph. He closes the front door to show me a poster describing the letters of the alphabet in sign language, hoping to communicate.) I had not recognized this as a living space from the outside. A single bed is jammed into a squat, dark lean-to pieced together with scrap in which you wouldn't be able to stand up straight and there is no window. People ask why they put him out back all alone, Flor—their mother—worries, but she defends their family arrangement; she set up a bed in the front room for Joel, but there he is anxious all night, hearing the small noises from the street. We continue on our tour of the backyard, and Flor shows me the barrel upon which she builds a fire to cook beans or stew or roasted corn, which would smoke up the house.

Later, as we watch TV, Flor volunteers that no, she does not like the *novelas*; women who do nothing but talk about men. She elaborates that when she watches, 'I feel that I am sinning.' She does not watch *Lucha Libre* or anything 'that wounds the soul'; she believes it is satanic. Flor tells Loniel not to watch either, that such programs are sinful. She admits mischievously though that when her youngest son comes home and turns on sports, and everyone else clears out, she sits down and they happily watch. She tells him, don't worry, when we have some money we'll buy our own TV.

We are having lunch, each sitting in a rocking chair facing the TV, though it's not on. I notice there is no dining room table, just Teresa's desk with her pedal sewing machine (her electric one is broken) under the window. There is a very tiny cat with a tiny face. It mews pitiably as we eat. Flor repeats, 'I am Christian.' She relates how she was told in a dream that the telephone number of the Christians is Jeremiah 33:3. She describes visions she had the day the pope died. As her words gain momentum, her voice assumes the hypnotic, loud intonations of a preacher, and she quotes the Bible. The kids stay quiet, retreating into their own thoughts (Teresa attends church each weekend day, and her mother also goes Tuesdays and Thursdays). Flor declares that the year 2000 has passed now, and Christ is coming soon. She informs me that at their church, the United Pentecostal Church, 'Our missionary is a gringo.'

Later Flor discusses the time of the Sandinistas. I had been trying to ask Teresa about this; like the 1972 earthquake, the war is something that, though her generation hardly remembers it, defines society still. Flor recounts how other mothers sacrificed their sons, gleefully accepting cash payment in return. Or how her brother took his family to Guatemala to avoid taking up arms. But she stayed, and she prayed. Her oldest son was conscripted, but he never had to spill blood. His encampment was attacked and he took shrapnel, however, losing forever the control over one side of his body as well as his sight. Flor began and ended her story stating that, economically, the Sandinistas had benefited their family.

Teresa will travel back into the city with me—she received a phone call and is all of a sudden hurrying to iron a different outfit and powder her face—she's going to see about a scholarship for school. We are in the bedroom. She changes out of the ruffled skirt and top she has on and into a self-fashioned, full-length skirt and matching blouse with her signature detail of jewels sewn along the neckline. She is arranging her hair and whispers that it's a secret from her mom but she cut it; she has managed to hide the fact even though they sleep in the same bed. Her friend cut it and cut it too short, and her mom would be upset after all she's done to her to make it grow, like preparing avocado treatments for Teresa to wear while sleeping. I guess maybe Flor—who couldn't identify family members in the photo album because she can't see without her glasses and she can't find her glasses—really doesn't know.

Carolina Montiel (thirty-one)

Carolina is the first person I've talked to who says she has no complaints about her job. She goes out of her way to praise the company that employs her. The stories she hears from women who work elsewhere convince her

Carolina at her mother's house.

that the treatment she receives is better than most. Carolina has been there for a year and a half and says there are so many companies to choose from, there is no reason to withstand bad treatment. If she is ill, she is given time off, unlike her younger sister Gaby, who works elsewhere and whose boss would tear up her doctor's notes even when she was pregnant in order not to honor her sick leave. Gaby earns C$1,200 a month (US$71), despite working the undesirable night shift alternate weeks. Carolina has been trying to convince Gaby to quit that job, and after just so much humiliation, she has finally agreed.

Carolina used to work for the *chinos* at a company called Gatornica, where the boss would violently pound the table to make a point. The *chinos* advertise for females between the ages of eighteen and twenty-five, and prefer that you do not study, Carolina tells me with resentment. They also time how long you stay in the bathroom. I hear so many complaints about them that I ask for clarification from Emilio at the CZF. He explains that there are no Chinese companies here (in fact, Chinese textile exports compete with Central America's for a share of the U.S. market[25]), that Nicaragua does not even have relations with mainland China, but that Taiwan is seeking Central American support at the United Nations and because of this, the first foreign companies here were Taiwanese (Sr. Lacayo holds that it is because Violeta Chamorro's son was an ambassador there). When these companies first established themselves, no one in Nicaragua knew how to do the jobs, so managers were brought from Taiwan. There is still a popular association between working at a *maquila* and working for the Chinese. Emilio diplomatically states that the *chinos* had a different work ethic, which I imagine refers to what the workers report as harsh discipline, curbed with labor laws in the early 1990s and an increase in Nicaraguan supervisors.[26]

'I like what I do,' Carolina announces. She is an inspector, which sounds like a supervisory position, but Carolina assures me that just like *operaria* this is entry level, with a salary to match. Each brings its discomforts; while the others are sitting all day, she is on her feet. In fact, she says, perhaps her work is harder physically, as she uses her hands while the *operarias* have the machines to facilitate their work. Part of her task is to determine which pants are *de primera* and which *de segunda*, first- and second-class quality. Not very many fall into the latter category, but the ones that do the company will sell to the workers for just C$50 a pair (US$2.94), an example of one of the perks it offers.

And there are others. When bus drivers went on strike, employees who made it in were each given a piece of chocolate in appreciation and the company offered free transportation home, while other companies charged C$5 (US$0.29), double the price of a trip on a public bus. Or, when the city was going to shut off the electricity in the afternoon the workers were told to come in at 5:00 a.m. (one hurdle for Nicaragua to compete globally is this type of interruption in production). Then when the city decided to shut off power in the morning instead, all two thousand workers who had come in early were served a complimentary breakfast. 'It makes me proud [to work there],' Carolina states, although she also says that the company fosters this atmosphere so that they'll work more; the employees are told to make Nicaragua proud by exporting the best product, when really it's so that the company looks good. Knowing the subject of my investigation, she recounts the day they were allowed to stop work

Carolina at her mother's house.

at 4:00 p.m., were treated to refreshments, and given a talk about how CAFTA will benefit them. They were urged to sign a petition in favor, although she thinks that it will pass regardless.

Three years ago Carolina developed a dorsal ganglion cyst; the scars seem manifestations of work that is hurtful to the body. She has also developed asthma. I don't remember if I looked at her quizzically, after all of her praise for her employer, but she amended, everything is nice where I work, except for the ventilation. She does have health insurance through her work; if you don't, she inveighs, you are stuck on the public side of the hospital, where there are few doctors and less medicine.

Carolina brings home C$2,000 per month, or C$1,600 if things are slow (US$118 or US$94). She usually works from 7:00 a.m. to 5:00 p.m., Monday through Friday. If she needs extra money, she can skip breakfast and rush through lunch, and turn out up to 450 pieces in a day. "El mundo es de los intrepidos" (The world belongs to the intrepid), Carolina recites. Two years ago she and her husband split up. Being a single mom with two kids, she stands her ground and refuses to take extra hours, 'Fire me,' she dares. She needs to be home for her kids. If only I earned C$5,000 a month (US$294), she dreams. . . . But for now, her salary doesn't even cover basic needs. She owes the electric company, and right now their water is shut off, so that she can pay for school for the kids.

It seems a sad postscript to the Sandinistas' legacy of literacy, that so many families have trouble meeting the costs of sending their children to school. Uniforms, notebooks, and graduation ceremonies from one grade to another are too much for some, but what Carolina explains is that there is a not-so-voluntary 'donation' for the utilities that, like everyone else, the school must pay; the schools are therefore called 'autonomous' instead of 'public.' She owes the entire year for her daughter, at C$40 a month (US$2.35). Kessler, her five-year-old son, attends a semiprivate, church-run school that costs C$110 a month (US$6.47). Carolina says she's not religious, although she grew up *evangelista*.

And so, Carolina plans to leave for Costa Rica with her two children. She has already obtained a passport for both of them, at a cost of US$20 each. She has lived there intermittently for a total of four years since 1997; she would leave her daughter Kemberlyng (a name she says she found in a Russian magazine) with her then-husband. As a domestic worker she saved US$1,500 in the year 2000, and bought her house with cash. Now her urgency is regarding education. Kemberlyng is starting secondary school and will graduate in four years; Carolina wants to move into a higher earning bracket now so that she can provide her children with a college education. She says Costa Rica has a better atmosphere, but then she says that when she lived there in 2002 with her youngest child still a baby, 'I lived in dread'; children are frequently stolen, and a few days later a body shows up. They steal children for satanic cult rituals, Carolina believes.

Carolina herself finished high school. She would have liked to study psychology or law, but couldn't afford it. What she doesn't want is for her and her daughter to both work in the *zona*. Carolina, who is so well-read and has such a clear grip on her life; Carolina, who is thirty-one years old, says she has given up hope for herself, but wants to see her kids get ahead. As a child, she was sent out to work as a street vendor, and she tells me she would feel like a bad mother if her little girl had to do that, knowing from experience how at that tender age, when a girl is just beginning to show her womanhood, she is exposed to too much on the street.

Carolina's house is a block from her mother's, in Barrio Jorge Dimitrov (named for a Bulgarian), where the government resettled the family when Lake Managua flooded their old neighborhood. After a long struggle, property rights were regularized, and Carolina is happy to say that the plot she bought is now, without the house, worth US$6,000.[27] Despite owning her own home, she has reason to leave Nicaragua. A friend had mentioned to me that the police won't enter this neighborhood at night, and Carolina confirms the reputation with stories of drug raids. Before, she says, the delinquents were 'polite' and would only hassle an unknown who might happen through. Now they will rob anyone.

She planned to have just one child, and opines that Nicaraguans bear too many children; her generation received sex education and should know how to avoid pregnancy, but even still, her peers were already expecting by sixteen. She adds that it's as if poor people don't have the right to have kids, as it is nearly impossible for them to maintain their families economically. When she got pregnant the second time, she says, 'I did not have the courage to get an abortion, to face the situation.'

Carolina is the oldest of nine siblings. 'We are very close,' she says, puffing up her chest a bit. Of those who are in Nicaragua, all live in the same neighborhood; four at home and Carolina and Gaby in their own places. Three of her sisters are in Costa Rica. There, they live poor, she admits, but they live better. They have a washing machine, can pay the electricity, and give their children chicken to eat if they want it. She says it pains her that her kids ask and ask for things that she can't give. She knows McDonald's is overpriced and unhealthy, but Kessler begs her to take him. A hamburger costs C$50 (US$2.94); one trip for the three of them would be four days' worth of beans, rice, cheese, and tortillas. She resolved this the last time by splurging to buy pancake mix—'rich people's food'—and milk and eggs. As she remembers it, kids didn't used to whine so much; she and her siblings would be given one eleven-ounce soda to share. Her parents told them this taught them to be 'brotherly,' but she knew that it was because of money, and did not complain. Her dad was in the military, which afforded them a small stipend, and her mom worked too (and still does, as a cleaning lady at a cultural center near her home). Nowadays, she says, kids are 'bratty.'

I walk home with Carolina on the last day of the workshop at MEC. She says she likes to walk and she is unfazed by the camp of political protesters that take up a square block with their black plastic tent homes, unfazed by crazy busy streets, unfazed by mud, by cat calls from passing cars. She says she gets up at six in the morning to go for a walk around the Laguna de Tiscapa—a small crater lake atop a hill in the middle of the city—and that she also walks to and from work.

All of this Carolina tells me as we sit at MEC waiting for the rain to stop and on the way to her house. As we enter her barrio, she greets people left and right. A bus comes around the corner and bears down on us as if possessed, as they tend to. We meet her sister coming down the street with Kessler—they are headed to church and she gives him a few cordobas to donate. First we go to her mom's house. We make our way past the barking dog and barbed wire, hung just low enough to slice my eyeballs if

I don't walk carefully (later I learn that this is a clothesline, the barbs not meant as a security system but rather to keep garments from blowing to the ground), to sit on rocking chairs on the stoop, surrounded by plants; you wouldn't know that across the street is a drug house, and a few feet away a boy sits half-naked in the mud under a streetlight. Carolina's daughter is over at her grandma's and greets us briefly.

Seven years ago Carolina's dad left one last time for the United States. They never heard from him again. Acquaintances report that they've seen him there, but she doesn't believe it. Even after her parents separated, he was always an active father—rare here, she says, once a man starts a new family—and so why would he forget about us now? She believes that he was killed on the train tracks and now lies in a 'common grave for immigrants.' They tried going to the chancellery, showing his photo and asking around, but as people often change their identities to cross over, they didn't pursue it. He went to Pittsburgh twice, both times being deported almost immediately. Carolina would like to go the United States too, but only if she could go legally. With her mom sitting in the third rocking chair, she talks about her plans to leave for Costa Rica, which I had assumed must be a secret. She will be an undocumented migrant there; you go as a tourist, and you stay, she explains. You learn to live in fear, always furtive, and to go out as little as possible, which isn't so hard since you work every day but Sunday. They stop buses and since Costa Ricans look a little different from Nicaraguans, she states, they only check certain passengers' papers. She always avoided problems, somehow. Now they check here too, as more and more South Americans try to come through en route to the United States. In Nicaragua, she says, it's the *chinos* who can't blend in. She will leave for Costa Rica within two months.

From her mother's, we walk to Carolina's house. She recounts how at work she made a pair of size sixty pants on special order from the United States; they could have been a bed sheet for her, she laughs. She shows me around her house, the house she bought. I try to imagine buying this structure. It feels like a large shed because there is a considerable quantity of building materials piled up against the walls, stored until she can afford the next stage. She has already added a bathroom. Partitions provide a living room and two sleeping rooms, one of which has a bunk bed, the other a double bed. Carolina and Kemberlyng and Kessler all sleep in the double, as the children don't like to sleep alone. I think about how different 'alone' seems here, when even if the kids did sleep in their own beds, they'd be just a whisper away from their mom. The living space consists of a couch and two chairs. Carolina cooks at her mother's; it's cheaper to share the cost of food, and nicer to cook and eat together too. My principal impression of the place is the grayness, the unfinished quality. Before walking me home—it turns out the room I am renting is less than a kilometer away—Carolina changes from heels to flip-flops. I in my boots cannot see how women negotiate the muddy, slimy streets in open shoes.

I call Carolina a week later, not really expecting her to be available, but she picks up and informs me that she already quit her job and is planning to leave for Costa Rica on the twentieth of the month. One of her sisters who lives down there is going to help her with the cost of passage—between the passports and the bus she'll spend US$150 to move her little family. She adds that the kids' father has agreed to sign the necessary papers. We arrange to meet in front of the Colegio Cristo Rey, a school near her house, so that I don't enter the barrio alone, and because of the confusing street directions. It's pouring, again, so I wait under a porch where as usual I am told not to go alone where I'm going because there are thieves. Carolina and Gaby walk up and ask if I mind accompanying them on an errand. We walk and walk—how Carolina loves to walk is a favorite subject with her and her family. Where we are going is right back past the house I'm living in to an agency where her sister is to buy a month's worth of powdered milk for her baby, Robert Neil. It turns out they can't give it to her until Monday, but we sit in the waiting room for a while and chat, hoping the rain will cease.

Talk turns to men and family, and both sisters give me a full diatribe on the mechanisms of machismo. And it's not just their words that are feminist. They are both separated, to the disapproval of their mother. They in turn disapprove of her way: she spent twenty years with an abusive husband and after he left her, at thirty-two years old with nine kids, she never had relations with another man. They describe a photograph of her from the time when he left in which she looks likes she's sixty. For this, she is respected in the barrio. She taught her daughters that sex is dirty, that they should be happy if their husbands aren't drug addicts or thieves, and put up with the rest; that one lives for one's husband irrespective of anything. I recall the last time I was at her house, when Carolina was talking about her dad, and her mom brought over a poster-sized picture of him from the wall. Carolina says she wishes her siblings had followed her warnings, looked at her own life as if in the mirror, and not married and not had children young. Gaby adds that in their culture women are "brutitas" (idiots) for having kids, and lots of them, when they really can't provide for them. Carolina says she lost ten years of her life with her ex.

Gaby was just a few months shy of receiving a technical degree that would have placed her two years into a university program. She jokes that she was studying administration, but she administered her own life badly.

Gaby rocks her baby in his stroller while drinking coffee in her mother's living room.

She got pregnant and quit school. Robert Neil is now six months old. Gaby would be approaching her first anniversary of marriage if she weren't divorced. This seems a fact to be congratulated, as her husband was psychologically abusive; upon a threat of physical assault, she ended it. After having seen her father hit her mother, she says, she will never put up with that. As much as the details of their stories, it's their attitudes that are noteworthy. Carolina says Gaby is suffering postpartum depression and that she herself struggled with low self-esteem from the decision to give up on her marriage, but both of them are so vivacious—they give each other a high five every few sentences, in support of any particularly rebellious statement—that I can't see them as anything but successful. Carolina sums up her philosophy with two phrases. One, mentioned above, that the world is for the intrepid, and "Cada quien es dueño de su propio miedo" (Every person owns their own fear). They mention MEC, or El Movimiento as they call it, and I ask if this is where they learned that life does not have to be limited to cooking and cleaning for a man you don't love. MEC supports them, they admit, but they figured it out for themselves first.

Carolina talks. A lot. But she is thoughtful and informed. She recalls instances from her childhood; being hit in the face by a Somoza guard—then on their way out of power—as she, the eldest sibling, tried to keep them from stealing the family TV when they barged in one day while her parents were out. She points out that Gaby is buying this powdered milk (it is not provided by the government), while under the Sandinistas, though there may have been little to buy compared to the diversity of items that enter the Nicaraguan market today, basic necessities were guaranteed. Now they have the goods but they can't afford to buy them. Gaby is wearing a long-sleeved T-shirt from a "Sno-Lodge" somewhere in the States. I ask about it and they laugh and say they sometimes wonder if they're unknowingly wearing a shirt with an offensive slogan in English. I ask about all the people I see wearing second-hand shirts with American flags and patriotic U.S. slogans. Carolina calls them *matamáma* (mother-killer) shirts and says people feel allegiance to the United States because of 'the eighties,' referring to the 1980s and the U.S. support for the *contras*. She describes her ire at seeing on TV a Nicaraguan immigrant to the United States, now a politician there, announcing his pride at sending his son to defend the United States in Iraq. The father had left Nicaragua in the 1980s; to send his son to fight for the Sandinistas would to him have been a disgrace. Carolina asks now, defend the United States from what?

She disparages her compatriots who emigrate and forget where they're from, and sometimes forget their own language. Conversely, she saw the daughter of Cuban immigrants to the United States speaking on TV, and admired how her accent was so Cuban she might have been born there herself. Carolina, however, admits that in Costa Rica she forced herself to drop the *pues* (the adverb 'then' or 'well') that Nicaraguans insert throughout their speech, to use *usted* in place of *vos* (the formal instead of informal 'you'), and to try to stop putting 'the' before people's names or a description of them, as is also common here but viewed as uneducated by some. In Costa Rica, she also learned to turn the lights off. A man she worked for flew into a rage: That's why poor people stay poor; turn the lights off in rooms you're not occupying! Gaby gives me a look and taps her elbow, signifying that Carolina is stingy, but Carolina says she just learned what money is worth. She tells the story of her son losing C$5 (US$0.29) when she sent him to the store. Five cordobas is half an hour of work for her.

After we fail to buy the powdered milk, Gaby wants to buy some regular milk for her son. She asks Carolina if she can borrow money and Carolina pulls out a bill: five U.S. dollars. Strange to see. I was finally going to find out where Nicaraguans get dollars, and why. It's simple. They go to the bank and buy them, because they don't trust their own currency. She lent it to her sister—for my nephew, she said—only if she promised to pay it back in dollars too.

We go back to their mom's house, which their parents built with their own hands over a period of two years, causing her mother to lose the child she was carrying. The house is more solid than a lot of those that I've been in. They have a refrigerator, and Gaby has a fancy crib and modern stroller for her baby. We don't even go to Carolina's house this time; she says the water comes in when it rains—last night, it started dripping on her bed—and she would be embarrassed. We arrive wet and they make coffee and buy white rolls to butter. *Lucha Libre* is on TV, and around the table the conversation wends back to the ever-common topic of emigration to the United States.

Jamileth del Socorro Centeno Reyes (twenty-seven)

Jamileth intimidated and fascinated me, and I would steal glances at her during the workshop where we met. She looked both tough, like the girls who would threaten to beat me up in school, and refreshingly unfussy; skinny, so that her shoulders caved forward, in a miniskirt and T-shirt—reminiscent of a teenager in the 1980s—while the other women there wore tight, low-cut, see-through outfits. There was something harsh about her presence; she came off as someone who could be very mean, but then she introduced herself and when I asked if I could photograph her and her family, she was pleased.

Jamileth and Dora live next door to one another and figure largely in each other's photo albums. She took the whole week off for the three days at MEC, so she had Friday morning free. They instruct me to go to Dora's house and she'll walk me over. When I enter, Jamileth hands me an open bottle of Coke and a packet of cookies. She apologizes, says the Coke was cold at nine when she expected me. Even though I've just eaten two breakfasts—one at home and one served to me by Rosa Emilia upon arrival (hence my lateness)—I eat cookies and sip soda while three empty-handed children stare at me, because this seems like the polite thing to do.

Jamileth at home, with her brother looking through the window.

Their front door is in the back of the house; the other half is occu-pied by Jamileth's brother and his wife and child. Although it was their stepfather who helped to raise them, this place was left to them by their father. Jamileth and her husband and kids are sitting together watching TV. Because their room is tiny, the kids are piled on and around their parents. They all sit on two chairs in the middle of the six-by-six-foot living room; there is the TV on a stand, a table under the window, a stovetop behind them, and to the left a curtain that hides two beds against the far wall. That the five of them live here together bespeaks not only the closeness of their family, but the circumscribed activities of their days.

Jamileth remains an enigma. She receives me warmly and although

I didn't have her pegged as the motherly type, she introduces me to her three children and her husband, Edwin, who is clearly smitten by her; of everyone I photograph, they are one of only a few couples who have stayed married. While Jamileth refers to Edwin by his first name when talking to their kids, thereby distancing herself from the family relationship, Edwin is much more demonstrative and cuddles the kids as we talk. As we peruse her photo album, he comments on how beautiful she is, and when we discuss his tattoos, he raises his eyebrows with appreciation and reveals that Jamileth has one too.

Jamileth was selling raffle tickets and Edwin bought one and fell in love. He explains how at age fourteen he stole Jamileth, "Me la robé." This is a common expression in Nicaragua, and in this case, means that the couple eloped, albeit very young, but returned to the family fold soon after.[28] Jamileth and Edwin were married at fifteen, and at sixteen she gave birth to Roxana. Now there are also Jefferson (six) and Edwin (three). Jamileth, like many women I talk to, gives me a knowing nod and says, "Me operé" (I got an operation), indicating that they've chosen not to have any more children. Jamileth herself is one of six. Her mom lives three blocks away, and all of her siblings live close by. Edwin's family lives four blocks in the other direction. There are nine kids plus his mom, making for a family of ten. One sister passed away last year, and although it was sad, Edwin says, she was retarded and it is good that she is at rest. He doesn't mention his father and I don't ask.

After working in a shoe store, a pizzeria, and as a street vendor of sundry items and sweets, Jamileth is now employed at a *maquila*. She shows me a snapshot of herself at work; she is wearing a smock and stands behind a pile of what looks like the front panel of jeans legs. Her job is to attach the size label. She works Table #11 (there are fifteen total), which produces about three thousand pieces a day. She says the *maquila* produces ten thousand pairs of pants per day. She earns about C$1,350 (US$79) per month, depending on her production level. She could make up to half of that again if she accepted overtime, but she won't because of the kids. She works 7:00 a.m. to 5:00 p.m., and sometimes five to seven, Monday to Friday, and half days on Saturdays. She says *maquila* work is hard, especially for what you earn. She would prefer to work for herself, doing raffles, selling perfumes and clothes. I ask if being a vender isn't tiresome too, and she says no because you set your own hours.

A year ago, Jamileth spent two months in Costa Rica where her father's side of the family lives. She sold pillows. Despite the fact that in the news these last few days Costa Rica has provoked Nicaragua by sending armed troops down the ever-contested San Juan River that is their border, and

Above: Roxana sits just inside the door to their house.
Below: Edwin displays tattoo art for the camera.

is now supposedly taking Nicaragua to the International Court at The Hague, Jamileth and Edwin speak highly of Costa Rica. It's more orderly there, they explain; the bus drivers wear seat belts and uniforms and wait for you to sit down before moving forward.

Edwin washes cars at the Mercado Central Roberto Huembes. It is one of the larger markets in the city, part indoor and part outdoor, where people buy their food, tourists buy *artesanía*, and everyone goes to catch buses out of town. Although they thus have two incomes, supporting three children is a stretch on what they earn. Jamileth tells about when some gringos bought one of her dad's paintings—he sells them in the *artesanía* section in Huembes—and upon noticing that the women he portrays look exactly like Jamileth, and her being sixteen years old and very pregnant at the time, they presented her with everything she would need for her first baby, including the expensive kind of diapers, she added. And for a while, the kids had some godparents in Canada; pen pals through the church who would send boxes of school supplies and candy. Just before noon Roxana and Jefferson leave for school; they attend the afternoon shift. Usually Jamileth's mom or sister watches them in the mornings. Jamileth herself finished high school. A couple of times she mentions how she would like to learn English, but can't afford the classes. On Sundays she attends a computer class given at the Huembes market.

In addition to the ubiquitous photo album, oversized family portraits hang on the cardboard walls. There is a poster of Christ in the center and when I ask about it, Jamileth replies that it's just an "adorno," for decoration. They are not religious and don't go to church, they answer, although various mentions are made of church activities. Trying to keep me entertained, Edwin brings in his doves. Between him and his brother-in-law, they have four. They too are "adornos." He sets them on the table and admires them, commenting on their habits and appreciating their cooing. There is something strangely innocent about him, and I wonder about that in relation to the something dangerous and hard that I sense in Jamileth.

I notice a woman in the backyard doing dishes or laundry. It is her sister-in-law. The bathroom and wash sink are out back, along with her brother's kitchen. From what I've seen, outdoor kitchens and cooking over wood is more common than buying a tank of gas and cooking inside, as Jamileth and Edwin do. She explains that she can't afford to construct an outdoor kitchen, not to mention that one then has to build the fire and be at the mercy of the rain. The tank of gas costs C$160 (US$9.41) and lasts for three months. Edwin adds that Roxana will ask who cooked, and if it's her dad she'll ask for seconds.

Edwin's doves.

I visit for a second time a week later, on a Saturday after Jamileth has returned from her half day of work. It's pouring and has been for hours, as it tends to during the rainy season in Managua. When I arrive she is eating soup and watching TV, surrounded by kids—her three and a young brother of hers. She quickly puts her food away and offers me her chair. She sends her daughter out with a huge yellow-and-white umbrella—a new and happy thing in the company of old and dingy things—to buy me a soda and two kinds of cookies, so that I can try both. She won't let me pay, of course, and says that she doesn't like for me to spend my money, as I'm studying and she has been blessed to have work. "Donde hay niños hay bendición" (Where there are children, there is blessing), she explains. By way

Jamileth and her youngest son, Edwin (junior).

of example, she describes a four-month period when she and Edwin were separated—the longest they've ever fought—and simultaneously she was out of work. 'Alone with three kids, and I ate well,' she relates with wonder. Between friends and family, they were fine; her aunt next door would always feed them, as would an uncle who lives there—she indicates a lean-to in the yard that I hadn't even noticed—and would give her money.

Edwin is at work and so we talk more intimately. We talk about being alone. Rosa Emilia, for instance, has been for twenty-six years, Jamileth confides. Inspired by my conversation with Carolina and Gaby, I state that women no longer need believe that having been with a man or becoming a mother means that they are undesirable, nor that they must remain loyal to his memory to be virtuous. But Jamileth points out that only one in a thousand men is a good man: If you have kids from a previous marriage a new husband will most likely hit them, or worse. Better to remain alone. She says she and her husband rarely fight anymore.

Where I am sitting I catch a few drops of rain. I look up—there are two perfectly round holes in the corrugated metal, referred to here as zinc, common roofing material in Nicaragua. A bowl on the floor by the TV catches a more serious drip. I only stay a couple of hours, as it becomes clear that nothing is going to happen this afternoon except TV watching. They have cable and flip between a U.S. movie and an old Mexican one. The picture is heavily tinted green. Roxana gets sent out at least twice more, again to the *pulpería* (a neighborhood general store, usually established in the entryway of a private home), for toilet paper, and to Rosa Emilia for tortillas and beans when Edwin gets home. She doesn't seem to mind, even when she has to go back to clarify why she only got three pesos change. Edwin went to work this morning too, although with the rain he gets little business. Silent, aloof Jamileth caresses her husband's back and head as he eats and watches TV. I get ready to leave and ask how they will spend the rest of their afternoon. Jamileth says her Saturdays after work consist of doing nothing, just sleeping.

Roxana.

Gabriela Sunsín Jaime (twenty-one)

Like Darling, Gabriela spends her free time working. If this is a story about the *maquilas*, it is equally about the informal market, and their combined effect on people's lives.[29] Like Darling's mom, Gabriela's puts out a *fritanga*. In fact, Gabriela instructs me to find her by asking for her mom, Salvadora; everyone on their block knows her because they've been in business for years.

In this house live five of seven siblings (four girls and three boys, not counting the two who died; one as a child when a wall fell on him, the other a miscarriage). One sister lives next door and one brother lives separately with his own family. In this house also live the three children of two of Gabriela's sisters, who are separated from the fathers, as well as

Gabriela starts the cook fire.

Gabriela's mother and father (her siblings have different fathers; Fátima's passed away and Erika's is the only other one living). The house is constructed as one large room; the bedrooms partitioned off with cardboard or cement block, the center room nearly empty of furniture save the requisite full-length gilt mirror. There is a separate bedroom out back, where her dad naps and watches TV. In the room where Gabriela sleeps, there are two beds end-to-end, one for her and one for Erika and her three-year-old daughter, Adriana. We spend most of the day in the back patio, where a countertop and the cook fire form an L on a raised corner that is the kitchen. Barbed-wire clotheslines stretch the length of the patio, and the sinks and toilet stalls stand to the far side. In the evening, when we move to the front of the house to sell the food, I am struck by what a pleasant, finished space the porch is; painted pink with flowery white iron security bars, two rocking chairs wait to be occupied.

I think Gabriela dressed up for my visit; she's wearing a low-cut tank top and high heels, while her sister's in a skirt with a broken zipper and everyone has on rubber flip-flops. At the end of the day she finally replaces her shoes. At five o'clock however, when the bustle to get out the *fritanga* involves the entire household, the women disappear one at a time to change. Salvadora wears a red tank top, nicer but still with a rip down the side. Throughout the day Gabriela forgets to be proper for the camera, rolling her shirt above her belly to cool off—many Nicaraguans have this habit—as they are constantly fanning the fire. Salvadora reminds her to pull it down, tells Erika not to swear in front of me, and the three of them murmur just out of my earshot; money worries it seems, something the girls are tired of talking about but that their mom won't let go.

Gabriela says their mornings usually consist of washing down the patio from yesterday's food preparation (the patio is cement, unlike the mud I grew accustomed to at Darling's), washing clothes, and watching TV. Except for her mom. Salvadora gets up at four to make breakfast for those siblings who leave for work, she goes to the market to be back by nine, cooks until five, and sells until ten. From noon on, you can find us here, says Gabriela. The women cooking don't eat all afternoon, though there are periodic Coke runs. When Gabriela asks if this project will be on TV and I reply that I hope to publish a book, she comes back with, 'Here we hope for *gaseosa*.' Soda is anticipated and enjoyed with guilty pleasure by all.

While she is cooking, Gabriela's cell phone rings; it's a friend from her old work, she says happily, 'who always thinks of me.' This morning it's just she and I and Radio Güegüense playing in the background, until

Gabriela and her mom, Salvadora, prepare the fritanga.

her mom and brother return from the market. Tired. You know how the market is, Gabriela says, you get jostled around a lot. I had assumed only an outsider would experience exhaustion from moving among so many people each on their private errands. As the day wears on, she repeatedly uses the word *rendida*—completely drained—to describe how they feel. Upon dumping the bags of purchases, Gabriela's brother sits down in front of the TV and I realize that he's quietly peeling all of the green bananas (to be sliced and deep fried for *tajada*) and then prepping the cabbage for salad. I ask if he has a job and Gabriela informs me that he's a *comerciante*, or merchant; he sells CDs in the market. His body, like so many I notice in Managua, seems misshapen, twisted by manual labor and poverty. Her dad then appears briefly at his doorway in the back, and Gabriela silently takes him a bowl of food. I ask if he works too— no, he's retired. (Although Salvadora declares, 'You have to work every day; if you eat and don't make money, that leaves you at zero.') Later Gabriela's father does come out and clean some beans to be set for boiling, though not without scolding about some dirty dishes. The women ignore this, as they are powering to get everything done in time for the dinner customers.

Initially, I think about Dora and Darling, and how their families are not representative of those of all *maquila* workers; they seem a little less ground down and exhibit a little more humor and *cariño*, warmth. This family is rougher. But by the end of the day, and especially once the cooking is done and Salvadora sits down for a few minutes to rest her swollen feet and eat some *arroz aguado* (a plate of soupy rice that excites anyone given the option to eat it), her smile becomes a kind and beautiful arrangement of laugh lines and she has time to call her grandchildren over and hug them when they cry and get in trouble. The family jokes with each other, pretending to each contribute until they have enough for a two-liter bottle of Coke, and they repeat that they are the "loca familia Jaime" (crazy Jaime family), proving above all their solidarity.

Gabriela and Salvadora.

Gabriela worked for the same company as Carolina, but while Carolina personifies MEC's motto of "Trabajo sí . . . pero con dignidad" (Jobs yes . . . but with dignity), Gabriela just quit yesterday because she was tired of putting up with the bosses; bored with them yelling orders when she already knew what she was supposed to be doing and was doing it, she protests. She was an inspector there for nine months, working from 7:00 a.m. to 6:00 p.m. Before that she worked a full year out by the airport, which means, she explains, for the *chinos*, which means a more tiresome workday; 7:00 a.m. to 9:00 p.m., except on Fridays when you leave early, at seven o'clock, plus weekends when you finish at five. She would have stayed on with the *chinos* because the money was good (C$5,000, or US$294, per month), but they fired her after she missed two days for being sick, although they had been generous with leave previous to that. When she was working that job she got skinny and her mom didn't like it. She had been getting sick a lot and Salvadora urged her to quit the *maquila*. In a week she'll get another job, she says, although she hopes to find employment outside of the *zona*; she'd like to be a buyer for a store. Before she started working in the *zona*, Gabriela was in school, but it wasn't economically feasible for her to continue on to college. She has completed all of the MEC seminars (health, self-esteem, economic advancement, labor rights, mediation, etc.) and will now be raised to *promotora*. She is then eligible (because she has a high school diploma) to receive a university scholarship, all expenses paid to attend class every Saturday for eight months. Then she could get a job at a bank, Gabriela says.

When Fátima arrives from an outing with the three kids (her two boys and Adriana), her mom and sister introduce her as the one who's worked in the *zona* for seven years. And they had warned me about the kids, complaining that they are hyper, always talking and underfoot, and home by noon even on school days. Fátima doesn't help with the cooking at all; I don't know whether this is in acknowledgement of her work at the *maquila* or because she's not a good cook. In the evening though, she does help sell. All three sisters who I meet have worked in the *maquilas*. Erika put in a couple of years, but quit long-term after Adriana was born, as she would cry incessantly when her mom was gone so late. Erika used the same term as Gabriela to describe the problem with the work; "Me aburrí," I got bored of it, always tired, with dark bags under my eyes. Last Monday she almost went to apply in the *zona*, but her mom dissuaded her.

Fátima works Monday through Friday, and sometimes takes extra hours (paid double), sometimes not. She tries to explain to me about her work, though the terms she uses have different meanings for me: After four years at one job you can indemnify yourself, which means formally requesting to be liquidated with three months' pay. Now another three years has gone by—she's been at the same company the whole time—and again she will indemnify herself. Last time they gave her the money and eight free days, but this time she doubts they'll give her the time off, probably just the money. If she can stand to stay, she says, she'll do the same in another three years. For seven years Fátima has sewn pant hems. They pay more the bigger the hem, as the half-inch ones are supposedly easier. You don't get to choose, it's just whatever comes down the line.

I ask Gabriela what she thinks of her own future and that of her country. She answers generally about hoping that things will get better, that they will see less of the tragedy they've experienced in the past, but that the kind of government they've got doesn't help much. I ask more specifically about the *maquilas*, and despite her comments earlier about how wearisome the work is, she says, 'I think it's good.' The majority of Nicaraguans depend on it, and more people are employed there than any other kind of work, she believes. If it were not for the *maquilas*, people would depend on nothing, Gabriela concludes. But the hard work and low pay, I counter, and she agrees, with a different sentiment than the one she started off with: 'One loses hope that things will change.' She unplugs the radio and plugs in the blender. Only then do I notice the TV noise underlying the radio; her brother is inside watching baseball in English. All the while that we talk, she is quickly moving from task to task. Everyone knows exactly which duties are theirs; they do not vary from day to day.

After the cooking is done I follow Gabriela into her room where she irons a fresh shirt for the social activity of tending to customers, and she shows me a picture of her boyfriend; a tinier-than-wallet-size photo. Adriana gets hold of it and smears cake on it by accident; when Gabriela wipes it off, the ink comes up too. I can tell that if I weren't there, Gabriela would have shown how upset she was, but as it is, she just tells Erika what happened. Gabriela and her boyfriend work for the same company. As she's telling me this and trying to get her clothes ready for the evening, after she's successfully kicked Adriana out, the little boys keep piling back in through a hole in the cardboard door. Lack of privacy is a constant.

When it's time to sell food, the neighbor lady comes over—Fátima says she helps out every evening—and asks me what I am studying. Socioeconomics? Domestic violence? I explain that my project is related to CAFTA. She becomes confrontational and describes how she gathered signatures against it, that as women they decided it will not benefit them; wages are so low already, why bring more work like that? Watching the street traffic go by, Gabriela is reminded of the gringos who walk by periodically, wearing ties, 'Mormons, we call them.' She's never talked to

Fátima on the front porch.

them, just seen them. Gabriela says she hasn't been to church in a while, but theirs is *evangelista*, called Ríos de Agua Viva. It turns out she lives three blocks from Dora and Darling, in Reparto 'Chick,' as she wrote it when she gave me her address. Just as happened one afternoon at Darling's, all of a sudden the kids are gathered and the pets are called in; gangs of boys can be heard fighting in the distance. Gabriela says if they have their *fritanga* outside when it happens, they take that in too. It's this barrio versus that one, she says gesturing with her chin.

Two Saturdays later, I arrive just as Salvadora is leaving for the Mercado Oriental with her son. Usually she goes every day, but Gabriela reports that they haven't been making food much this week, as her mom's been sick:

swollen feet again. Everyone hugs and kisses me and says they thought I wasn't coming back. I'm starting to sense jealousy from the different women I'm photographing; they ask me how many times I've gone to see the others, they ask when I am coming back. Quite opposite of academe's worries that I'd be prying, I think for them it is delicious to receive this personal attention, to have someone ask and care what their life is like.

Somehow I feel the poverty more this visit. As good as this family is to me—first sending one of the kids out for a Coke and piece of cake, then making me coffee, offering to buy me an ice cream, dragging a rocking chair from room to room so I can sit down wherever we are, always smiling, always welcoming—there is also an underlying harshness to their behavior, interactions, bodies, and home. Underneath the public face I feel the ugliness of their lives. Gabriela is not going to look for work until January now. Between washing and cleaning and cooking every afternoon, she is busy; although if they haven't been doing the *fritanga*, I wonder how she's been spending her time. The whole family gets by on two salaries. Some of them are out this morning picking out a new television set. There are two in the house already, but they are small. A new TV costs at least C$3,000 (US$176).

I ask Gabriela if she prefers cooking or *maquila* work. 'I prefer [to go out and] work because it's more tiresome here.' The smoke is one reason she says this. As we talk and Gabriela cooks, I am constantly sidestepping billows of it. Ashes float in the air. The walls are covered in thick black slime. When I wake up the next morning, my hair smells intensely of smoke. To start the fire, she arranges wood and plastic bags on a little pile of ashes from breakfast preparations and pours gas on it. High flames jump up immediately. Darling had commented that her family doesn't do this because the food retains the taste of gas, but here they continuously feed the fire with it, poured from an old soda bottle. The cooking oil also arrives in a reused cola bottle. Her dad returns from his errand to the "mini-super." He unloads rice, sugar, oil, and a few other items that are cheaper there than at the open-air market, and makes a beeline from the taxi to his back room. Later I hear him yelling and I ask Gabriela what's happening. She explains that he's yelling at the TV, playing with Fátima's youngest, Kevin, as they watch *Lucha Libre*. She calls him "mi papi," with tenderness and respect.

Oscar, Fátima's seven-year-old son, is serious and considerate. But Kevin, five, doesn't know when to stop, and throws himself about with unchecked force. 'He watches *Lucha Libre* a lot' was one explanation, and, 'We want to take him to a psychologist.' They can't control him. Meanwhile, Adriana is sullen and mischievous. At one point she pulls her

Oscar.

mom's pants down in front of me. Everyone laughs, although she is told firmly not to do it again. The kids rule the environment. Gabriela's sister who lives next door has five kids, from three years old to adolescence. The oldest stops by with a one-month-old baby who belongs to one of her sisters; now Salvadora is a great-grandmother.

Gabriela mops the cement patio. She has two bags of neon-green liquid, to make it 'smell nice.' She has me sniff the laundry detergent as well, which exudes equally intense chemicals, and asks if it doesn't smell good. She said last night it was raining so hard they had to get up in the middle of the night to deal with water coming into the bedrooms. As Gabriela clears a space to iron Kevin's T-shirt, she blurts, 'Thank God I know how to do all of this; clean, iron, cook. . . . But I don't know how to be a good girlfriend.' She reveals that she has been in a fight with her boyfriend for a week now. 'I put up with too much,' she explains. I ask if she wants to get back together with him, and receive a conflicting answer. "Cómo no" (of course), she says, but she continues, 'We fight all the time, and it's boring.'

I say I'll come back, but I'm not sure I'll be in Managua long enough to fit in another visit. I ask if she has e-mail, and she says no, that's difficult here. When I see Darling a few months later, she mentions that Gabriela is pregnant.

Conclusion

One aspect of globalization is the linkage it creates between people who remain distant from each other geographically. We in the United States buy, take home, and put on garments cut and sewn by Nicaraguan *maquila* workers. We wear their working conditions on our bodies. They breathe the fibers of the fabric into theirs. Is this low-wage, dead-end factory work or a sustaining, liberating job? The lives of the women I met in Managua don't answer that question easily. The women's narratives sketch impressions not only of the work that produces those T-shirts that we buy at a markup (T-shirts that often return to the developing world to be sold secondhand and in bulk), but also of the context created by it: the daily customs and personalities that emerge, the home life, the coming-of-age, the third shift in the informal market.

Although many of the workers seemed ambivalent about the prospect of CAFTA, of all the industries portrayed in this book, the free trade zones will probably be most directly affected by the agreement. The continued presence of the *zonas francas* in Nicaragua, however, depends on the global labor market. *Maquilas* can disappear overnight—the equipment is not difficult to transport—if wages become lower across the ocean. Emilio Noguera, the labor consultant at the CZF, said, 'We do not want the *maquilas* to represent hope'; still, they are seen by many as a stepping stone, both nationally and for individuals, toward better jobs. For now, and for many, these jobs are the most stable option, though they do not come with any promises.

San Lucas. Adrian milking.

TWO

Cattle

Introduction

MATIGUÁS IS IN THE PRECISE CENTER OF NICARAGUA, IN THE STATE of Matagalpa. Coffee-growing mountains lie to the north, cowboy flat-lands to the south. It is the interior of a small country in which the Pacific and Atlantic coasts predominate in the national consciousness. Matiguás is known for its dairy and beef. Three-quarters of homes there are rural, half again more than the average in Central America.[1] Yet agriculture employs at least one-third of Nicaragua's economically active population[2] and accounts for about one-quarter of its gross domestic product. Farm commodities represent 50–70 percent of Nicaragua's total exports (over 60 percent of that amount is coffee).[3] During the 1980s, land redistribution was a significant aspect of the Sandinistas' agenda,[4] with the dual goals of economic development for Nicaragua and a more equitable division of resources, which they hoped would create a society where socialism would be possible.[5] Now, fifteen years after the dismantling of that framework, large landholders are regaining the territory that they believe was redistrib-uted unfairly. 'For the farming sector in the municipality of Matiguás, the nineties have been a decade of slow and unequal economic reactivation, after nearly ten years of conflict.'[6]

I went to Matiguás because the cattle industry provides important export commodities for Nicaragua and is specifically addressed in CAFTA. The globalization that I found there was latent. It was an Eden in some ways: beautiful countryside whose inhabitants are healthier and safer than in other areas I visited. Yet the global market has a strong presence, felt if not always understood, and global culture is a constant current through life. The means of production and therefore class structure here have been

All of the photographs in this chapter were made in the municipality of Matiguás.   73 determined by foreign companies and market trends for many, many years. And now, most families include members who have emigrated or those who long to go (and who represent a potential export market). The farmers know that it is a simpler kind of cheese and a lower grade of beef consumed here than exported, and they know that they sell their milk to the same company from which they then buy processed dairy products. They know that they have to meet certain sanitation requirements to sell to this company. They know that in other countries their industry would be subsidized but that here they are on their own. And they have high hopes for what this new opportunity will bring.

"Ganaderos van a ser ganadores del CAFTA" (Cattlemen will be winners with CAFTA), predicts Miguel Alemán Robleto,[7] an investigator at Nitlapán (a research and development institute at UCA). He suggested that I photograph in Matiguás, an area where most everyone is a dairy farmer. Nicaragua negotiated well for beef and dairy, assuring that industry a decade and a half to ease into CAFTA, Miguel explains. Livestock is a growing business. In 2002–3 beef and cheese exports increased by around 10 percent, contributing US$20.5 million in that year and thirty million in 2004.[8] Miguel introduced me to the manager of the local branch of the Fondo de Desarollo Local (Local Development Fund, or FDL), a nonprofit loan institution for farmers that is also affiliated with UCA. Through the FDL, I met families to photograph in Matiguás, staying with each one for four days. As is illustrated in the table on page 78, these families were medium and large producers, which allowed me also to interview their hired workers, representatives of the rural proletariat.[9] Subsistence farmers are not represented in this project.

Ever since Spanish colonizers settled in the region in the mid-1800s, foreign influence and cattle raising have held sway in Matiguás.[10] In the early 1900s, the rubber and precious wood were exploited, bringing migrants— and North American companies—to the region and establishing means of transportation. In 1928 the municipality of Matiguás was created and simultaneously the North Americans introduced the businesses of coffee and cattle. Large haciendas were the principal local authority, monopolizing indigenous lands. The cattle industry expanded in the 1940s, when the demand for beef in the United States spiked after World War II.[11] At that time, original hacienda owners were displaced by more modern producers. In the late 1950s, Nicaragua gained facilities allowing for the export of frozen beef to the United States.[12] In this and the following decades, U.S. demand for beef continued to swell, due in large part to the popularity of the new fast-food burger chains. Subsistence farmers were displaced, and as ranching requires fewer hands per acre than other large-scale agricultural industries, it does not provide enough jobs to support the rural proletariat that it creates. Again in the 1970s, the industry was boosted; the companies Prolacsa and Nestle established a plant in Matagalpa to produce powdered milk for the Central American market and invested in the infrastructure of the region (in order to sell liquid milk, a farmer must have proximity to a road). 'The more comfortable *campesinos* and those located on the principal routes of the *acopiadores*, [at this time] are benefited and achieve security.'[13]

Those not benefited by these processes—due to land too low-lying to grow coffee and too isolated to sell milk—became wageworkers and later the Sandinista support base. This uneven regional development plus the worldwide recessions of the 1970s led the government to establish a system of loans and technical assistance to promote the export of beef. It was an attempt to prevent social unrest, but it was not enough. "By 1978 Central America's herd of ten million provided the United States with 250 million pounds of beef a year, representing 15 percent of U.S. beef imports."[14] What did occur during this escalation of the industry, according to author Robert Williams, was "qualitative change in every phase of beef production,"[15] bringing it up to international standards. Over time, the United States changed the nature of the industry in Central America, with the fast-food restaurants creating a market for cheap beef while U.S. cattle ranchers simultaneously demanded quotas on imports. "Usually, a U.S. government agency or international development bank in Washington provided a grant or low-interest loan to a Central American government agency or development bank, which, in turn, would be responsible for administering the grant or loan."[16] Modernizing changes benefited large holders; *campesinos* with small herds were not able to compete.

Robert Williams also notes that rapid changes in the Matiguás region led to early peasant support for the FSLN. The 1963 census listed the municipality as growing the most beans in all of Nicaragua, as well as having the most cattle. The following decade saw a boom in the international beef market, and the farmland devoted to pastures increased from 39 percent to 94 percent, meaning *campesinos* were losing their crops.[17] In the early 1980s, with the triumph of the Sandinistas, co-ops were established and some agrarian reform took place, but by the middle of that decade, enough citizens were in disagreement with the policies that a counterinsurgency gained strength. Farms were abandoned as people fled or joined the armed forces. The infrastructure of the region was all but destroyed—roads gone and companies unable to function.

In 1990 the Sandinistas were voted out and land ownership was again reorganized. Property titles that had never been legalized were contested on various fronts. Many land grant beneficiaries never achieved solvency as independent producers and sold their land back to the *finqueros* (large landowners).[18] Jack Spence contributes an alternate scenario to this complex history: "[L]and invasions began immediately. The invaders were ex *contra*, or gangs organized by confiscated former owners."[19] The new government reduced technical and financial support, leaving a hole that would slowly be filled by nongovernmental organizations (NGOs). Then in the late 1990s, El Salvadoran cheese factories established themselves in Matiguás and improved the price paid for milk. Infrastructure in general and conflicts over land began to heal.

In Matiguás, just 10 percent of homes have potable water, 20 percent have electricity (just 12 percent in rural areas), and fewer than 40 percent have latrines. There is one doctor for every five thousand inhabitants.[20] And yet there are more *finqueros* in this region than other agricultural areas of Nicaragua. Orlando Valverde of FENACOOP compares it, for example, to the Masaya region, where he says there are more small farmers, who live at subsistence level on about five *manzanas* each (one *manzana* is about one and three-quarters acres). He criticizes the inhabitants of La Patriota, a small town in the Matiguás region, for practicing monoculture. He says they received money from the government to establish dairy production, and due to that aid have become successful in it.[21] Orlando also warned me that people in the countryside might tell me that they support CAFTA, but in fact they do not understand the issues. The researcher Laura Enríquez similarly posits an apparent discrepancy between personal economic benefit and political choices in the same population. Writing on why *campesinos* would have voted out the Sandinistas in 1990, she found that variances in individuals' experiences created subgroups within the population, which in turn affected voting,[22] thereby prohibiting assumptions regarding the relationship of social station to political behavior. What I found was not only support for CAFTA, but diehard dedication to the Liberal Party that traces back to the war experience: I did not meet one person in this region loyal to the Sandinista party.

INTERVIEW WITH FONDO DE DESAROLLO LOCAL

FDL has been in this town for eleven years now and has eighteen employees, Oscar Antonio Peña Soza recites proudly. Just strolling through town, I'd noticed storefronts for numerous small lenders, and Oscar, a loan officer at FDL, confirms that in the last two years many have sprung up. Most, however, are more interested in commerce than agriculture, which he deems a riskier proposition. His opinion is that easy credit has complicated townspeople's lives; they take out one loan to pay another, never truly owning anything, never actually earning a living. The region and the industry are undergoing a change right now, Oscar says; every year more milk, more beef, and more crops are produced thanks to supervision of the cattle by the *acopiadores* (companies that receive milk from many farms), while increased technical assistance from the outside ensures, for instance, that cattle have salt and minerals year-round and hay in the summer, the dry season in Central America. Still, many farmers do not feel competent to face the changes CAFTA may require. Oscar relates their worries: Some say CAFTA is too demanding in terms of the quality they will have to produce to compete. And while agriculture is subsidized in other countries, which insures producers there some income, here we depend on the rain, they say, so how will we export enough? Some producers I spoke with worry that strict United States hygiene rules, already enforced in Nicaragua's slaughterhouses, might be applied to the countryside, making their work more difficult. However, they also hope that CAFTA will raise the price paid for products exported to the United States.

An article unencouragingly entitled 'Nicaragua has a long way to go in terms of quality' nonetheless highlights a small but important niche market: migrants. Farmers here send *platano* products, *yuca*, and other crops to homesick Central Americans in the United States. Cheese could be another one of these commodities.[23] The region's *queseras* are usually

San Rafael. Pablo Damian milking in the corral.

SOCIAL DIVISIONS AND DESCRIPTIONS
OF AGRICULTURAL PRODUCERS IN MATIGÚAS

Social sector	Stories	Characteristics	Proportion of total population	Control over land
Campesinos without land[1]	Fanni and Francisco/ Jovania and Juan	Source of income: wages. Either live on boss's property or own a very small plot that does not provide enough to live on.	40%	0%
Subsistence *campesinos*[2]	none	Only labor is familial. Produce just enough to live on. Own 1–30 *manzanas* (*mzas*).	30%	15%
Campesinos-finqueros[3]	Adrian	Produce in excess of subsistence level. 15–100 *mzas*. 6–12 cows/10–30 total herd.	20%	25%
Finqueros[4]	Pablo Damian (bottom end)/ Don Ramón[5] (top end)	Family lives on *finca*, but 1–3 hired workers required too. 100–400 *mzas*. 40–50 cows/at least 100 total herd.	7%	20%
Agrarian enterprise[6]	Don Lucas	Does not live on *finca*. 100–1,000 *mzas*. At least 100 cows/200 total herd. Often all labor done by hired workers.	3%	40%

Table adapted for this study from page 30 and subsequent definitions in chapter 2 of *Municipio de Matiguás: Potencialidades y limitantes del desarrollo agropecuario* by Levard, Marín, and Navarro. Reprinted by permission of Nitlapan at UCA in Managua. Information was gathered in the second half of the 1990s.

1. Either descendants of peons from haciendas, people who have lost their lands, or beneficiaries of the agrarian reform who were not able to establish themselves and sold their land to return to the rural proletariat.
2. This group is made up mostly of peasants who own land thanks to the agrarian reform and other transformation in ownership during the 1980s and 1990s. It consists of two different subgroups: *campesinos* with a small piece of land, which

they work intensively (10% of total population), and *campesinos* with more land who do not have the capital to work it to its maximum benefit (20% of total population).

3. This group also includes two subgroups, the first focusing on agriculture and cattle, the second more specifically on cattle. The first is similar to the second set above, but has the means to work the land more profitably. Its members represent only 5% of the total population and are often descendants of a long line of *campesinos*. The other 15% owns a little more land, usually inherited from larger landholding parents but sometimes beneficiaries of agrarian reform. This second group focuses on cattle and grows only what is needed for the family.

4. Also mostly landowners for generations, they tend to have either much land in inaccessible but wet mountainous areas or less land along the road. The family is ensured a decent quality of life and the possibility to further invest.

5. Unlike the rest, don Ramón and Douglas are not principally dairy farmers; in terms of capital they may exceed this category.

6. Contains three levels: first, those who come from oligarchic families; second, families who made their money as merchants and invested in land; third, people involved in politics who bought land cheap during land redistribution.

---

cottage industries, often consisting of a lone individual who lives too far afield to sell fresh milk and so makes *cuajada* (farm cheese), which they transport to town once a week. In Matiguás there are also larger cheese factories that export mostly to El Salvador, but to the United States as well, according to Oscar. They don't try to sell the same type of cheese domestically as that exported to the United States; it's too expensive for the local population. It is packaged here and trucked away. One of the largest milk buyers in the region is Parmalat, an Italian company. It pays more than the *queseras* (C$130–140, or US$7.64–8.24 per forty-liter milk can, called a *pichinga*), but its sanitation standards are higher as well. Producers with fewer resources therefore must sell to the cheese makers; indeed many choose to, as the *quesera* not only gives them the whey after making the cheese, which allows a farmer to raise pigs, but will give them an advance sum, to be deducted from subsequent payments throughout the month. Some producers sell to both Parmalat and a *quesera* to assure that in times of high yield, they will still be able to unload their product.

In the winter, when there is plenty of grass for the cows to eat, production goes up and prices go down. Oscar calls this season the "golpe de leche," or milk slam. He takes me to one *acopiador* in Matiguás that serves as a middleman between the producers and Parmalat; it receives on average sixty-five hundred liters of milk per day here, plus four thousand in the town of Paiwas, and four thousand more in Muy Muy. This milk is for domestic consumption, not export; Oscar half jokes that the farmers sell their product to Parmalat, it is shipped to Managua and processed, and then it is sold back to them as *crema*, cheese, powdered milk, and other dairy products. For one *pichinga* of Grade A milk, Parmalat pays the farmer C$160 (US$9.41), or four cordobas per liter. Grade B (higher in impurities and acidity) is worth C$145 (US$8.53), and Grade C yields C$120 (US$7.06). Dairy farmers would prefer to deal directly with Parmalat, but there is always at least one middleman; more than one local has made a fortune running an *acopiador*. It is for this reason that thirty producers in La Patriota set up their own *acopiador*. With it they hope to maintain a stable price for milk. They have a generator in case of power outages and have borrowed huge tanks for the milk, for which they supply the maintenance and which they can purchase at a devalued price after ten years. They truck the milk to the city of Jinotega, and sell it to a middleman there, who sells it to Parmalat.

San Lucas

OCTOBER 19–22

I tumble off the bus in the town of Matiguás, dusty and smaller than I'd expected, which becomes apparent when I hire a taxi to the FDL office and it's just a few blocks from the market. Although I am clearly not a customer—in the waiting room sit local agriculturalists—the manager receives me and quickly passes me on to Oscar. It is not until months later that I will understand that Oscar made my stay in this area the smoothest segment of the project, arranging my visits with three thoughtfully considered cattle-raising families. He shows me the way to the hostel Hospedaje Dulce Sueño, where the bank manager lives during the week. I am due back at the bank tomorrow by 7:00 a.m., so I while away the afternoon wandering the streets of this tiny town. As I sit on the plaza at dusk, drinking orange soda from a heavy glass bottle, a man approaches and introduces himself in English. He lived in California for fourteen years and has returned to his hometown to spend time with his elderly parents. He tells me where his house is, in case I have any trouble. I am charmed by the plaza—even though the cathedral is modern and plain, and in the center of the square is a hulking cement structure—because of the role it plays in the life of a town. I am charmed by the children who approach me giggling, thrilled to exchange hellos instead of crazy on glue fumes. I am charmed by everything that is not Managua.

The next morning I climb into the back of FDL's pickup truck, with Oscar and a driver up front, and ride the few blocks to the home of don Lucas, the first client they've chosen to place me with. It's not yet seven, but he's already gone out. The woman who comes to the door tells us he's at the market; we take off but don't find him so return and sit in the truck until she invites us to wait inside. Two of his daughters, both in

San Lucas. Fanni in the kitchen doorway.

their twenties, run across the street to buy a two-liter Coke, which they serve to us in small glasses with ice. The driver goes out two more times to look for don Lucas, the second time with luck. I don't know how the project was proposed, but don Lucas enters the house, goes into his room for a backpack, and we're off. He will spend the night at his *finca* (ranch or farm), and I will stay for three. During the ride to the *finca*, Oscar explains that don Lucas is a longtime FDL client who has made smart investments with his loans, such as the *sala de ordeño* that he has recently built (literally translated as 'milking room,' this is a more sanitary environment in which to milk the cows, with a cement floor and facilities for scrubbing down). Oscar lists don Lucas's properties: the *finca*, comprising about five hundred *manzanas*; his home in Matiguás; and a house in the village of La Patriota (the largest town in Muy Muy Viejo, the zone where don Lucas's *finca* is).

Don Lucas is the wealthiest of the *finqueros* that I visit: 'quite comfortable' as Oscar puts it. But he also explains that don Lucas is a modest person who could buy luxury items and does not. Miguel at Nitlapán had said that the *finqueros* in this region are "menos ricos y menos vinculados con el poder nacional que los en la costa" (not as wealthy as the wealthy of the Pacific coast and less connected to national politics). This may explain the bare-bones living on the farms of this comparatively affluent sector. Oscar says that before the 1990s there were few houses in La Patriota, but the *finqueros* made small landholders cash offers that they couldn't refuse and now it is a prosperous village populated by the families of large landholders. He notes that the present inhabitants of Muy Muy Viejo have put their FDL credit to good use. A market woman in Matiguás had likewise described La Patriota as *puro finquero* with *todos montados* (everyone's a property owner, and they're all on horseback). There are stores in La Patriota, and the *finqueros* ride in for supplies or, like don Lucas, have a home in town as well as in the mountains. We drive by the *acopiador* of which don Lucas is an associate, where all of the surrounding dairy farms send their fresh milk every morning. It collects about thirty-five hundred liters of milk a day, which it trucks to the nearby small city of Jinotega. There it is pasteurized, and most of it is made into cheese. Don Lucas surmises that it is exported to the United States, but he is not sure.

More than in other areas, the infrastructure of this part of the country was destroyed by the war, and although that was fifteen years ago, many of the roads have only recently been repaired.[24] Because of the heavy fighting and dying that happened here, that period remains more present than elsewhere. In Matiguás I saw graffiti from the elections that ended the insurgency: "1990 Viva Violeta." A low wall along the smooth new highway that we now travel sports its own graffiti, "Viva Hugo Chávez"; it was donated by the Venezuelan government. Then we ride for a long while on a rough unpaved road. Our driver proudly recites the Toyota ad for his model, "No manéjame, maltrátame" (Don't drive me, mistreat me) as we dive in and out of streambeds. In the backcountry, it seems like there are as many schools as houses, every single one painted blue and white for Nicaragua. I will think of them later when Francisco (who is a hired worker on the farm) explains why "toditos los campesinos" (all of the peasants) support ex-president Alemán. We cross the Muy Muy Viejo River—the name is funny every time, Old Very Very or Very Very Old, depending on how it came about—which runs between mountains overlaid with grassy meadows, and huge trees scattered along their bases.

Despite the junglelike flora, this land is beautiful in the domesticated way that European landscapes are; it has in fact been transformed over time from cattle ranching. I am told that in the dry season, the lower areas are brown and barren.

We pull up to a house at a fork in the road. Other vehicles are parked as well; from here one goes on foot. I bid farewell to my FDL guides and fall into step with don Luke, as I think of him. We walk along a narrow dirt road, which in the summer is passable by vehicle but now has mud patches a foot deep. Sometimes we jump from one dry hump to another, but sometimes it's wet from top to bottom and we sink. We are not on don Lucas's land yet, but he teaches me about what we are seeing nonetheless. *Platano enano* and *yuca* plants that people grow for their own consumption. Two different kinds of grass for livestock, one that they graze and a wider leafed grass—called *pasto de corte*—planted by more prosperous farmers who then harvest it for hay during the dry season. I see some coffee plants and don Luke says that prices have recovered somewhat and a few people do grow it exclusively. We also see fields of the root crop *quequisque*, which has been mentioned with awe a couple of times by farmers in this area. Two young *campesinos* planted this vegetable on a whim, but when it brought in triple the price they expected, they dedicated themselves to growing it. Everyone who tells this story does so not with jealousy, but pride in the new idea. Don Lucas says the *quequisque* is grown for export, but I'm not sure he differentiates between international export and selling one's goods at any market (as opposed to family consumption). As we walk, I feel the relief of the absence of filth—the trash that accumulates along every street in Managua, and an overall sense born of the slums that the very presence of humans scars the earth; that the spaces we carve out for ourselves are by definition ugly.

The *finca* didn't have a name until don Lucas needed a loan and the bank dubbed it San Lucas, which suits the owner just fine. It stands about five kilometers from La Patriota—two of these by foot—far enough to make you know you're cut off from communication. We trudge for forty minutes, and I reach our destination sweaty and winded as I am carrying my backpack, full of books I won't read and clothes I won't wear (don Lucas's is empty; he will bring fresh cheese in it to his family tomorrow). We are hungry for breakfast and upon arriving are handed a sweet oatmeal beverage; my resolve not to drink the water vanishes immediately. Don Lucas's wife and children all used to live on this land, but now only his unmarried sons live in the house here and he looks in once a week. He says life is good up here; the heat is less intense than in town, as are the mosquitoes, and in the dry season it stays greener. He lives in Matiguás because his wife is not well (she has a weak and nervous constitution that was pushed to the limit by a family tragedy that also helped to push the family off the *finca*, Francisco's wife, Fanni, explains later in a sympathetic tone) and because his daughters are finishing secondary school. The only time when don Lucas did not feel comfortable on the *finca* was during the war. A number of times he mentions the fighting that took place on his land. The Sandinistas had a base in La Patriota and would take over his house; during the war years he lost thirty cows. You could see the rockets from the front porch. Most of his sons were still too young to fight, but two of them were around fifteen years old, and he would take them into hiding to avoid their being conscripted.

Don Lucas was born on a nearby *finca*; when he married he purchased his own plot—of one hundred *manzanas*—and has slowly expanded it over the years. He tamed the land and he built the house; it is thirty-six years old, so it's a "Somocista" house, he jokes, as it was built under that regime. 'We are all Liberals,' he tells me, referring to the other *finqueros* in the region. The Sandinistas wanted to break up land that was not theirs, don Lucas states: 'When there is destruction, there is no progress.' 'How I have suffered for what I have,' he says. "En el tiempo de Somoza fue más bonito . . . no habían ladrones porque se aplicaba la ley" (It was better in the time of Somoza . . . there were no thieves because the law was enforced). Now don Lucas carries a gun—he sticks it cavalierly in the back of his pants—all of the *finqueros* do. He has shot twice at thieves. Fanni explains that if you have a gun, no one comes to bother you, and that you have to have one because everyone else does.

Don Lucas has eight children; there were nine, but his oldest son was murdered in a long-running dispute with a neighbor over property lines. Four of his sons live on the *finca* (the other four kids are in Matiguás): Lucas Jr. (twenty-three) and Guadalupe (twenty-seven) live in the main house, as they are single, while Adrian and another son have their own parcels of land. Adrian is newly remarried, and although his father has apportioned forty-five *manzanas* to him, he still keeps his dairy cows with his father's and comes over every morning to direct the milking. The other son works separately and I do not meet him, although his house is pointed out across the hills. Additionally, there are six hired workers who live at the *finca*: Francisco (thirty-eight) and Fanni (twenty-three) are the principal caretakers (they live in the main house with their three children); Felipe—just a kid at seventeen—stays in the main house as well; another couple lives up the hill (I can hear their children playing, but they do not come over); and an elderly man passes through during the day, as he goes about his tasks of caring for the property.

Around five o'clock dusk begins to fall. Felipe chops a fallen log, and Francisco and Lucas Jr. watch and converse. Guadalupe, or Lupe, who is deaf, passes through with a bottle of liquor. Fanni is still at work in the kitchen, and her six-year-old twin girls race all around. Don Lucas circulates, chatting with everyone. I am preoccupied with where I will sleep (in a long back room along with don Lucas), brush my teeth (in the backyard), and bathe (in a small shed where the laundry sink is). By eight at the latest, everyone is in bed. There is not much else to do once it's dark, and don Lucas quips, "Antes se nacieron muchos chavalos" (Before, many kids were born).

Fanni awakens first, to make coffee for the men and start grinding corn for the breakfast tortillas. One by one, the workers gather in the smoky

San Lucas. Lucas Jr. milking.

kitchen and wait, then quickly slug down a mug and head outside to milk the cows. Some have set up the tins before the others come out. It's dark yet but quickly lightens. As they are milked, the cows constantly urinate and defecate. The guys wear rubber boots for wading around, which they attach spurs to for riding as if they were cowboy boots. They also strap one-legged stools around their waists to be able to sit and stand repeatedly. Just as I put tablets into my water to drink it, brown-tinted and iodine-flavored, so they rinse the small cloths they use to clean the cows' udders in iodine-spiked water before milking. Although officially they should use a different rag each time, and wash their hands, they do rinse with water first, then the iodine. Another rule that they follow is to delegate certain workers to tie up the back legs and babies, while others to do the milking. Lupe is usually assigned the former, a brutal task to my eyes, as he hits the calves and twists them by the head to pull them off their mother's teat and tie them to her front leg. The cow's back legs are tied together so she can't kick, and then she is milked.

Depending on the age of the calf, it is separated from its mother earlier or later in the day—the younger ones being allowed more hours to nurse—and kept apart all night. Thus, by the early morning, the cows want to be milked. The gate dividing mothers from babies is opened just enough for one calf at a time to fit through. It runs directly to its mother, who sometimes calls out to it but sometimes not, and starts to nurse. One calf persists in trying to milk the wrong mother, who butts it violently; when it tries another, Lupe pushes it out of the corral to teach it a lesson. The usual routine is to allow the calf to suckle for just a moment, then pull it off and sit down to milk. Finishing, in one smooth motion the person milking gets up with his full pail and pulls both ropes off the cow so that she is free and her baby can finish breakfast. I am informed that there are nursing young all year round, but many cows give birth in November, and then there will be double the number there is now, milked in the same yard, with the same number of workers. The twins, affectionately referred to as Mecha and Carmencita, bring down tall plastic cups half filled with coffee, which the men hold under the udders to top off with frothy warm milk.

By 7:00 a.m., two full *pichingas* are ready to be strapped onto the burro, which Felipe leads on horseback to the *acopiador* in La Patriota, arriving there no later than eight. San Lucas produces more than two *pichingas* of milk a day, earning C$3.29 (US$0.19) per liter. Don Lucas owns more than three hundred head of cattle, half of them young steers raised only for slaughter. The breed of cattle is a native mix, he explains; wealthier farmers might breed with foreign bulls, but not him. Don Lucas asks me if CAFTA will benefit dairy farmers, as if I were not also searching for that

Above: San Lucas. Lucas (Jr.) straining the milk. Below: San Lucas. Francisco and Lucas (Jr.) loading the fresh milk to be carried to the *acopiador.*

answer. He suggests that perhaps it will help to control price fluctuations in his product that are a result of rising gas prices. 'Well,' he comments, 'not everyone can always win.' He seems content with whatever fate holds for him. Still, he has plans. With his newly built *sala de ordeño*, if he has his cattle tested for disease he can achieve government certification, thus fetching a higher price for his meat and dairy.

Like all *fincas*, at San Lucas they grow what they can of what they consume, primarily the corn and beans. Other people, "los que tienen más lugar," those with more space, plant *yuca*, *plátano*, *guineo* . . . but really don Lucas prefers the work of cattle to agriculture, he says. Sugar and rice are the only products they buy in large quantities. Outside the house stands an elevated wooden shed where the corn is stored in metal barrels so the rats can't get it; they put away about three barrels of beans a year and twelve of corn. Fanni prepares three square meals a day, consisting of beans, rice, tortillas, sometimes chicken and always fresh cheese. There is little variation from breakfast to dinner or from one day to the next. For me it is far too much food, as I am not engaging in physical labor for twelve hours a day the way they are. Most everyone in the country is lean and strong, as opposed to in Managua. Here, almost nothing is deep-fried, and they consume few sweets or sodas, save the heavily sugared fruit and grain drinks that Fanni makes. At first I felt the food was purely for sustenance, not pleasure, but by the end of our stay I appreciated the fresh tortillas and homemade cheese, unrivalled in the rest of the country. I also felt the nourishment provided by eating food grown from the same ground you stand on, and although it may be psychological, I could understand how this would bind people to the place where they are from; it's a small circle made.

On his second and last day with us at the *finca*, don Lucas takes me on a tour on horseback—or on *bestias*, as they call them around here—to the highest point of his land, from which one can see the property line: the Muy Muy Viejo River. He names all of the surrounding hills and waits expectantly for me to photograph each one in turn. There is the one where the fatal mudslide took place—we can see the scar on the mountainside. The *acopiador* is named in commemoration of that date. Then he takes me to see the schoolhouse that sits on his property, and next to it a chapel that he in large part funded, both from his pocket and by requesting money from the church and local businesses. We can hear the singing before we arrive; it is a Wednesday afternoon and a young *campesino* is preaching to a small group. Don Lucas expresses his anger that the people who use it have not taken the same initiative to put on the finishing touches as he did in building it. He then tells a complicated story of how he lobbied the municipal government to repair the water pipeline to the school, thereby benefiting the houses on the *finca* as well, and causing consternation among fellow citizens. Additionally, three months ago they installed solar panels at the house, so now they have electricity; they display to me the blinking control panel in the bedroom that has a twenty-year warranty. There are just a few light bulbs and no outlets; they run the radio on batteries and keep the adapter required to plug in appliances locked in a cabinet.

You don't wash clothes by hand where you come from? You don't make tortillas from scratch? Fanni is incredulous. Sometimes it seems that if my objective were to search out a corner of the earth where globalization is *not*, this would be it. There are a few plastic toys, the option of ramen noodles for a quick meal, and factory-made clothes, but no other sign of it. In La Patriota, the story of globalization is an old story: television. Hour after endless hour, young girls sit close to the screen transfixed by music videos blatantly imbued with sex. Naked bodies pulse with great monotony. How they relate these scenarios to their own lives and expectations I can only imagine.

During one of the natural lulls in the rhythm of the day's work, the guys gather on the porch, as they are wont to. I've been asked so many times now how to get to the United States, if there are jobs there, if I will take someone with me, if they will need a visa, that I'm not surprised when it comes up. But out here, it is a different permutation of the matter. Where are you from? Which direction is New Mexico? I wasn't sure how to answer that question, but what they wanted was for me to point in the cardinal direction. I was surprised that *campesinos* wouldn't know where north was, and I didn't know either. One guy volunteered a guess and gestured: It must be in that direction, because on 9/11 when all flights were grounded, the larger planes that usually fly that way didn't pass overhead. And why is it that some of the migrants to the United States return with money and some don't? And, do you dream? Don Luke contributes that he once dreamed he saw a snake while he was picking coffee beans, and the next day one crossed his path. Soon everyone else goes back to work, and I watch the *congos* (howler monkeys), transfixed. I can hear Fanni making her way through the laundry. She is responsible for the clothes of all eight inhabitants of the house.

Last night after dinner, don Lucas immediately excused himself from the kitchen, where we gather for meals, because the smoke was too intense—my eyes water and turn red and I'm too hot. Fanni spends the majority of her eighteen-hour day in the thick of it. Like so many kitchens in Nicaragua, the ceiling is blackened with ashy slime. Above the fire, strips of pigskin are slowly cured. Once for lunch she cut squares of it and boiled it in with the beans to produce chocolate-colored pieces of soft smoke.

San Lucas. One of the twins on the porch, her father
Francisco at left, and Lupe in the background.

I watch her make our food. It is so simple. The only seasoning is salt or sugar, used generously. Tortillas are made from corn. Cheese is made from milk. Everything starts in her hands in its natural state. The corn kernels are soaked overnight in water, ground into *masa* (dough), patted into a flat circle, and cooked. The fresh cheese requires a tablet that curdles it; then after letting it sit awhile, add salt and knead. The labor required is not only physically demanding, but never-ending and monotonous. Fanni takes to making me fresh chili salsa every day, with lime and peppers from the back-yard. She sends her son Gilbert (eight) up the grapefruit tree to pick fruit for me. I think she gets vicarious pleasure from my pleasure, my leisure, my experience of novelty.

Fanni is sick of making tortillas, and she is only twenty-three. Aside from the milking routine, the men do different tasks each day (shelling corn, fumigating fields, planting grass for fodder, mending fences, fishing, chopping firewood or rescuing a calf from a mud pit), but Fanni does the same thing: housework. And no matter how diligent she is, she can never finish, never get ahead, she can never expand her horizon. She is sweet and giving, but her dissatisfaction is a thin scratch from the surface. Still, Fanni is the one to explain to me why Lucas Jr. has not been given land by his father; how could he run a *finca* alone? 'He has not settled down.' The contribution of a woman to the enterprise is recognized. But don Lucas pays Fanni C$300 (US$17.65) a month (the amount I budget for two day's worth of expenses in Managua) while he pays Francisco C$900 (US$52.94). Fanni describes how if a woman is hired to sow hay or shell corn, she is paid half of what the men are paid. It's not a devaluing of women's work, I conclude, but a devaluing of women. To get by, Fanni also sells small items out of their bedroom window, which opens onto the porch. Neighbors and other workers stop by for bread, cigarettes, candy, and cooking and cleaning items.

Their room has two beds in it; I had been assuming whenever I saw this that the parents sleep in one bed and the children in the other. Fanni surprises me by explaining that she and her daughters are in one, and Francisco and Gilbert in the other. She and Francisco have been together for ten years; if you do the math, you'll figure out that she was married (although never formally so) at age thirteen. Gilbert was born when she was fifteen. I piece together Francisco's history; there are children from a previous marriage, and a great gulf when he gave ten years of his life to the war. Their family has been living at San Lucas for three years. Fanni has a fourth-grade education. All of her siblings are in Matiguás, except for one in Costa Rica.

I can witness what people's lives look like, but not necessarily what they consist of. I can only know what they tell me, and—especially as regards themselves—this can be misleading. In one afternoon passed chatting with Fanni, sitting on the porch, being fed cookies from her store, I am overwhelmed by tragedy. She relates in detail the shooting of don Lucas's son (she did not witness it, but has heard). She gets out her photo album, and when we stop at a picture of her mom at a baptism, she elaborates that she has a sister who can't talk: some guy 'took advantage of her' so now she has a child whom Fanni's mom is raising. Then an aside about a local kid who got kidnapped and held for ransom (which makes me glad all of the brothers have guns). The photo of Francisco's two children from his first marriage; one of them fell ill and died. Fanni tells the story of her sixteen-year-old sister who was recently *cachada* by a man in his thirties who already has a wife.[25]

Suddenly it is four in the afternoon and I am due at Adrian's house to meet his wife. In contrast to Fanni's story, she is eighteen, was married only five months ago, and wants to wait to have children. Adrian is twenty-seven. She has covered the walls of their home with wedding photos, and he stops by the house to show her wildflower seeds he has collected to plant in the garden that he is laboring over. Like Fanni, she gets intensely bored during the day, but in her case because she does not have enough to

San Lucas. One morning, Lupe reaches into the cook stove and pulls out a fistful of ashes; he takes them out the back door and sprinkles a cross on the ground. Fanni explains to me that when the day dawns yellow, this protects you from getting sick.

do. She spends her days alone with Adrian's two little boys from a previous marriage. She chose not to finish school.

Lupe, *el mudito* (the deaf one), as the others refer to him, huffs and grunts and constantly tries to communicate in a language of signs and sounds that his family has learned but that I, without their shared history, cannot decipher. He is highly conscientious of others; as if trying to earn his keep, he provides sufficient chairs in every room where we gather, sometimes placing them right behind you so that you may sit without moving an inch, like royalty. He brushes a mosquito or tick off of you if you are unaware of it. He is especially attentive to his father. When a hand is needed, Lupe accompanies his brother or another worker on jobs around the land, as well as taking part in the milking every morning. He had a wife, but she ran away in the middle of the night to marry another man. This personal detail is an exception; it would be unheard of and uncomfortable for me, as a foreigner and a woman, to truly "enter" the lives of the men here, and more so to document them. Lucas never allowed me to. Felipe is shy but obliging. When I ask him about himself, he reveals he quit school a year ago, having reached the second year of high school. He is from Matiguás, but his mother and father went to Costa Rica and did not want to take him along. When I say that life out here in the country is pretty good, he disagrees. It's hard, he says, because he's without his parents.

Francisco is different. When he smiles, in his eyes is a warmth and recognition that transcends human difference. The barrier I feel with many *campesinos* is less with him, though he does not volunteer conversation either. On my last evening at San Lucas, we talk politics. Francisco emerges from the shadows to the spotlight when inspired to relate his war experiences, and he reveals incisive beliefs on Nicaraguan politics. The conversation began because of a 1982 U.S. Army mess kit hanging on the kitchen wall, used by Francisco for ten years in the field, "luchando para libertad" (fighting for liberty) with the help of the United States. Francisco expounds: The Sandinistas aimed to oppress people just like the regime in Cuba does. They are communists. They came in and were killing people, forcing people to fight in their army, and taking away what little we had. What choice did the *campesinos* have, he asks rhetorically, but to arm themselves and resist? Under the Sandinistas, one could not benefit from one's own labor. Fanni gives an example: If you were headed to town to sell a chicken, the Sandinistas would be in the road, would check you, would take away the chicken. You could buy it back if you wanted to, but more likely you would accept the ration cards that would not stretch enough to feed your family.

San Lucas. Francisco talks to one of his daughters while he eats breakfast, the skin on his hands wrinkled from milking.

Francisco took up arms to protect what he thought was right and what is his way of life. The Sandinistas appropriated land from families who had established their *fincas* with sweat and blood. No, they did not redistribute this land to the poor, but kept it for themselves, Francisco replies. He went to war because what was happening was unjust; he went out of indignation that *finqueros* were being killed and their land taken from them. Maybe, I think, he went because if those who suffer to become solvent property owners are punished, there's no point to the grinding work from the bottom up. Under the Sandinistas 'we couldn't be *tranquilo* like we are now,' Francisco concludes—'we' being *campesinos*. Francisco speaks for this group and numbers himself among them; he is content with his life right now. It is good. He does not own land, but he is happy with his situation. His family lives in a substantial house, not a shack pieced together. His children eat well and have potable water.[26] For these *campesinos*, the political leader now is Alemán, the same one I had disregarded as corrupt and a criminal, unable to understand how he is still a force in Nicaraguan politics. Parents used to have to cooperate to raise the schoolhouses, the walls and roofs made out of leaves. Now the schools are constructed with enduring cement block and painted neatly. Now there are health clinics and paved roads in the area. Alemán brought that. He is under house arrest now, but Francisco says there is no proof that he laundered that money. They will vote for whomever he supports in the next presidential election. The sitting president, Bolaños, can be praised for policy-level changes in the government, but this is trifling if—as Francisco sees it—he has done nothing for the people.

In the few days that I stay at San Lucas, the men seem to take turns making the journey to town, whether La Patriota or Matiguás. For this they spiff up. On the *finca* everyone sleeps in their clothes, so it takes one minute to roll out of bed and into the stables instead of fifteen, which in the pre-dawn is significant. Open flies—broken zippers—are as socially

San Lucas. Drinking fresh milk.

acceptable as T-shirts rolled above bellies. But not for town. One night Lupe comes home drunk at 1:00 a.m. There are two bars in La Patriota, and Fanni says the men do sometimes go drinking, but do not do so at home—"a echar sus traguitos . . . pero, por ahí fíjase"—which makes it acceptable. Most evenings are spent sitting quietly, the rhythm of conversation one of familiarity and routine and perhaps downright physical exhaustion.

San Rafael
OCTOBER 25–28

The FDL had trouble finding twenty-somethings to place me with. The majority of farmers established enough to be granted a loan are older, which is why I wound up mostly photographing families that included grown sons. Pablo Damian (twenty-seven) was to some extent an exception. Although he works in tandem with his parents—his mother, Luz Marina, is the official owner of the land, and his father, Pablo Absolom, is also a client of the bank—it is he who runs the *finca*. He has received three small loans from FDL to buy first land and then cattle. He has amassed 115 *manzanas* of land and fifty-six head of cattle that produce 50 liters of milk a day, which he sells at C$3.25 (US$0.19) each (earning the equivalent of about US$9.50 per day, not including the periodic sale of bulls). Despite the fact that his young family lives in extreme poverty, Pablo Damian's own background contains middle-class elements. Although his parents are separated, his father was wealthy before the war, and Pablo Damian lived with his mother in the city of Matagalpa and attended school through his second year of college.

Five years ago he started out with twenty-five *manzanas*. As plots adjacent to his become available, he purchases them; on my last day with him, he left before I did to see about selling cattle in order to buy another piece of land. He has thirty-five female cows that will produce twenty-five off-spring this year. When he purchased the property, only part of what is now the central room of the house existed; he has added two bedrooms and a kitchen. It is constructed with a combination of cement, wood, and bricks, and is spacious with high ceilings (common in this area). Bricks last longer than wood, Pablo Damian explains. He is apologetic for the unfinished conditions under which they live, but explains that he is slowly building his dairy operation first. Pablo Damian used to rent land to graze his cattle. After seven years, they had multiplied to the extent that this was no longer profitable. Now he owns land but fewer cows, and produces just half as much milk. The house sits on the Carretera a Matagalpa, the highway to

Outside the kitchen of San Rafael.

town. It is a dirt road, but sees a fair amount of traffic nonetheless. Buses go by, the passengers craning their necks to get a glimpse of the gringa on his porch. Nearly everyone calls out a greeting to him. He used to be a cattle broker too, which is how he knows just about everyone. I ask if it doesn't bother him that they stare. He says no, he looks at others too. Maybe in more civilized countries they don't stare, he says, but here we do.

The backyard is deep green shade, variations on the banana plant every few feet, wide leaves providing full coverage. Pablo Damian explains that he plants trees to be conscientious of the environment as well as for a garden. One of the trees has long beanlike pods. Malinche it's called, he says. Sometimes it sports brilliant red flowers. Each tree is beautiful to look at during its own time of year, according to Pablo Damian. A discarded tractor tire is the perfect height to be his favorite place to sit in the backyard. If you turn around to face down the hill away from the house, all you see is trash. If you face forward, you are looking at the square cement tub where clothes and bodies are washed, where buckets of water are drawn for the kitchen. This is the only household I've seen that does not have a cement wash sink (again, the priority is land and cattle). Sandra (thirty-three) does the laundry on three stacked flat rocks, not high enough to reach waist level, which for me proves not only difficult, but uncomfortable. When

San Rafael. Sandra bathes the two boys in the backyard.

the faucet is turned on to fill the tub, it sprays water, turning the backyard into a mud pit. When it rains, water comes into the kitchen and the floor becomes equally difficult to navigate. Otherwise, the kitchen is like most others I've seen. The counter is a flat board with a groove slanting toward the end that rests in a slot in the wall, ingeniously serving as a drain to the outside. In the corner, the fire is lit atop a wooden stand treated with ash to resemble cement. Firewood is collected on their property and stacked near where the horses are parked.

There is a single light bulb in the house. It hangs from the living room ceiling, so in the kitchen Sandra makes the coffee in darkness before day-break. In the evenings, the family gathers underneath the light bulb, with

Pablo Damian lying in the hammock directly below it. One year ago the government installed electricity. Since they do not use electric appliances, the family pays the minimum fee of C$35 per month (US$2.06). The light is left on all night, and it shines into the room where I sleep. The only reasons I can imagine that Pablo Damian does this are (1) because he can, the novelty of having light and the luxury of using it blithely; or (2) fear. The night that his mom sleeps over, he leaves the house open as they chat into the night, explaining that usually he would shut and lock the doors at an earlier hour out of caution. Pablo Damian always takes his gun with him when he goes up to the *finca*, as he calls the corral where he milks the cows. When I comment, he relates shooting a snake the week before; the gun is not to harm other people, but for protection against whatever might come our way. Our first day out, we cross paths with two policemen carrying machine guns, accompanied by two *campesinos* with a spear and a machete. They are on the trail of a thief who stole a couple thousand cordobas from a neighbor.

On my first day there are three dogs; then there are two. One spends half its time at Sandra's parents' place, she explains. The dogs are skinny, and watch every move you make while you eat. Once a day they are fed whey, and the one time we eat chicken, we give them the bones. The dogs are shooed out of the house every time they come in, and they are always coming in. But they earn their keep by helping to herd the cattle. There are also five goats and about ten chickens living around the house. The goats are for eating on special occasions, selling when you can, and general farm adornment. The chickens sleep in the trees, climbing a log ramp that is carefully placed for them to use. At dawn, they line up to toddle down. My last day on the farm, I am fed one of those chickens, and two of the sixteen eggs that Sandra had shown me—lifting the chicken with reverence from the nest fashioned in their bedroom—along with vegetables, which I had seen none of for days, except for a wilting cabbage that she seemed to guard for her children. Otherwise we eat some combination of beans, tortillas, rice, and cheese for every meal. I am served at a table, Pablo Damian perches in the kitchen, and I never do see Sandra eat anything. When Luz Marina visits, she sends her son to buy sweetened white bread for me at the store across the street, and when we take a horseback ride to Pablo Damian's father's *finca*, we eat guava and *anona* fruits from the trees. When the trees in their garden give them bananas or oranges, they eat those.

Whenever Pablo Damian is in the house, little Pablo Damian (three) and Dámisis (eighteen months) surround him. Little Pablo is usually referred to as "El Negro," as his skin is darker than his brother's, whom

San Rafael. Pablo Damian holds his baby, Dámisis.

they call "Jacobito," after a grandfather whom he resembles. Pablo Damian is especially attached to the little one, and in the evenings lies with the baby on his chest in the hammock. But when the boys misbehave, he calls to Sandra, and she comes to discipline them. They both yell at the kids a fair amount, but Sandra also goes out of her way to include them in her daily chores, teaching them how to help and never tiring of the constant verbal repetition that they demand. Sandra says that with two, she is done having children. Her grandmother gave birth to fourteen and her mother twelve (though Sandra is one of only two girls). Damian is one of three children (with the same mother anyway) and thinks that is the perfect number, but he does not plan on having any more either. In their economic situation, they couldn't support them, he explains. He goes on to say that because they live on the *finca*, the kids eat okay—they have milk—but beyond that . . . he drifts off. Sandra is thirty-three, to Pablo Damian's twenty-seven years, an almost shocking reversal of the norm. Sandra's sister, for example, has already been married six months and is not yet fourteen.

Although Pablo Damian only seems to bark orders at Sandra, she looks adoringly at him. Sandra's family has a *finca* nearby. They always knew each other, but he was just a boy when he moved with his mother to the city. Three years ago, when his oldest son was born, he quit the university (he says he prefers life in the country). They are not formally married, because to make that decision, Pablo Damian explains, is to bring God into it, and so one had better be sure. He spends most weekends in Matagalpa with his mother, leaving Sandra and the kids at the *finca*. Indeed, when Luz Marina visits, he spends far more time conversing with her and doing chores with her than he does with Sandra. But he does not seem to feel the need to control Sandra, and since she is always able to produce what he desires on the spot and keeps the kids in line, I never see this tested. Sandra moves energetically through her tasks. She likes to cook. She does not shuffle nor exude the humbled air that so many women here do. But watching her, I can't help but compare her days to Pablo Damian's. He sets out every morning into the majestic hills, takes in glorious views, breathes fresh air, meets all sorts of different people. She is confined to the dingy, smoke-filled kitchen and muddy backyard. Poor and rural have very different meanings depending on gender.

Pablo Damian's father ran off with (*se cachó*) his mother when she was fourteen. By fifteen, she was pregnant. He does not seem to approve of this, nor enjoy the fact that he has four half-siblings. He lived for eight years on his father's *finca* before moving into the city with his mother. Because of my experience at San Lucas, I assume that Pablo Absolom would have given his son some of his own land when he started a family. Pablo Damian is quick to correct this: His mother has been the one to support him, to teach him how to milk, how to run a *finca*. Indeed, the day she visits she is busy helping to brand a calf, roast corn kernels, and gather ingredients for *nacatamales* to sell in Matagalpa. Pablo Damian does not forgive his father, repeating a couple of times that although their *fincas* are intertwined, his father will not sell him the tracts of land that lie inside of his. His dad's *finca* is named San Rafael. His own doesn't really have a name yet, so on paper he too calls his San Rafael. Pablo Absolom stops by to visit nearly every day, and they have each lived at each other's houses when they could not be in their own.

San Rafael. Sandra in the kitchen.

One afternoon we ride to Pablo Absolom's house to visit, as well as to see more of the two San Rafaels. We climb almost to Pablo Damian's bean patch, which is atop the furthest hill, then turn and cross his father's land, which consists of two hundred *manzanas* for nearly that many cattle. It is an enchanted forest; plants upon plants, forgotten corners, moss and vines create green walls. Hundred-year-old trees, always noble, spread branches in flat networks above. Pablo Damian halts abruptly. The gate we were headed through has a large wasps' nest on it, which I had not even seen; we must go around, cutting a fence to slip through. We pass a worker's home—a single room with no windows. One, two, then three and four children crowd the dark doorway. Then we arrive at his father's house. Pablo Damian explains that it used to belong to his grandfather, a very wealthy man. 'It gets used up,' he says referring to his father's inherited fortune.

I can imagine the elevated veranda, now grey and heaped with recently harvested corn, in grander times. It still looks grand to me, although really it could be an abandoned house, the wood so worn, square holes cut in plank walls for windows, as in any modest structure. Pablo Absolom says his youngest child is seventeen, although Pablo Damian indicates that some of the boys hanging around on the porch are his father's too. One is named Pablo. One of his daughters left to join her husband in Arizona almost two years ago; they talk often on the phone. As did his son, Pablo Absolom makes a comment about how people in the United States must be more civilized.

Pablo Damian asks numerous times if I have noticed how nicely kept up his *finca* is, nicer than his father's. People have begged him to sell, he says. It is indeed a beautiful piece of land. The earth is black: a sign of fertility, he informs me. Every pasture has water. He says he has purposefully left many trees standing because during the summer months of March and April the cows need shade, 'poor things.' We pass a perfectly straight cedar tree, a *cedro real*, says Pablo Damian, who volunteers that in a financial pinch he would sell a calf before cutting it down.[27] During those dry months there are hardly leaves on the trees, and cattle get thin— hard to imagine now, in October, when the only thing not green is the sky. Without supplementary feed and minerals the animals sometimes

San Rafael. Pablo Damian on the veranda at his father's finca, behind him one of the boys who lives there.

die.[28] Pablo Damian is able to keep his livestock healthy all year because he grows grass to keep a reserve of hay, plus has the resources to provide salt and minerals to the stock year-round. Whenever we pass a planted field, he points it out with pride. This is true on every *finca* that I visit. Pablo Absolom too has us ride home out of our way to admire up close the wide green leaves sown with care.

Both Pablo Damian and his father grow what they can for subsistence. Pablo Absolom explains the process: first you prepare the land by burning; after the first rain of winter (the rainy season), which begins in May, you plant; the next step is herbicide and from then on weeding with a machete. "Sale carita," he concludes, meaning that much labor is required. Still, Pablo Absolom concludes, he's sixty years old and over time has noticed that "lo que uno cosecha se rinde," (what one harvests, provides), whereas when one buys a pound of beans, for example, it is quickly consumed. But the beans are not ready yet; it is the corn that I witness. It has been recently harvested and has usurped Pablo Damian's living room; I climb over mounds of it to reach my room, my feet sliding out from under me. Two *campesinos* are hired to sort and store it, making it dangerous to walk through the house for the flying corncobs. The smaller ears are thrown into a separate pile from the larger ones, the former to be eaten first and the latter to be stacked carefully for use throughout the rest of the year (unlike at San Lucas, where the corn kernels are stored in metal barrels, here the ears are stored whole and poison is put down to protect them from rats). Before the corn is stacked, the outer husks are removed and burned. I stand with Pablo Damian, watching the blaze. He says it looks like the eternal fires of hell, and asks if I read the Bible. Both he and Sandra grew up Catholic, but do not attend church now; he is not interested in the responsibilities of being a member. I tell him that I do not believe in God, and after that he mentions periodically that he does indeed believe and he follows His rules.

At 5:30 every morning Pablo Damian heads out with the empty *pichingas* and the pail slung over his shoulder to drive the cows into the corral for milking. Before daylight savings, he would have to ride the two kilometers in the dark. Now it's light enough for me to make my way through the deep mud on foot, sliding as if I were walking on ice (a comparison that they wouldn't understand), crossing streams, and opening gates. Pablo Damian's milking routine is a smaller operation than at San Lucas. He works alone, and so while he says he receives top ratings from Parmalat for hygiene and purity, he does not rinse with iodine nor have someone else to tie the cows' hooves. He is proud of the speed with which he can finish the task, and says the reason is that he's been doing it since he was six years old. As he lets the calves into the corral, he yells their names

San Rafael. After draining a lump on the cow's udder with a pocketknife,
Pablo Damian explains that she must have been bitten by a wasp.

over and over so that they will learn them. Some already have: "Chavala,"
"Solito," "Maravilla," "Peluza." It's important to give animals names, he
believes. Pablo Damian knows the characteristics of each cow—this one
gives the best milk, that one has short udders (forcing him to hold the
bucket up between his knees instead of placing it on the ground). As he
milks, he allows his *bestia* to roam; he feels sorry for it being tied up all the
time. One day, while searching for a horse gone missing, he nearly misses
the Parmalat truck that passes for the milk between 7:30 and 8:30 a.m.

He waits to strain the milk until he's back at the house, where Sandra
can assist. She also pours off a pail for their own consumption. He asks

me if it's the same at the other *fincas* I've seen; like the *maquila* girls, he is curious about the insider's view I have been granted. There does come a point where I just don't need any more photographs of cows being milked. Even though this family represents a different economic situation than don Lucas and his sons, especially in the context of the local community, the general impressions of lifestyle and living conditions are similar. Still, I continue to accompany Pablo Damian up the mountain every day; I wake up early anyway, and the morning would be long without this excursion. It's nice to go out walking through the high grass, to be at the corral with a view of the sunrise and the bands of hills and clouds in the distance, before 6:30 when the sun strikes and the air heats. At this time of day the *congos* howl like mountain lions. Something is always a little different too, whether it is the policemen looking for the fugitive, a visiting neighbor to whom Pablo Damian tries to sell cattle, or his dad dropping by to chat and lend a hand. They gossip about the romantic intrigues of one of Pablo Damian's brothers, about cows, about acquaintances. One day I ride his horse up to the corral, and in spite of Pablo Damian's tirelessly chivalrous comportment, he asks me to walk back so that he can ride with the full *pichingas*; he will not risk the day's milk with an untested rider.

Sandra's father sells his milk to the *quesera* across the street from her house. All through the morning a steady stream of young boys on horseback ride up to vend their family's daily milk. Doña Eta will make fresh cheese and *crema* to sell in Matagalpa. Doña Eta runs a store out of the front of her place, which looks more like a city house than Pablo Damian's; it is made of cement block with a floor and window bars, surrounded by a garden. She says we can come by to see the cheese being made. Pablo Damian is nervous about this proposition, but acquiesces; in Nicaragua, he says, it's better to maintain distance from your neighbors in order to keep everything easygoing. Pablo Damian is near to obsessive in his concern that everything always remain *tranquilo*. When I first arrived he immediately set the tone of casual openness: I am to feel comfortable, and I do, but it is apparent that underneath his desire for friendliness, he is nervous. He needs constant affirmation from whomever he is speaking with. "¿Verdad que es bonito aquí? ¿Verdad?" (It's pretty here, isn't it? Don't you think?) But perhaps for him I serve as a neutral mirror that will not reflect back to anyone else in his world, the way one is sometimes prompted to confide in a stranger. He asks how I view his land, and if I perceive him as introverted. He wants to make sure I know he is a serious person and is considered as such by his community. But his insecurity makes it impossible for him to feel comfortable being photographed candidly or to answer personal questions. When I mention that Sandra is older than he, hoping to hear how they met or what their relationship is like, he goes on guard immediately, jumping to explain that while some men marry older women for their money, this is not the case with him. In the evenings he is different: less macho, less insecure. We trade stories, his of raising cattle and mine of U.S. culture, climate, and traditions. Pablo Damian studied business administration and completed a computing certificate, and he conducts himself differently than the other *campesinos*. Still, his kids don't seem to know what books are, and his own gulfs of ignorance lie just outside the realm of his immediate experience. In that realm, however, he is well versed. He can perform casual surgery on cow udders, maneuver angry bulls, and move through the countryside with ease. As I prepare to leave, he says with a questioning tone, hesitant to be so bold, that he hopes we are friends.

People ask where I am from, and when they hear "los Estados" (the States, as they refer to the United States here), their eyes light up like those of kids who have just been told I live in Candy Land. Even Pablo Damian, who has property and seems to enjoy taking care of it, would like to try his luck in the United States. In every community, there are a few people who have gone and come back a decade later to buy a *finca* and an expensive pickup truck, to live between two homes; everyone knows how much money they brought back, everyone wants that. Pablo Damian won't go illegally, but if he could get a visa to go work for six months, he could come back and buy more livestock. When I talk with him about CAFTA, Pablo Damian suggests that it is a good thing because it will afford more communication between the United States and Nicaragua. His father agrees, commenting that CAFTA will create *zonas francas* all over the country and then people will have jobs. Right now there are no jobs. I suggest that they will be low paying, but to him this seems trifling compared to vast unemployment. He also mentions that it is "comandante Ortega" who is against the agreement. I can imagine that if the citizens here spent ten years fighting against Daniel Ortega, they will be in favor of whatever he is not. When I tell people that my project is about the repercussions of globalization and CAFTA, it is sometimes unsettling for them to realize that I believe these themes are to be found in their own homes. The very individuals affected by globalization are as little able to formulate it concretely as are the theoreticians.

In our conversations about politics, Pablo Damian's main concern is that Nicaragua be democratic. It was doña Violeta who brought democracy to Nicaragua, he says. Like Francisco at San Lucas, he prefers to be poor, work for what he has, and be assured that it is his. This is his definition of democracy. War and rationing are the opposite, and Nicaraguans do not want to return to that, Pablo Damian states emphatically. He was too young to go to war, but he remembers his cousins and other family members being involved. They joined the opposition; the alternative was to be forced to serve under Ortega, and to be forced is never good. The same philosophy is applied to agricultural reform. As was Francisco, Pablo Damian is indignant that the Sandinistas took land from large landholders. The rationale of taking from the rich to give to the poor is not one that they apply to their experience. What they saw was land being seized from people who had worked hard for what they had. He eyes my camera and uses it as an example: Would I want someone to confiscate it and share out pieces of it to different people? He also describes a nearby *finca* run by a Swiss man who arrived with ample funds. It is beautifully run, and Pablo Damian explains that it gives him pleasure to see what he loves to do done so well. Before the Sandinistas came to power, Pablo Absolom was worth a lot of money, and his brother three times that. Pablo Absolom first lost the cattle that were not kept directly on his land. He sold off one of his two *fincas*, to keep from having it confiscated, and put the money in the bank. But when the currency was devalued, he lost his savings too. Now Nicaragua faces another round of presidential elections, with Daniel Ortega once again the candidate for the FSLN. Pablo Damian worries that his own lands will be taken if Ortega wins. As for Alemán—whom he credits with the electricity they finally received—while Pablo Damian believes

San Rafael. Pablo Damian, on his front porch, admires a dead bird.

wrongdoing should be penalized, he wonders why all of the deaths caused by Ortega went unpunished.

"¿Conoce el pájaro muerto?" (Have you ever seen a dead bird?) On my last morning at San Rafael, Pablo Damian brings me a soft, still bird body. It was in the woodpile; its neck must have been broken by shifting logs. It is something that he thinks I should be familiar with, like any number of factual elements of his life about which I have exhibited ignorance. Indeed, if I was unacquainted with the *anona* fruit, why not banana or tomato as well? He cradles the corpse in his hands, opening and closing the wings that I may observe its markings. It is sad and beautiful, he comments. Then he tosses it across the fence without further reflection.

Matapalo
OCTOBER 30–NOVEMBER 2

Between treks into the countryside, I recharge my batteries (literally) in Matiguás at the Hospedaje Dulce Sueño. By my third time through, it seems like people in town are becoming friendlier. This impression is perhaps prompted by Berta's comment upon meeting me that she'd seen me around. Indeed, I'd walked by their house a couple of times before ever being introduced to the family. Berta (twenty-five) is the wife of Douglas (twenty-seven), who, in partnership with his father don Ramón (who everyone calls Moncho), is a cattle dealer. When Oscar from FDL told me the name of the client he had chosen to put me with next, I dutifully wrote down "Dula," which is how it is pronounced here. Like Jimmy (pronounced "Yimi") and Evelyn (written "Eveling"), names in English are common but sometimes hard to recognize. Oscar prepped me, explaining that the son lived on a small plot of land near town in a house so modest we would not be able to spend the night with the family. In actuality, Douglas does not live there, but in a cozy house in town with his parents, great-uncle, wife, and only child, Douglitas (five). Matapalo is the family's second *finca*, purchased primarily as a holding ground for cattle after they are purchased and before they are transported to the slaughterhouses. The family's own cattle are raised on their principal *finca*, further from town, called El Paraíso, which consists of 150 *manzanas*. As soon as I arrive, the whole family piles into the back of the pickup, along with extra chairs and food to cook, and we head out to spend Sunday in the country. This is the first family with whom I have spent leisure time.

The *matapalo* is a kind of tree, of which there is one on this property. Less than five kilometers from Matiguás, it is just twenty *manzanas* in size. Land here is expensive: US$1,000 per *manzana*, as opposed to at El Paraíso,

Matapalo. Don Ramón's living room in their family's house in town.

for example, where it is worth about US$600 per *manzana*. The family has plans to build a two-story second home out here so that they can come out for a few days at a time. Presently, there is only a shack—indeed too small for any sleepover guests—where the hired workers, Jovania (twenty-three) and Juan (twenty-one), live with their two-and-a-half-year-old daughter, Miurel. Don Ramón has been a "negociante de ganado toda la vida" (cattle dealer all his life), and where to keep the cattle has always been a problem. He buys them one to five at a time, but waits until he can fill a truck, which takes at least sixteen head, before making a trip to the slaughter-house.[29] When others rent land to you, he says, it is often the least desirable piece, where the cattle escape and the pastures are inferior in quality.

There are also dairy cows at Matapalo, but they are permanent residents (although the beef cattle also receive the JRC brand). Though his primary business will continue to be beef, don Ramón plans to build a *sala de ordeño* here. Juan is in charge of the operation—he has given all of the cows at Matapalo names—which produces at least fifty liters of milk a day. A local man rides by on his bicycle every morning and buys it (at C$145 per *pichinga*, or US$8.53) to resell in town.

Don Ramón's wife, Daisy (whose name I looked up for her, both of us learning that it means Margarita), and Berta are just as comfortable in Jovania's tight hut as they are in their own cement-block kitchen. This only surprised me later, when Berta showed me her bedroom, with matching beds for herself and her husband and her son, painted walls with cutout images carefully pasted up and a TV/DVD player. From an old radio Jovania has hanging from the wall, Daisy chooses a religious station playing hypnotic incantations at top volume—indeed, they are Catholic and today is Sunday—and Berta turns it down behind her mother-in-law's back. Over the next few days I will observe this a number of times.

Douglas and Berta married seven years ago. Her family lives on a *finca* at the entrance to El Paraíso, and Douglas would park his truck there to ride in. They married soon after meeting each other. He acknowledges that he

Matapalo. In the kitchen of the Matapalo house,
a plucked chicken waits to be cooked.

would like to have another child, but Berta says that neither of them want any more and that she'll get the operation as soon as it's allowed, which is when she turns thirty. Daisy—*mamita*, as they say for grandmother here—explains that at three months, Douglitas stopped nursing; later, when Berta tells the same story, it is not an anecdote but a traumatic experience that left both her and her husband afraid to try again. Douglitas got so skinny, she worries. She is afraid another baby would get sick too, and a sick baby, she says, just cries and cries and can't tell you what's wrong.

Berta is one of eight siblings. Douglas has one sister, plus the half-siblings from his dad's first marriage. Don Ramón was one of fifteen children. In his words, he did not get one day of schooling. Neither did his wife. But he taught himself to read; it wasn't very hard, as he has a good memory. This is apparent from his success as a businessman. His father owned a few dairy cows, but concentrated his energies on agriculture. At a young age, Ramón knew that lifestyle did not suit him, and started the business he is in today, a business that requires keeping a fair amount of cash on hand, and constant hustling. Daisy worked as a seamstress for twelve years upon moving into Matiguás with the family. She suffered severe back problems from this, had to have her spinal column operated on, and now she can barely help Berta with the cooking. Don Ramón was disappointed that Douglas chose the country life instead of finishing his studies (he stopped after primary school). Now all of them have their hopes pinned on frail, overprotected Douglitas. He in turn wants to go to Mexico and sing with Vicente Fernández. Don Ramón says sadly but with conviction that Douglitas will study and move away. I wonder why he is determined for that to happen, when it means the end of a lifestyle that he has worked so hard to establish.

When we pull up in front of their house in town, having left Matapalo just before the rains moved in, men in long yellow slickers are waiting for us. Don Ramón is annoyed. This is why we should never leave the house empty, he explains. He and Douglas immediately speed off with the men to see about some cows. They buy five and deliver them to Matapalo before returning home. Meanwhile a friend of Berta's stops by and we sit in the kitchen drinking coffee. In contrast to the rest of the house, the kitchen walls are unpainted. Like in many other homes, the metal roof shows a constellation of perfectly round holes open to the sky. They use both open fire and a gas burner, depending on how much cooking they will be doing. Later, even the men who are always rushing off to do business are sucked into a *telenovela*. I am beginning to miss the information overload of life in the United States and try to imagine how this life in Matiguás would be for someone who had never attended school.

Jovania in the doorway of the house on the
"finquita" Matapalo. To the left, the kitchen drain.

Early in the day and sometimes again in the afternoon, don Ramón and
Douglas drive to Matapalo just to check in. On Monday morning they drop
me off there to spend the day with Jovania and Juan, who have worked for
the family for two years. Initially they were out at El Paraíso. Now Jovania
is happier, on "la finquita," because she can visit her family more easily;
she often rides into town on Saturday morning and spends the night. This
way, she can also attend evening Mass. Jovania is Catholic, as is everyone I
have met in this region. She holds, however, that most people around here
are *evangelistas*. Both her brother and her brother-in-law have converted.
While it seems strict to her that women are not allowed to wear earrings

and must wear skirts instead of pants and the men always in button-down shirts, she knows that her mother 'thanks God' that the men found this religion, "antes eran bolos," before they were drunks, and now they do not drink at all. She and Juan have been together for five years. It happened like this: She was living in Managua and came home to Matiguás for a visit. Their fathers worked together, and once they met, she never returned to the city. She liked Managua, but she was also glad to return to where she's from. And life is better here, as one is free to be outside; in the capital, one must shut oneself in with fear. She bought a little piece of land in Matiguás and her dream is to be able to build a house on it. Juan will continue to work the land, coming home every two weeks to be with her in town. At

Matapalo. Jovania bathes at the water pump.

her parents' place she has a real bed waiting for her, not like out here where the three of them share a cot (what most people sleep on, a collapsible wooden frame with fabric that pulls taut between the two sides).

Jovania never went to school nor did any of her three siblings, which surprises me since they grew up in town, but, she explains, "Somos pobres" (We are poor); hers is a family that works other people's land. Juan comments that his father owns 'a lot' of land: sixty *manzanas*. Because he has older brothers—I ask how many they are and he hesitates, unsure of the exact number, and ventures ten—he has to work for a wage. He is paid C$40 a day (US$2.35), seven days a week (Douglas informs me that, unlike himself, on Sunday the workers are responsible only for milking the cows and then are off). Jovania explains that Juan gets paid C$1,150 (US$68) once a month.[30] She is paid nothing. Don Ramón's family grows their corn and beans at El Paraíso, and Jovania and Juan grow theirs here. Juan hopes that in time he can produce enough to sell the excess. But he also thinks about looking for other types of jobs. He could be a mason, but there is no work in Matiguás. He would like to go to Chinandega, on the Pacific coast, to work the shrimp boats, where the work is hard, the hours long, and the pay good. I am surprised to hear this, as like other *campesinos* I've met, his work seems integral to his identity. He states that winter this year started on the twelfth of May, which is when they had their first heavy rain. "Se pone alegre a uno," a good storm makes one happy, as the next day will be the first day of planting—as long as one's land is prepared.

Miurel follows one or the other of her parents as they do their daily chores. Or she plays happily with an empty two-liter soda bottle, or entrances herself running her hand along the seat of a plastic chair to produce a squeaking sound. When she hears music on the radio, she sways her hips, trancelike, then runs for a baby doll to rock to the music. She follows her father and me as he wheels manure from the corral into the fields of grass that reach twice my height. We are deep inside this labyrinth, when Juan stops and listens. I never would have heard it, and can't make out what she's saying, but Jovania is yelling something to him. When we get back, he goes into the house and brings out a shotgun, and walks toward the *ceiba* tree. A hawk had flown overhead; they wouldn't eat it, but it's a threat to the chickens. We are too late and it is not to be found. I follow Juan as he fixes a fence, something that consumes a fair amount of time on *fincas*. He uproots a slender tree, which he identifies as an *indio desnudo*, naked Indian tree, to use as the new stake; he is planting it near a stream, and a dead post would rot, while this one will take root. As he works, Juan asks me if most people in the United States know how to read. He was able to complete the first year of high school before his dad pulled all the kids out of school due

*Matapalo. Jovania prepares corn in the kitchen
with her two-and-a-half-year-old daughter.*

to the long walk home in the dark. Juan has a higher level of education than
most in his station, and clearly has a passion for school.[31] He mentions an
English class that was offered once in town that he was not able to take.

I head back to the house where Jovania is cooking. She prepares a feast
for me: *huirila*, a tortilla of baby corn; scrambled eggs that have bright
orange yolks—"huevos de amor," she explains: love eggs, as opposed to the
forced industrial variety—and we eat squash, slowly baked over the fire in
sugar. All the while fuzzy chicks zigzag underfoot, making far more noise
than their size should allow. First Miurel and then the pig tread on one; I
try to move slowly in my big boots. "Ushe, ushe," Jovania says to the pig to

get it out of her way, making the same sound as Fanni at San Lucas had. I wonder how it strikes Jovania that she earns no wage for her long days of work, that she spends so much time in this dark kitchen, and repeats the same tasks day after day. She explains, "Así me criaba: trabajando" (That's how I was raised: working). I have arranged for a taxi to come for me in the afternoon, and as we drive back toward town, we pass a little boy walking somberly down the road, a dead chicken dangling in each hand.

The next day I accompany don Ramón and Douglas as they make their rounds to look at cattle. The first *finca* we go to is on the road to San Rafael. It belongs to other middlemen: those who travel into the mountains to buy one cow at a time from *campesinos* who do not have the means to deal directly with the slaughterhouse. Don Ramón and Douglas stand and study the cows because they buy them "a la vista," by sight, and can make mistakes that cause them to lose money when they resell. It is not an exact science, and I get different answers to questions about how much money they make, but the outer limits are C$300 and C$800 (US$18 and US$47) per cow, between C$3,000 and C$9,000 (US$176 and US$529) per trip to the butcher.[32] A dairy cow is worth more, and a bull still more.[33] All of this leads to the interesting discovery that the beef being exported to the United States is all from male animals; as don Ramón puts it, the good meat, the healthy, fat bulls, go to your country. The only females that get butchered are old, or those that for some other reason do not give good milk or cannot breed. This is the beef that stays in Nicaragua.

As we wind through the gentle, green mountains on a road where truckers come around the bend taking up a lane and a half, Douglas plays Tigres del Norte songs. In this old shell of a pickup truck, he has installed a CD player and displays a large collection of burned CDs. He declares that the music most listened to by Nicaraguans is Mexican *ranchera*. Douglas and his father, however, wear baseball caps; it is great-uncle Virgilio, whom they simply refer to as "Tío" (Uncle), who never removes his cowboy hat. We are on our way to their second engagement of the day, and Tío comes with us to *pasear* (come along for the ride) he says, although he brings his machete as if to work. They are to buy some cattle from Daisy's brother-in-law, and we leave Tío at the relatives' house while we go out to the pastures. When we pick him up he has a bundle of firewood under his arm—for his coffee, he explains sheepishly. He is in the kitchen, and the men tease him: 'Is lunch ready yet?' Everyone laughs, and I am reminded that the men in this family, sweet and gentle as they are, are very traditional. Back on the road, we pass a trucker parked at a curve. He has strung his hammock underneath his rig and is resting. Around the next bend we come upon a wayward semi, lodged into the front porch of a house. A

*Matapalo. Don Ramón, Douglas, and a cousin stop
at a roadside stand while out looking at cattle to buy.*

couple of kilometers later, a pickup full of *pichingas,* parked askew, contemplates a dead calf crumpled in the road. Douglas comments angrily that some people don't keep their livestock off the highway. The road is "bien incómodo," quite uncomfortable, he emphasizes. Then, on the way home, we get a flat tire. At one point in the journey, Douglas pulls over without any notice, and points to a hilltop. That is where El Paraíso begins. They proudly delineate the boundaries and make sure I see exactly where they mean.

Once a year they sell between fifty and one hundred of their own young bulls to the slaughterhouse at C$4,000 to C$7,000 (US$235 to US$412) each. They raise the bulls at El Paraíso, adding to their value as they eat and grow. Whereas Juan is the single permanent worker at Matapalo, there are five living at El Paraíso. Additionally, Douglas makes the trip out about once a week. An hour on horseback to arrive means that don Ramón cannot easily go anymore. When it rains, the way is rough, but usually Douglas goes and comes back in one day. Sometimes Berta accompanies him; indeed, they lived at El Paraíso until one year ago, when they moved into town so that Douglitas could go to school. The house there has running water and electricity. Douglas says wistfully, "Vive feliz en la finca" (One lives happy on the *finca*), with fresh chicken, eggs, milk, and cheese. But last February, little Douglitas started first grade. That afternoon as I am sitting in the kitchen with Daisy and Berta, he dutifully approaches his mother with his notebook so that she may check over his careful cursive letters. When the men return, the women crowd the front door to see what they need and wonder if they'll be off right away again. When Douglas is finally home for the evening, Berta sets his dinner before him and stands behind his chair as he eats. She does not seem servile; rather she is spending the time with him that she can. As they do not look forward to more children, and Douglitas has already started school, I wonder that twenty-five-year-old Berta's days do not seem to stretch out long and empty before her. From talking to Douglas, I do gain insight into one aspect of her contentedness. He is above all an attentive son, father, and husband; the night before he did not attend the town Halloween party, and states that he does not like parties and doesn't drink very much, although sometimes he enjoys watching bullfights and cockfights, plus the eight days of fiesta in honor of San José, the patron saint of Matiguás.

We are sitting in the living room, and don Ramón gives me a tour of the family photographs that hang on the walls around us: the graduation, then the wedding of Douglas's younger sister, who has been in Miami for just two months now. She and her husband were granted six-month tourist visas; Daisy explains that they will travel and reenter when that time is up in order to avoid illegal status. Douglas adds that his sister plans to stay for two years in order to return home with savings. On her second day in the United States, she found work; a friend helped her land a job as a cashier, where she earns US$500 per week. With her degree in business administration, she had been living in Matagalpa and earning the equivalent of that amount per month. While one often assumes that educational level is a product of a family's economic class, these two siblings vary greatly. Douglas says that he made the conscious choice to work the land instead of pursue his schooling. But he also explains the disruptive effect the war had on his education, as the family took refuge on the *finca*. Many in his generation lacked a 'normal' childhood, he says. This is ironic considering the vast increase the Sandinista government effected in the percentage of the population who could read.[34]

Despite her professional employment, Douglas's sister chose to migrate to the United States to work. He too would like to go. When we meet, one of the first questions he asks me is, If a good Christian has a U.S. citizen invite them, isn't it easy to enter the States? I imagine that he has been formulating this idea since Oscar knocked on their door and asked if they would mind hosting a photographer from the United States for a few days. I repeat what other Nicaraguans have told me—having a letter of invitation does not necessarily facilitate being granted a visa. As Pablo Damian had asked the same question, and Douglas seems to enjoy his work just as much, I wonder whether it is for adventure and perhaps as a rite of passage that these young men dream of taking the risk. It must be hard to remain behind as so many other members of your community travel and come back with exciting stories and significant cash.[35] Douglas explains that it is the only way to accumulate a sum of money large enough to invest in livestock. He asks, Everyone there drives a new car, right? Everyone in the United States has a university-level education, don't they? They ask about cooking practices and I explain that if there is a fire inside of the house, it is probably ornamental and not used for cooking. Another common question is, Are there poor people in the United States?

My last day with the family is November 2: Día de todos los santos. Don Ramón's parents are buried in the town of Río Blanco, forty-five minutes to the east, and Daisy's are in Matiguás, so the family will visit both cemeteries to clean and decorate the graves. I ask Douglas if he'll be accompanying his parents, and he replies, none too happily, that where they go, he goes; he's the chauffeur. Don Ramón came to Matiguás fifty years ago. Back then, one had to travel for a week by burro or ox to buy supplies in Matagalpa. Back then, the town consisted of undeveloped hills. Don Ramón explains that because his father did not leave him any land, giving it all to his brothers, he bought El Paraíso himself. Douglas continues the story. For a while, the family had a house in Río Blanco, near El Paraíso, but when the war came, don Ramón took his family and fled to the mountains. To avoid combat they lived for ten years on the *finca*, losing their home in Río Blanco. During this time, don Ramón's father passed away. The bridges between El Paraíso and Matiguás were not passable, due to rain and wartime destruction, and so *los viejitos*, who had lived most of their lives in Matiguás, were buried in Río Blanco. Douglas was just young enough not to be pressed into military service himself, nor did they see any combat on their land. They did lose cattle to the Sandinistas' hunger,

Matapalo. After cleaning and decorating Don Ramón's parents' gravesite for Día de todos los santos, the family relaxes at the Río Blanco cemetery. From left, Douglitas, Douglas, Berta, and Tío Virgilio.

however. "Ahora vivimos felices" (We live contentedly now), Douglas says, displaying the same sentiment of fulfillment as did Francisco at San Lucas, in having land to work, food to eat, and freedom of movement. Douglas attended a country school from the age of seven to fifteen, but he says getting an education wasn't easy then, with everyone armed and afraid. "Antes no había esa juventud en las calles" (Before, one did not see young people in the streets), as they were all hidden in the mountains. I comment on how different it is here than in Managua, where people his age did not talk to me about the war. Of course, he says, there was no combat there. "Cómo mataban gente . . . los campesinos" (How they killed people . . . the peasants).

   Don Ramón does not tell me much about how he passed the war years, just that they were hard; how many people died and how many fled, some not to return until the change in government in 1990. Communism is no good, he says. "Hay todavía gente engañada" (There are still people who are deceived), he reasons, to explain the continuing existence of the Sandinistas. There are always needy people who long for what others have, he goes on. His experience of the movement that was to liberate his country from dictatorship matches everyone else's in this region with whom

I've discussed this: They march onto your land with guns, tell you to leave, and then take everything you have. You chose between losing everything and dying, and so you just walk away. I ask don Ramón if those who sided with the Sandinistas were from here or were outsiders; he must have understood the question on a national level, although I meant locally, because he answered that Cuba implanted the ideas and it grew from there. But in these parts, "Toditos somos liberales, gente democrática" (All of us are Liberals, democratic people).

We are traveling the same eventful highway to Río Blanco, and the whole family is aboard. The same truck driver rests in the same hammock (his truck is broken down and he is waiting for a part, I am informed). Three people lie stretched out on the pavement, calmly waiting for something. A calf wanders the middle of the road, licking its fur, unaware of the fate of its brother. Douglitas and his mom take turns with a hand-held electronic toy; incessant videogame noise competes with Douglas's *ranchera* music. Everyone except me has dressed up; I did not have clean clothes, as the town has been without water for days due to the heavy rains of hurricane season.

Entering Río Blanco, everybody cranes their necks to find just the right plastic flower arrangement for don Ramón to buy for his parents' graves. When we stop for one, a woman with a baby approaches the window. It's Douglas's half-sister. Later he mentions that there are four siblings in that family, and that don Ramón gave them a *finca* as well as purchasing a house for one daughter who is a teacher in Managua. The whole family admires Río Blanco; here the houses are better and the streets are busier than in Matiguás. There is more money here. Indeed, after visiting the cemetery we eat lunch at a restaurant where the tables are arranged around an old swimming pool converted into a huge dance floor. We are the only customers and our food takes forever, but don Ramón only likes to eat where "gente decente" go, decent people, *finqueros*. They excitedly show me the small plot of land that was don Ramón's first *finca*, when Douglas was the size of Douglitas, his father says affectionately. I am surprised that Río Blanco bustles the way it does; I had assumed that the further down the highway from Managua, the more forgotten. Another phenomenon I have been noticing is the presence of foreign aid. Here there is a metal sign stretched above the main road: 'Donated by Japan.' They paved the road up to the new market, which, when we pass it, does not exist. The people never wanted their market far from town, up a steep hill.

Back in Matiguás now, waiting for my bus back to Managua, I squat in the dust bowl-*mercado*-bus stop. The *campesinos* stare at me and do not understand my accented words when I say which bus I am looking for.

Two young guys strut and preen. Girls in tank tops serve sodas. A family works the counter of their food stand. They all ignore the sight of a white horse eating out of a dumpster. The strange thing is, it doesn't look skinny or sick or scraggly or abandoned as so many of the animals here do. Though horses should never look like that, delicate and prized creatures that they are. Then the animal lifts its head to expose a festering red wound covering one side of its muzzle. Smaller spots on its back become noticeable. It is too disgusting to look at directly. The horse wanders to the middle of the highway and cars calmly avoid it. That is when I notice a rainbow arcing overhead, although it has not rained. Finally a bus comes blaring through, running the horse off and distracting me.

Conclusion

International demand for beef has had a strong hand in shaping this region of Nicaragua, and international demand could direct further growth in the dairy industry here. Although this rural area lies distant from the highly modernized life of cities and wealthier nations, its inhabitants look to that world for opportunity and to share in the richness of U.S. consumption. To a large extent, the nature of the cattle industry, if not its very existence, is subject to foreign influence. For example, U.S. sanitation regulations dictate the way in which these Nicaraguan dairy farmers and slaughterhouses do their work.

A hundred years ago, U.S. companies began doing business here. Later, beef brought such a high return that no one would grow beans for local consumption. Now an Italian company is the best customer for milk. Migrants and television tell stories of what can be obtained: there is no separating yourself anymore from the global market. That mammoth can determine a man's fate: Will he be a farmer or work for a daily wage (is a small plot of land competitive)? How much will he be allowed to sell (quotas determine not how much he can produce, but what will be allowed for import elsewhere)? Miles off the grid, producing two tins of milk in a day, these dairy farmers pin their hopes on something called CAFTA. Yet it is not known whether exporting dairy products to the United States will become an obtainable goal. It is not known whether new, lower tariffs could allow imported powdered milk to displace the real thing. Still, the promise of free trade bringing higher prices and more demand raises hopes that the dairy farmers of Matiguás will be able to make a living doing what they do.

The iconic entry to the Ingenio San Antonio.

THREE

Sugar

Chinandega

Soaked in sweat, constantly pursued by a brutal sun, hassled on the street, I am at the same time enjoying the most sensuous fruits and witnessing customs that are not only aesthetically fulfilling but only make sense in the context of the chaotic streets that surround them. Glimpses of a continuum that I cannot partake in nor truly live, but only steal temporarily in a glance: the blue-lit photo studio crumbling inside a gigantic red building; a chapel lit by candles, crowded with people facing a gruesome Christ—wrapped in a gold-sequin loincloth—each lost in their own requests.

I am in the stately city of Chinandega. The region has a reputation for being hot and dusty, destroyed environmentally by large-scale cotton growing years ago, and now, because it is surrounded by volcanoes and their fertile soil, sugarcane— another of the world's crops charged with a history of extremes. The volcanoes: from the bus I stare fixedly awaiting a glimpse, granted by a break in the foliage, of the perfectly symmetrical gray loners. They are commonplace for Nicaraguans, commemorated in paintings and flags and logos. Above them their smoke hangs motionless, otherworldly; they seem to have a strange effect on nearby clouds, as if their gravity is stronger than the rest of the earth's.

THURSDAY, NOVEMBER 10

There are three people who are always in the reception area at the funky, friendly APRICO office (Association of Private Sugarcane Producers): the receptionist, who up until now has given me more useful information about the sugar industry than anyone else, an old man who makes interesting conversation but whose

All of the photographs in this chapter were made in the town of Chichigalpa, the nearby San Antonio sugar mill, or the fields surrounding the mill.

speech I find difficult to understand, and a woman who looks like a man, who welcomes me with warmth and kisses me goodbye. The receptionist's little daughter immediately puts herself on intimate terms, asking my name and serving me coffee. Another older man wanders through and tells me that if I eat a Nicaraguan ear of corn, I won't need any other food for two days, only water. And the executive secretary, Ruth Betanco, who with few questions graciously arranges introductory meetings for me at the two largest sugar mills.

The wires are down on one of Chinandega's main streets. It seems a permanent condition. At first I avoided them for my life, but now, as I walk, I nonchalantly sidestep the tangles. Spilling out of doorways and from a shuttered house, blasting at the Internet café and in stores and buses, if it's not Latin pop it's eighties pop—nowhere else in Nicaragua have I heard so much Madonna, We are the World, *and Whitney Houston. One of the dark interiors glimpsed from the sidewalk turns out to be a workshop—holding a screw to make the round holes, a man weaves a cane chair. In Chinandega I sleep on a cane bed and sit in a cane rocking chair.*

The HR manager at the Monte Rosa sugar mill tells me to be careful, Chinandega is dangerous. Don't walk around after nine—especially beyond downtown. There are gangs. It's less safe than León, he says. I ask why—it feels small-town safe, though it's true that Chinandega has appeared often in the national papers with news of grisly murders—he says he doesn't know, especially as this region supposedly has less unemployment than any other. But he also thinks Chinandega is dirty, which he attributes to all the commerce that passes through town.

At dusk I stroll the perimeter of the parque central, *unnerved by the cacophony of the grackles in the trees and the creaking swing sets. From up close I study an alligator as it sleeps in a small cement pool surrounded by fencing. Walking home in the dark, I see, for the second Saturday night in a row, a big church wedding: the lights spilling out, the tiny white and black figures poised at the altar, the rose-petal-strewn red carpet lying now in the past.*

MONDAY, NOVEMBER 14

On the bus between the capital, Chinandega, and Chichigalpa, a town near the Ingenio San Antonio, the vendors yell and squeeze by each other in the aisle, comical in number. From the head of the bus a man earnestly hawks a remedy for all ills. Mostly, though, they are girls in their early teens who spend their days repeating "paletas de chocolate" or "agua helada," their voices intermingling until they trail off and they just stand staring into space. Some are so sweet, whether girlishly endearing or motherly, offering each rider a treat as if they really care that you have it and are content. We're packed on the bus, mostly school kids classic in their navy and white uniforms. Three girls giggle when the money collector squeezes through, his belly bulging in a white tank top, with yesterday's stubble

The plaza in Chichigalpa.

and a spider-web tattoo. The vendors stay on the bus until the last second, until it's already moving, at the edge of the parking lot or even to the outskirts of town, when they head down the steps to the next bus, still calling out, attempting to tempt with "naranja dulce . . . ."

The town of Chichigalpa, which I am always passing through and never stopping in, is enchanting: one church caving in, another with trees growing out the top, crowds of young people in the streets and almost no cars.

The San Antonio sugar mill is idyllic and suffocating: pastel houses and trim lawns, uniformed happy children, and the sunset behind the gargantuan factory, its ash sprinkling the residential streets. To live there is to live on an island, outside the rubric of society. As the vice manager informed me and they themselves said, *year-round employees tend to stay with the mill for their entire working lives. I meet families in which three generations or more have done as much. The entire town of Chichigalpa is intertwined with the mill; at some point in every conversation comes a mention of the person's relationship to San Antonio—her dad is a bus driver for them, his other job is in the hospital there. . . .*

THURSDAY, NOVEMBER 17

I am living under a string of twenty-one volcanoes (five active). Daily, ash floats down. It's no cause for alarm, however—people wave it out of their faces, mildly annoyed—it's from the mills: the zafra *(sugar harvest) has begun.*

Introduction

Because the soil in the Pacific northwest of Nicaragua has always been fertile, the history of the region is an agrarian history.[1] The area was a pre-Columbian settlement that after colonization became home to *campesinos* and larger haciendas devoted to livestock. Because of the well-watered, well-drained, flat and fertile terrain, the haciendas grew and began to invest in local infrastructure. Toward the end of the nineteenth century, plantations were pressing to expand by privatizing land from the traditional communal system. By the first half of the twentieth century the region had established the characteristics—such as unequal distribution of property—of an agro-export economy. By the second half, cotton was king. It busted in the 1960s but boomed to its peak in the late 1970s: global prices, pesticide use, and then war dictated its production.[2] In the rebuilding of postwar Nicaragua, sugarcane all but replaced cotton. What did not change was the deeply polarized class structure of the region.

Cotton replaced livestock, cotton replaced farmland, cotton pushed *campesinos* off their land (farmers would go into debt trying to compete with big producers and eventually go bankrupt), and so finally, cotton contributed to the proletarianization of the region. Those farmers became the quarter-million migratory workers who harvested the yield of this monoculture in Nicaragua, and those workers became some of the first to form a popular movement that would feed the Sandinista revolution.[3] Cotton became profitable due not only to its value on the world market but also to pesticides; it would become unprofitable for the same reasons. In the 1980s, pesticides came to represent 50 percent of production costs, eliminating many pest-eating pests and helping the boll weevil increase its resistance to a level thirty times that of its cousin in the United States.[4] One of the explanations for the epidemic of kidney failure that now takes

A bus transports the sugarcane cutters to and from
the fields at the Ingenio San Antonio.

the lives of hundreds of agricultural workers in Nicaragua—primarily in
the sugarcane fields of Chichigalpa—is that they are living out the conse-
quences of this past contamination.

Chichigalpa is a municipality within the department of Chinandega,
which is also the name of its largest city. The town of Chichigalpa harbors
Nicaragua Sugar Estates Limited, which dominates it culturally, environmentally, and economically. Nicaragua Sugar Estates was founded in 1890
and includes the sugar mill Ingenio San Antonio (ISA) and the rum distillery Flor de Caña, producer of the national drink. It is an important part of
the holdings of the Pellas family, one of the wealthiest and most powerful

in the country; the Pellas group businesses and distributorships include Toyota, Credomatic, Victoria Beer, IBM, and the Central America Bank. Although in my interviews I do not hear any bitterness toward the family, the magazine *Envio* interpreted the Nicaraguan media's lack of coverage of the hundreds of dispossessed sugarcane workers marching to the capital in 2004 and 2005 as disinclination to lose the advertising dollars of the aforementioned companies.[5]

Close to the sea, the region has easy port access, but the most extraordinary thing is the volcanoes. "A chain of volcanoes running through the western lowlands from northwest to southeast enriches the soil of the region through frequent dustings of volcanic ash."[6] Chinandega is also known for being hot, and sugarcane grows well in subtropical and tropical climes. A superior transportation network supports the industry. Almost all of the sugar produced in Nicaragua comes from Chinandega, and just over half of it is produced by ISA. In the year 2000, Nicaragua harvested over four million tons of cane.[7] The sugar industry as a whole employs between seven thousand and twenty thousand people. Including indirect employment (for example, service providers such as sugarcane transporters, machine operators, suppliers of fertilizer, agrochemicals, gasoline, etc.), the sugar industry generates jobs for thirty thousand to seventy thousand people. The number of citizens who benefit might be fivefold, assuming each of those people supports a family. Sugar exported to the United States brings in the highest profit, at US$23 per *quintal* (about 100 pounds). On the world market it is worth less than half of that amount. The raw material—the sugarcane—is cut by the *paileros* (sugarcane cutters) for about US$1 per ton. There are too many factors to compare here the economy of sugarcane to the refined sugar from varied sources that is delivered to grocery stores in the United States, but according to the U.S. Department of Agriculture, in 2005 the price for a pound of sugar there was US$0.44.[8]

More than half of the world's sugar comes from sugarcane (the rest from beets). The plant takes twelve months to mature and can be harvested for five years, beginning the same year it is sown, before the cycle must begin anew. The sugarcane is cut and loaded onto trucks in the fields and lifted off the truck at the mill. It is washed and cut into pieces. The juice is extracted from the cane by grinding (the plant residue, or bagasse, is sent to the boiler) and the sugar is extracted from the juice by heating, crystallization, and centrifugation. Raw sugar is the result, the product primarily traded internationally. Remelting and purification are required to achieve refined sugar.[9] One important byproduct is molasses (3.4 tons for every 10 of sugar), which is utilized, for the external market specifically,

Cutting sugar cane.

in animal feed and ethanol.[10] Another byproduct is the bagasse. In 1998, ISA was consuming two million gallons of petroleum per *zafra*, while in 2004 they required nearly zero;[11] electricity is cogenerated from the woody pulp, so during the *zafra* the mill is fully supplied and the excess energy is marketed to the national network. Off-season they exploit the six million eucalyptus trees that are cultivated to this end (though in the opinion of Dr. Sergio Rueda, a urologist at San Antonio and at the Hospital España in Chinandega, who treats many of the workers suffering kidney problems, this allows the company to claim they are reforesting, when in actuality they are burning up the soil's nutrients). In a further attempt to diversify, ISA runs a shrimp farm on the side. The *zafra* lasts for about

180 days between November and May, in which time ISA produces about five million *quintales* of sugar. While perhaps fifteen thousand *manzanas* (one *manzana* is about one-and-three-quarters acres) sown with sugarcane belong to San Antonio, it rents surrounding lands as well as buying cane from local producers, thereby, in essence, spreading across tens of thousands of *manzanas*. ISA commands great economic resources and is one of the most technologically advanced *ingenios* in Central America.

In the 1960s, San Antonio "was the largest producer of raw sugar for export in Central America."[12] In 1983, the United States cut its sugar quota from Nicaragua by 90 percent.[13] The state confiscated the *ingenios*, and for five years the Soviet Union was their largest customer. Exports to the United States began to grow again in 1990 with the end of the Sandinista government. Reprivatization began simultaneously and was complete by 1993, although land ownership disputes continued. In 1994, a report issued by the Comité Nacional de Productores de Azúcar proclaimed that sugar alone accounted for over a quarter of land cultivated for export. They complained, however, of institutionalized effects of the nationalized period such as overemployment and a culture of inefficiency that distracted from modernization.[14] One significant change that ISA underwent was moving workers' residences off its land; the *ingenio* gave land to two thousand

The mill at San Antonio.

people, allowing them to dismantle their on-site homes and rebuild in a nearby neighborhood. The workers who now suffer from chronic renal insufficiency (CRI) charge that the company made this decision after discovering how many cases of illness were emerging.[15] Antonio Vargas, a contractor, tells me that the company had to move the workers off after the nationalized period because Sandinistas who were no longer employed there insisted on remaining in the company houses. Others maintain that the move was made to increase the acreage available for cultivation, and they blame ISA for displacement as well as the contamination of the area's water supply and the resultant death of thousands of workers.[16]

San Antonio maintains a hospital on its property, attending to workers and their families. In addition, it has schools, a Catholic church, and various sports fields on its grounds. ISA claims to be the first agricultural company in Nicaragua to offer pensions to its workers and to pay a percentage of their families' food bills. I detected, however, a gulf separating the permanent employees of the company and the contracted or temporary workers. There is a hierarchy even among the former. Manual laborers are on the bottom, then operators or technicians, and on top the engineers. One man I spoke with, who has worked at ISA for eleven years and been studying for his engineering degree for five (with ISA paying half of his tuition, as long as he makes good grades), remains a laborer, the same status as the sugarcane cutters, he indicates. He complains that the company has month-long training courses for the engineers, but for the rest of the workers it provides only one-hour sessions, and with this it claims that it prepares its personnel.

Private, independent producers grow about half of the sugarcane that ISA mills. Like any other farmer, the producer must find his own financing and negotiate a price with his customer, the *ingenio*. The *ingenio* might advance the producer money, but the contract, according to one producer, is unilateral, with the mill getting the better deal. The producer does receive a bonus, though, if he supplies sugarcane with exceptional yield. There are different levels of producers, some with very little land and some with a lot. Compared to the rest of Central America, Nicaragua has few producers (650), and 2 percent of them grow 62 percent of the sugarcane to be sold to the mills, on large tracts of land.[17] The *ingenio* buys and processes the raw material to produce the final product (raw or refined sugar) as well as the secondary products. It is the *ingenio* that will market the sugar—and thus directly gain or lose under CAFTA—although the producer's income will also fluctuate with its price. It was through APRICO, which is one of the larger associations of sugarcane producers, that I was able to photograph in the fields as well as make contact with ISA.

Paileros adjust their arm and hand protection before getting back to work.

Most of the sugarcane is cut manually (it is explained to me that a machete cuts more cleanly than a tractor and means hardier regrowth, but some observers wonder if it isn't simply cheaper), and ISA's annual report explains that the *paileros* are hired by contract because they are migrant workers and there is a high turnover.[18] Others charge that by going through a middleman, the *ingenio* intends to liberate itself from liability to these five thousand men.[19] One former worker, Alexander García, points out an advantage to this arrangement; you don't have to show up every day. He specifies; after payday, turnout is very low due to hangovers. In a November 2005 article, *La Prensa* reported on worries within the sugar industry that the seasonal workers would be lured to neighboring countries that pay more than the amount offered to cut sugarcane in Nicaragua.[20] The sugarcane cutters are different from other agricultural workers—whose minimum wage is US$46 per month[21]—as they are paid on the basis of individual production. ISA insures that the contractors follow the *ingenio*'s safety guidelines, including providing protective equipment and distributing protein crackers and drinks with electrolytes to the *paileros*.

But this may be too little too late. As of February 2007, according to an organization of those afflicted (Asociación nicaragüense de afectados por insuficiencia renal crónica, or Asociación de afectados por IRC), nationwide 2,417 people had died from CRI,[22] 80 percent of them in Chichigalpa.[23] Some say it is a public health epidemic; already in 2001 the mayor of Chichigalpa noted that it was one of the principal causes of death in the region.[24] An estimated two to three thousand people are ill with this irreversible disease. Dialysis is the treatment and transplant is the cure. Both of these are financially unattainable here, although the government has set up a clinic devoted entirely to CRI patients.[25] A restrictive diet, medication, and lifestyle change can help, but even when a person stops working, a damaged kidney can only deteriorate further. 'It reduces the kidneys to the size of a bean,' reports a *Nuevo Herald* article.[26]

CRI is a gradual and progressive loss of the kidneys' ability to excrete wastes, concentrate urine, and conserve electrolytes; this occurs over a number of years as the internal structures of the kidneys are slowly damaged.[27] The disease is usually at an advanced stage by the time the symptoms are detected. One of these is an elevated level of creatinine in the blood (over 1.2 mg/dL)—hence the colloquial name for CRI, *creatinina*—which indicates that the kidneys have not excreted it and are therefore malfunctioning. The Ingenio San Antonio began requiring workers to undergo a medical exam before rehiring them each season, a controversial step because if their level is above 1.2 they are denied a job by the very company that has perhaps caused their illness, and to which in some cases they have devoted the majority of their working lives. Additionally, those whose *creatinina* is at an advanced stage have so little energy that they can do nearly nothing. Not only do they join the ranks of Nicaragua's unemployed (officially at just under 4 percent, though nearly 50 percent have no steady job[28]), but their lives are reduced to an oppressive monotony.

Sometimes *paileros* who only worked a short time fall ill, sometimes engineers do, sometimes their wives or children do. The *ingenio* uses this as an argument that their practices in the field cannot be at fault. But this could also be evidence of large-scale contamination. At ISA a work-safety manager alleges that the phenomenon is the result of unregulated chemical use by the cotton industry, as well as seepage from the volcanoes into the water and the hurricanes that stir it up. But the massive scale of this illness began to be noted in the late 1990s, and the cultivated area and capacity of the sugar industry has only grown since then.[29] Many observers blame the workers' lifestyle for their illness. Dr. Sergio Rueda says that the *paileros* work fourteen days straight and on the fifteenth day, they drink. But he compares them to professional athletes, with the exception that the cutters work at high noon. And he mentions the danger in the company practice of paying time and a half per ton when they need a larger quantity of cane that day, instigating the *paileros* to work faster and longer. These different means of overexertion, all related to dehydration, may increase the *paileros'* vulnerability to kidney disease.

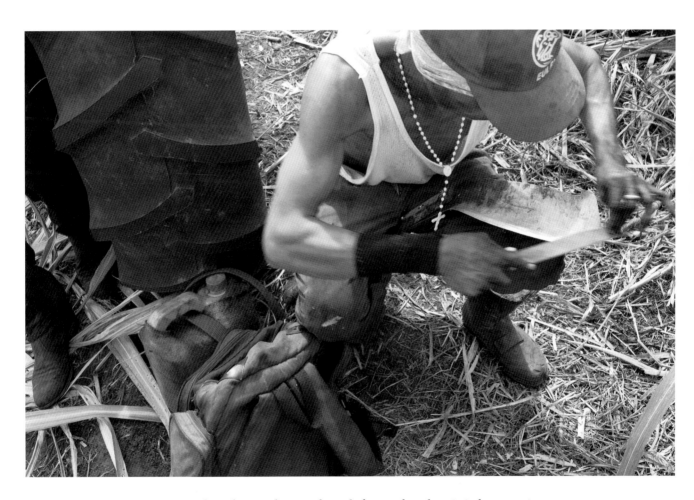

Workers sharpen their machetes before work and again in late morning.

Officially, the cause is unknown. There is a dearth of official studies, and no conclusive knowledge has emerged. The disease does appear to be multicausal. Locals believe the root to be toxic chemicals used, if not now, then in the past, at ISA. "Everyone who gets sick has in some way been linked to the San Antonio mill, not because we are the causers of the illness but because we're in the area where the problem exists," says managing director Alvaro Bermúdez, quoted in the *Miami Herald*.[30] Between 60 and 70 percent of local income indeed comes from this *ingenio*.[31] Drinking water is of specific concern. One in eight wells is polluted with substances that are banned in other countries. These same contaminants (DDT and DDE among them) were found in high concentrations in 99 percent of women who gave birth in Chinandega, and pesticide concentrations ten times higher than any acceptable level were present in their breast milk.[32]

The Ingenio San Antonio acknowledges the problem but sees it as a public health issue. Beginning in 2003, Law 456 has been in force, recognizing CRI as an occupational illness. This means that workers or their widows can collect disability pensions from the government, though they still do not have the right to compensation from the company. Apparently the realization of these payments has been marked by inconsistency and noncompliance, as well as legislative questions as to whether the illness is related to the type of work one does or one's place of work—whether only the *paileros* can collect, or anyone who worked at the *ingenio*. The government claims that the latter may be more than the social security system can handle. Either way, the pension provided is not sufficient for dialysis treatments. One of the primary requests of the Asociación de afectados por IRC is that the company restore the area's drinking water, cleaning up the surrounding bodies of water and the environment in general.[33]

Back at the APRICO office, Antonio Vargas picks up a printout and informs me that yesterday sugar was at US$8.47 on the world market—an excellent price. That means that somewhere else had a bad harvest, he says. Last year it went down to US$7, but this year maybe it will be US$14 or US$15. CAFTA is going to be good for them, he believes, because the United States pays the highest price for sugar (US$23/*quintal*). Right now the quota is two hundred thousand *quintales*; maybe that will double, he says (the quota sets the quantity of sugar that may enter the United States before the prohibitively high tariff is imposed). On the other hand, Nicaragua imports almost no sugar. As in practically all other sugar-producing countries (and there are more of them than for any other staple), it is protected by the government; here this takes the form of prohibiting imports via high duties (55 percent) and authorizing price-setting for the

Cutting sugar cane.

domestic market.[34] Nicaragua consumes half of what it produces—70 percent of which is destined for sale to the public, 20 percent for industry, and 10 percent for smaller businesses[35]—at about double the international price. Thus, the sugar industry makes its profit internally. Exports to the United States make up 2 percent of total demand.[36] The rest is distributed in the following manner, Antonio explains: five million *quintales* are sold domestically at US$20 per *quintal;* then come the preferential markets, one hundred thousand go to Chile for example, at US$13 or US$14; and five million more are sold on the international market at US$8 or US$9.

Some say that protectionism leads to overproduction, which leads to low prices, and that a freer market would mean truer dollar amounts on the international market. The current international market price is inadequate, as sugar costs US$20 per *quintal* to produce, and so others argue against removing subsidies. In a market study done on the heels of reprivatization, the author concluded that due to fixed prices, the sugar industry could not know if it was competitive internationally.[37] The Comité Nacional de Productores de Azúcar argues that protection has not made the industry inefficient and concomitantly that the sugar industry is big enough in Nicaragua that to destabilize it would damage the national economy.[38] Compared to other types of agriculture, sugar is more developed technologically, thanks to this political protection.[39] Presently, the sugar industries in both the United States and Nicaragua have enough political weight to ensure the status quo. It is generally agreed upon that correcting the world market cannot occur in a bilateral or regional agreement but must be done through the World Trade Organization.

Most countries produce enough sugar to satisfy three-quarters of their internal demand. Therefore only one-quarter of sugar production (or about 27 million tons annually worldwide) is sold internationally.[40] "Sugar is the most distorted commodity market in the world. . . . The biggest producers, and subsidizers, dump their surpluses on the world market for whatever price it will bring. As a result of this pervasive dumping, so-called world market prices for sugar have averaged barely half the world average cost of producing over the past two decades."[41] Central America supplies 1 percent of the world's sugar.[42] And while Nicaragua has the fewest *ingenios* of the Central American countries (at four), in 2002, sugarcane and its industrialization represented 6 percent of total exports and 2 percent of the gross domestic product.[43] Eighty percent of Nicaragua's sugar exports to the United States are produced by the Ingenio San Antonio.[44]

Because the price of sugar is controlled, it does not lend itself to free trade agreements.[45] Still, the U.S. sugar industry is concerned that CAFTA sets a precedent for duty-free foreign imports that might threaten its domestic market in the future. The Nicaraguan sugar industry will probably see only a slight change, and that change is likely to benefit the *ingenios* more than the producers or workers. This is due to the Sugar Compensation Mechanism written into the treaty. It allows the U.S. government to discontinue imports from Central America if it perceives that the U.S. market is threatened, but the United States must pay the foreign exporters for the amount of sugar that they would have been able to send under the quota. Oxfam calls this hypocrisy because while CAFTA demands the opening of Central American markets, the United States protects its sugar industry from what that organization calls "the product that has the greatest export potential for the region."[46] For the purpose of this project, it is important

A pailero, skin and clothing blackened from the burnt cane, pauses in his work.

to remember that Nicaragua will see little of this growth; most will fall to the highest-producing country, Guatemala. During its initial year, CAFTA was to allow Central American countries a 78 percent increase in duty-free access to the U.S. market; by the end of fifteen years it will be III percent, and will then continue to rise in small annual increments.[47]

The Central American Sugar Association argues that the impact of the higher tonnage of sugar allowed into the United States under CAFTA will be "minuscule."[48] The Office of the United States Trade Representative agrees: "In the first year, increased sugar market access for Central American countries and the Dominican Republic under this agreement will amount to *about 1.2 percent of current U.S. sugar consumption,* growing very slowly over fifteen years to about 1.7 percent of current consumption" (original emphasis).[49] U.S. sugar industry officials do not agree, and before President Bush signed the treaty, they gently reminded him that this industry is present in nineteen states and that a presidential election was nearing.[50] Meanwhile, Sinforiano Cáceres of Nicaragua's National Federation of Agricultural and Agroindustrial Cooperatives argues that cheaper rice, maize, and beans will be allowed to compete with Nicaraguan producers, but not sugar: The powerful sugar industry is less interested in exporting to the United States than in maintaining its subsidized domestic market.[51]

"[E]ven before the conquest and the massive reductions in population, the capacity of the land to produce crops had always been greater than the demands made upon it." As mentioned in the overview, Nicaragua is less densely populated than its neighbors, and so for the span of modern history the culture has been shaped by an agro-export economy.[52] Peter Rosset, executive director of the Institute for Food and Development Policy, stated in an interview that 'the primary historical attack on food sovereignty has been monoculture.'[53] The poor are pushed to less fertile land or go to work for often very low, often seasonal wages for the export crop that displaced them. Monocultures are not sustainable forever, whether due to market vagaries or natural limitations. The rural people who can no longer provide for themselves, who lose their land and then the wages that replaced it, are at the bottom of the economic structure. Interestingly, although the social context varies greatly, it is not only in developing countries that the population is dependent on imported food.

Antonio Vargas
SATURDAY, NOVEMBER 12

Today is the second day of the *zafra*, the cutting of the sugar cane. The machine starts cranking slowly: the men grow accustomed to working in the sun again, the trucks grow accustomed to hauling, the mill to receiving the *caña* and turning it into sugar.

I am visiting a plantation called El Parche; ISA rented the land and contracted don Antonio Vargas (who has brought me here) to hire the cutters and deliver the product. An engineer from ISA works with him. The engineer asks me to note along with my photographs that the cane they are cutting today was an accidental burn; it is three months shy of being mature (the ideal is 320 days), and that is why it appears inferior. This cane will only serve to generate power or run preliminary tests at the mill. At this stage of the harvest, things are running at about one-third capacity.

Photographing, crouching among the plants, I smell burnt sugar. The workers' hands become blackened from the charred cane. Now, on the heels of the rainy season when the early mornings are wet with dew, they burn tomorrow's allotment after the cutters finish their workday. Later, when the cane is dry and there is wind, they will burn in the pre-dawn. They set the fire on the perimeter in an attempt to maintain control, the flames moving down the rows, dulling the knife-sharp edges of the green leaves, which would otherwise prohibit the workers from moving among them. The fire also drives worms and insects out, provoking the many clusters of darting sparrows above us.

Every afternoon at two o'clock, don Antonio goes to a meeting at the *ingenio*; depending on the status of the mill, they will want between eight and ten thousand tons the next day. The cut cane can sit for two or three days before being processed, although it suffers a bit. The thirty-five thousand *manzanas* that are currently planted will satisfy ISA for the duration of the *zafra*. For six months the *ingenio* only halts if there is a machine break or a miscalculation in the quantity of cane it can process that day, Antonio notes. The *paileros* work the early part of the day, but into the night trucks armed with huge lights still scoop the sugarcane from the fields.

Antonio provides the bus that collects the workers before first light. They are transported to the fields where they are assigned their *rayas*, the distance that they are to cut: fifty *varas* (or forty-two meters) each. On days when the *ingenio* wants more sugar, they get more *rayas*, more rows. The workers are paid according to the weight of the material they cut. On average, in a day a *pailero* cuts eight to nine tons; for each one he is paid C$12 (US$0.71).[54] Every two weeks the ISA engineer pays Antonio, and Antonio pays the workers. Today they are being given their shin guards. I ask if it happens often that they cut their legs. 'Always,' says the engineer.

When it's 104 degrees Fahrenheit with wind blowing dust, the *paileros* will be working. And during the *tiempo muerto* (literally, dead time), Antonio still employs anywhere from 100 to 200 men, clearing weeds and tending to crops such as peanuts and rice, which can grow before the *caña* overshadows them. The off-season is the rainy season, and it is "off" because the fields become so muddy that a truck cannot traverse them, especially a truck loaded down with sugarcane. It is at that time that herbicides and fertilizers are applied by airplane; Antonio assures me that these do no harm to humans.

The beginning of the *zafra* is tiring. No one is used to being in the sun all day and it is hard not only on the workers, comments Antonio, but on everyone. *Pailero* José Alberto pauses to drink water and sharpen his

José Alberto working at El Parche, a property rented by the ingenio.

machete. His words match his cutting style: angry. He scowls and tells me that Nicaraguans are good at bearing up under the brutal sun. He says in the United States, work like this probably does not even exist.

I ask Antonio about El Salvador's recent efforts to attract Nicaraguans to work the coffee harvest, and subsequent worries about a shortage of agricultural workers here. In El Salvador, he says, they are afraid to go to work because of the *maras* (gangs). But he does not believe this will create a problem for Nicaragua's sugar industry; the workers are locals and they don't emigrate because they find work at home. He believes that the people who migrate to the United States from Nicaragua are more skilled—plumbers and construction workers, for example—not agricultural workers. The immigrants in agriculture in the United States are Mexicans, he says; Central American immigrants don't work in the fields.

Presumably Antonio lives comfortably, but on our ride back to town he displays acceptance rather than frustration over poor road conditions. Sometimes there is money for repairs following the rainy season, sometimes there is not; this is a poor country. His tone seems to indicate, 'We're all in this together.' As we part and I say, 'See you later,' he responds that he hopes so, but that in this country cork sinks and lead floats and so only if nothing befalls either of us. . . .

Noel Téllez Ríos
SUNDAY, NOVEMBER 13

I arrive early at the Chichigalpa bus stop, where Noel is to meet me. He is already there, which shows the kind of person he is: considerate and quietly responsible. He buys some oranges and gets us into a taxi, which he directs to the first road in Reparto Weell (named after some Danish people—he thinks—who donated money for the barrio). We leave paved streets behind and drive the dirt, though uncharacteristically the *taxista* does not complain. Rainy season has ended, just like that, and mud is no longer an issue, though as I write this, it's thundering and I'm hoping the *zafra* will not be held up. Almost all of the houses are constructed of block, which, true or not, now signifies a middle-class neighborhood to me.

When we arrive at Noel's home, his wife Esperanza is still getting dressed; she emerges, quite young and pretty, wearing the same red flowered dress that she has on in the photos they show me of their daughter's *quinceaños* last year. Martha, Esperanza's brother's ex-wife, is cooking. We sit down to chat. Esperanza serves me a glass of juice. Noel disappears to arrange for a neighbor to bring by the Sunday meal of soup in a couple of hours.

*Esperanza, the wife of foreman Noel Téllez Ríos,
in the pulpería that they run out of their home.*

Noel works the six months of the *zafra*, then three months weeding the rows, and three unemployed. He is a foreman in the field—an overseer as well as the boss of seven other overseers, all of whom work for contractor Antonio Vargas. He did cut sugar once upon a time but informs me that he has been in his current capacity since November 10, 1973. Since 2002 he has worked for señor Vargas instead of for the *ingenio* (which means he no longer has benefits like health care, a uniform, boots, and meals—although Martha says, and he later confirms, that the *ingenio* doesn't offer these anymore). He rides with the workers on the bus, which leaves at 5:00 a.m., and returns with them in the afternoon around two or three o'clock. He forms the *paileros* into teams and directs them as they work.

Don Noel is in charge of 130 men, at least 15 workers per overseer. Each man is paid according to the weight he cuts. It is the overseer's job to know who his strong workers are, apportion them larger plots, and pay them more. I think of Antonio Vargas's remark about how Noel learned to read and write, and that because he's a serious, responsible person, doesn't drink, and has proven himself, the workers respect him, and that's why he's a supervisor. Every afternoon, seven days a week, he goes to church. Noel is an *evangelista*. For the last three days he has not gone, however, because of getting too much sun.

Noel's sixteen-year-old daughter blows through, having just finished one of her finals—school is about to let out for summer break—but she and I don't cross paths again. Don Noel sees his son every month to three months; he attends boarding school and spends Sundays at his grandparents' ranch, nearer the school (his parents sent him there to keep him out of trouble). Noel's father cut cane all his life—Noel grew up on the plantation, Esperanza adds—and now Noel too lives his life under the sun in the fields; he wants his own son to study. Although it might appear to be labor that one would do when young and for only a few years, Noel says some men cut for a couple of decades.

Martha works at the *ingenio* as a housekeeper—Monday through Saturday, 6:00 a.m. to 5:00 p.m.—for one of the engineers who lives on site. The only thing that bothers her about this is that her boys are on their own before and after school. She is separated from their father, who does not contribute his fair share, she asserts. He was an engineer at the *ingenio*, until he got sick from chemicals on the job. He has CRI and now he doesn't work.

Before 2000, many workers lived at the *ingenio*, and most locals seem nostalgic for the days when housing, utilities, and cooked meals for the workers were provided. Martha recounts how they also had electric wells. And no, they did not raise workers' wages when they lost these benefits. Doña Ruth at APRICO simply said there were many, many problems. Noel and his family explained that it was a losing proposition financially for the *ingenio*. Where the houses used to be, now sugarcane is planted. Now don Noel goes barrio to barrio, knocking on doors to contract workers. It didn't used to be like that, he said. Before, when the *ingenio* offered benefits, the workers came soliciting. In the same breath, though, he pronounces that there is not enough employment.

The workers displaced from the *ingenio* now fill Reparto Candelaria. There are gangs there, I'm warned, though at Noel's the barred door hangs

*Young men stop by don Noel's home to collect their
machetes for the commencement of the zafra.*

open and there is a parade in the street of kids playing, going on errands, and attending an evangelical sing-along. Noel says the insecurity is a result of the inhabitants having moved here from all over. Every few minutes we are interrupted by a knocking, and someone—Esperanza, Martha, don Noel, Martha's boys, a visiting friend—yells out, 'What did you need?' The neighbor calls their reply: Eggs, beans, bleach, do you have soup? The family runs a *pulpería*, and it seems to generate a fair amount of business: Esperanza can't leave the house much, and Noel is constantly pushing himself up out of his chair.

Throughout the afternoon young men stop by, and don Noel supplies them with their "plumas." I know *pluma* to mean pen, but in this context it apparently means machete; they use a style termed the *australiano* (which has a curved tip to draw over the cane after cutting it). He also gives them a sharpener, which they will use at the beginning of each workday and again in late morning. When they start work, he will give them their shin protectors and a sheath for the machete blade. After two or three months, they will have worn out the machete and will be supplied with a new one.

Carlos Roja rides by on his bike, and Noel calls to him to come visit. He has been an overseer for two years, he tells me, and cut sugar before that, for seven years. We sit quietly on the porch, he and I uncomfortable around Noel's dog, a shorthaired, chop-tailed fighter dog with a jerky shoulder. A number of times the current headline is mentioned—a Nica in Costa Rica savagely attacked by two guard dogs. The kid was from Chichigalpa, and his funeral is today.

The Sugarcane Fields
WEDNESDAY, NOVEMBER 16

I walk with Noel in the dark and we wait with the workers as the world takes shape. When the bus pulls up, it is a big yellow bus, and so the workers lining up to board seem for a moment like dutiful schoolchildren. At least it is a bus; leaving the *ingenio* yesterday the taxi followed a flatbed pickup with workers glomming on like barnacles, colorful and lively for their perilous ride.

Upon our arrival at the fields, a number of guys take their shirts off and stash them in their backpacks, donning old clothes. One unfastens a gigantic silver watch and stows it. Next, most eat. One man complains that he woke up late and didn't have time to prepare breakfast. After a silent moment, one of the others asks "¿Qué, no tienes mujer?" (What, you don't have a wife?)

Before the burn, the sugarcane plants are startlingly green, and their tufts of white are so high. The plants we move among have dead leaves, the earth beneath scorched. Today we are on the grounds of the Ingenio San Antonio. I can hear the refinery mill and see its plume of smoke. Two days ago at El Parche, sparrows flitted about—an unsettling number of them, but they were sparrows. Today birds of prey circle tirelessly. One of the overseers explains that when the cane blazes, snakes and foxes burn. An irrigation ditch runs the length of the field. The water stinks and runs opaque. It is not destined for the grounds we are on; in this location irrigation is mechanized.

Crowded on the bus to the sugarcane fields in first light.

The contractors supply the workers with *bolis* (a Gatorade-like liquid in a bag), fortified milk, and a special biscuit. One of the workers mistakes me for an inspector, come to ascertain that their water jugs are wrapped to keep the contents from heating, which the workers are told increases their likelihood of falling ill. Most of them are in their twenties and thirties, a few older and a few adolescents of fifteen and sixteen years. "Pobre gente" (poor people), comments don Antonio, again, as we watch them work in the sun. One of the *paileros* has explained to me that if the bosses believe the group can finish their allotment for that day, they push them to keep cutting until around six in the evening, but if there is no way then they stop at four.

Workers head into the fields, each carrying his own water supply for the day.

To keep the sweat that runs down his machete arm from loosening his grip, one worker sports a winter glove, another a sock with the foot cut off, and a third a rag around his wrist. Others bind their hands, aching from repetitive motion or early season blisters.

A pickup truck full of *policía nacional* passes through; they explain that the *ingenio* requests their watchful eye by day and that by night they patrol in town. They buy a drink from the woman who sits all day selling her C$1 (US$0.06) bags of juice. I had been happily surprised by her presence at the back of the bus this morning—another female. Although later in the day I discover a clutch of women under a tree, selling snacks and sodas. Doña Mercedes of the juice affirms that she sells more out there than she would in town, even taking into account that the sugarcane cutters buy on credit. She shares proudly that her son is soon to finish high school and of her high hopes that he go to college.

When they are done, each worker pulls his fresh change of clothes from his bag. They are rowdy and happy as they wash down with water from their drinking jugs. The towels some brought were not to mop sweat but to dry off after this impromptu bath. The guys strip down to their underwear and finish spiffy, in baggy belted-below-the-boxers pants. Many procure cigarettes, so unappealing in this heat and dust that I am reminded that they are young men who want to look tough.

We sit by the side of the road and wait for a good while. Now everyone is quiet. Tractors and huge trucks loaded with sugarcane rumble inches from our toes—the earth seems to shake deep down with their noise—lifting the dust so that when I get home, I find that my legs are dirty under my jeans. We can't leave until everyone is done, so the effects of the bathing are reversed when most of the workers leap to help those who had more to begin with. No one seems to find this frustrating, and no one complains as we sit longer still while the last group takes their time washing. I feel that four o'clock has come and gone, but come to

*Before getting on the bus back into town at the end of
their workday, the paileros wash their tools and themselves
by taking a mouthful of water and using it as a spout.*

find out it's only 2:30 and that today they did half to two-thirds of the work they usually would.

I cannot say I was not exhausted and sunburned after that day; that I did not wake up sore the next, at an hour when I knew those workers were already back at it; that I did not drink an entire gallon of water without ever having to search out a bathroom; or that my experience did not more closely resemble that of the overseers, who sat in the shade along the field's edge. But at day's end I was also struck by the feeling that these guys worked hard but were not broken. They were jubilant at going home, again bringing to mind school kids as we boarded the big yellow bus, eating sugar cane, enjoying the completion of a good day's work. There is nothing wrong with physical labor, always part of existence; what seems unjust is that others benefit from their work more than they do.

María Lourdes Ríos (twenty-something)

THURSDAY, NOVEMBER 17

Because I am a photographer, the officials at Ingenio San Antonio elect María Lourdes Ríos—a confident young woman in charge of the on-site museum—to give me a tour of the grounds. She's in her twenties and lives

Maria Lourdes's home in the Reparto Sacuanjoche on the grounds of the Ingenio San Antonio.

at the *ingenio* with her boyfriend's family. He is still finishing his studies, while she works here and has also opened a clothing store in town. They live in one of the sweet pink houses in the Reparto Sacuanjoche (named for the national flower). She meets me at the main office and we walk first to her house so that she can change into more comfortable shoes for our expedition. We amble through the various neighborhoods—Reparto Calzada, Reparto Nena (named after a member of the Pellas family)—we see the hospital, pass the abandoned movie theater, peek into the church, and visit with the man who oversees hygiene issues. Lastly, María Lourdes shows off the incipient museum. Mostly, we chat about her view of life at the *ingenio*.

It used to be that five thousand people lived on the grounds. As the *ingenio* needed more land, she recites, it removed them and gave them houses in what is known as the Reparto Candelaria in Chichigalpa. As we stroll through streets lined with houses like the one she lives in, I ask what worker housing was like back then: the same as these, she says. She may believe this, but I do not. She estimates that currently two to three hundred people live on-site. Upper-level managers live next door to the mill in order to be available at a moment's notice. I wonder how their families feel. Protected? Trapped? It has been difficult for me to get from town to the mill, as a taxi costs three times what it does around Chichigalpa; and from the mill to town, as they are scarce in the late afternoon. María Lourdes surprises me by commenting that you might hardly know your neighbors; I had imagined a lack of privacy, but she feels no constraint on her personal freedom and views it as an advantage that the company performs upkeep on her home.

María Lourdes tells the story of the Sandinista period at the mill. Before, the *ingenio* had a movie theater, fabulous gardens, a recreation center for workers and for employees; it was nicer. Production dropped under the Sandinistas. A lot of housing was destroyed or allowed to deteriorate. Strong unions tried to control workers. For her, this experience and the subsequent realization of a miscalculation parallel the history of the country. In war, everyone loses. Discussing housing, María Lourdes says ISA had to remove the workers, as they had been instigators of the revolution that took the business away from the family.

But María Lourdes does not volunteer information about the war. When we walk by the movie theater, now in ruins, she says nothing. In 1993, the Pellas family recovered their property, and at that time workers lost a lot of benefits. The company was putting more resources into the workers than the work, she concludes. María Lourdes says that the workers realized that they had made a mistake and that their quality of life

The Adela cinema, on the grounds of the Ingenio
San Antonio, fell into ruin as a result of the war.

had gone down overall. ISA now provides more benefits than the other *ingenios*, María Lourdes proclaims, deeming their practices innovative: You receive a ration card with your paycheck and an assigned time to pick up your provisions, of which the company pays 60 percent and subtracts the remaining 40 percent from your pay. The company store used to stock everything from bicycles to food, but now it deals only in staples, as buying on credit became a vice for many. ISA also pays social security, provides meals for those who live off-site, and organizes recreation opportunities. But as with the school on ISA grounds, I understand 'employees' to not include the contracted *paileros*.

Carlos Lionel Canales (twenty-four)

There are no photographs in this book of Carlos Canales. We speak only once and he comments about working as a mechanic at the mill, but he will be either sleeping or at work until I leave and so there is no time. Carlos is don Noel's neighbor, father of two small daughters, one of seven siblings (five living). He is wearing a white tank top, his tattoos exposed. He is educated, sweet, and open. We are joined in our conversation, sitting on the front porch of her house, by his mother and brother. His brother is the second man I've met in this masculine milieu with toenail polish and tweezed eyebrows. Carlos graduated from high school and his brother completed a bachelor's degree.

During the *zafra*, everyone at the mill alternates working nights for a week, then days for a week. The mechanics work twelve-hour shifts, seven days a week. This week Carlos is to report at six o'clock every evening. On Saturday he will work from noon to 6:00 p.m., thereby resetting his schedule to begin again on Sunday morning. Working the "day" shift usually means staying until ten or eleven at night; one does not leave a job partially finished. Carlos's record is a thirty-eight-hour shift. Right before the start date of the *zafra*, they really have to push, and something always goes wrong, he comments. When they have to stay, the *ingenio* does provide meals. Other mechanics are very specialized, but Carlos works a lot of different areas, especially at night when the staff is reduced.

One of the first things that Carlos mentions are the accidents on the job caused by exhaustion or haste. 'Many people have died.' For bosses, twenty minutes is a lot of time to lose, and an hour too much. The old guys, he says, always remind us to advise each other of where we will be. Carlos relates a horrifying story of a man being crushed when the machinery was started up, the other workers unaware he was inside. Carlos also mentions the accidents that occur when workers show up inebriated, and he shares another story of dismemberment. In sum, "El trabajo es bastante delicado" (The work is quite delicate). Others say that working in the mill is easy, he says, but he disagrees; sometimes, when he's feeling exhausted, he wonders how to stop working there.

Carlos worked for one *zafra* as a *pailero* when he was sixteen years old. Never again. At nineteen he started at the mill, working for C$1,000 (US$59) twice monthly at various unskilled jobs. But every season his name was absent from the hire list and he had to reapply. He approached the engineer to ask why, and when they recognized his education and perseverance, they offered him the job he has now, as mechanic. He earns C$2,000 (US$118) twice monthly, from which is deducted C$150 (US$8.82) for the food provided by the company and the same amount again for social security. Regarding the health care, Carlos complains that he pays every month for attention he rarely seeks, and when he does it is impersonal, rushed, and often irrelevant: prescriptions for what's covered by your health plan, not what you actually need.

Last *zafra*, Carlos was at home for an entire month due to back problems. The doctor approved him to receive pay during that time: C$80 (US$4.71) per day, considerably less than his salary, so when he wasn't better after a month and the doctor offered to give him another week off with pay, he declined and returned to work. Soon after that, the front of his body was burned with hot oil. He went home, his face blackened and blistered. He was given four days rest, unpaid. The doctor told him, 'You work with your hands, not your mouth, and the blisters are on your face.'

Carlos just recently graduated from high school. When he started to work he had reached his fourth year; three years later he asked for permission to complete the fifth and final year. ISA granted him Sundays until 2:00 p.m., but the classes went until 4:00 p.m. And because of his schedule of alternating weeks, he would miss every other class. Plus he would arrive after working all Saturday night only to fall asleep in class. On the other hand, Carlos believes that 'that mill is like a school,' as he was taught his trade on the job; the *ingenio* will teach those who are interested in learning, he concludes.

It seems to Carlos that ISA has fewer *paileros* than before, and he wonders if that is due to the disappearance of benefits—a principal draw used to be the cash bonus and bag of sugar proffered at the end of the *zafra*—or because of mechanization. Most people in Chichigalpa are going to work at Monte Rosa these days, the competing *ingenio*. It's hearsay, he admits, and he's never personally been there, but he's heard that they give you a day off, feed you lunch, pay higher wages, and divide the day into three shifts instead of two. He opts to stay at San Antonio because he doesn't have to travel as far to get to work. And despite this perceived loss of workers, ISA has been raising production levels impressively as well as advancing technologically.

Carlos concludes that the reason he works at ISA, in spite of conditions that are sometimes hard to bear, is that 'It's hard to find work here.' His mother tears up as she reveals that one of her sons died of CRI six years ago at age eighteen, after just two *zafras* as a *pailero*. Carlos adds his own story of a coworker who died in the field from drinking water hot from the sun. I think of María Lourdes professing, as she showed me the display of machetes in the museum, that she considers the *paileros* to be the heart of the business.

Chichigalpa

It's not even five o'clock but night is falling. I'm chilled—maybe it's dengue fever? Maybe it's because it rained this afternoon. The campesinos and cane cutters know that there is a date when the rain stops, so while rain was a constant in Managua, by now it's nearly absent. Today the air is wet—my clothes feel damp and I move through thick atmosphere.

The Hospedaje Flores is aptly named; it's the second-to-last building before the dead end that is the Flor de Caña distillery. Despite the pretty name, a very bad smell settles over town for a number of hours every day. I sit under gigantic banana leaves in the patio of the otherwise dismal hostel. This region has high malaria counts because the mosquitoes breed in the water used to irrigate the sugarcane. Family groups walking to mass this evening seem like an organized march through town. One is always caught up in a tangle of bicycles. No one says anything rude.

As night falls couples talk and sigh softly in the rooms on either side of me. Earlier, the manager played loud Christian rock despite the love-motel aspect of the place; perhaps why the proprietor seemed surprised that I wanted the room. And why no one mentioned it when I asked around for a place to stay upon my arrival, and one of my interviewees commented that it's not a place women or couples would go. But actually, it's lovely to hear people conversing in even tones for an

Main street in Chichigalpa.

extended period. Not the abandoned nights in the office I lived in in Managua or the silent campesinos in the sleepy hills of Matiguas, not the blaring TV of all the family hostels. Although how this stinking, filthy, pest-infested place could be considered romantic. . . .

SUNDAY, NOVEMBER 20

The heavy flannel curtain over my window keeps out the smell, which I discover when I lift it to see the morning and almost gag. I wonder if it's just being this close to the distillery, or if the whole town lives with this.

The humidity doubles when you're on the grounds of the mill. That and the ashes raining down only add to the surreal feeling that it is a world unto itself. This morning the daily whistle, long and low, of the distillery sounds seemingly at random. In the land of sugar, the zafra rules. During six months the factory needs feeding twenty-four hours a day. María Lourdes said you can feel the energy cranking from her house, the trucks rumbling by at all hours.

MONDAY, NOVEMBER 21

At a meeting of the Asociación de afectados por IRC, the only two people in their twenties just happen to be sweet, soft-spoken guys. This aspect of their personalities accentuates the quiet of their lives. As is one of the symptoms of their illness—the sensation of suffocation—so is their daily existence. They are burning up on the inside, silently closing on the outside. The loneliness of their prospects is all-consuming. Theirs is an unjust, unnecessary fate. Their patience with it makes it nearly unbearable to walk away, to leave them in their struggle against a force so much larger than themselves.

FRIDAY, NOVEMBER 25

Leaving the Hospedaje Flores, I tell the owner, César, that I hope to return in five years to witness the changes CAFTA brings. He is twenty-eight and is surprised by the projection into the far distant future. He says, 'I'll be old by then'—he nods toward the group of little girls who play in the courtyard—'and they will attend to you.'

Asociación nicaragüense de afectados por insuficiencia renal crónica "Domingo Téllez"

SATURDAY, NOVEMBER 19

Without asking who I am or what I'm looking for, presumably conscious that global awareness can change local circumstances, the president, Carmen Ríos, and vice president of the association whisk me directly into a room where the sickest man lies, dying. We stand over him and they bombard me with information. There is a stifling odor that I assume is from the ill. Unsolicited, Carmen explains that it is the water from the *licorería*, from the *ingenio*; that for five hours every day, this is what they smell.

The association wishes to analyze the water in Chinandega, but they do not have the funds. They do, however, possess what appear to be authentic internal ISA memos regarding test results that conclude that the water is a cause of CRI. So many stories about the *ingenio* and so many theories! Here they suspect that the forty-year-old pipes being used by ISA are leaching residual toxins into the water. They add that the *ingenio* displaced the workers because it recognized that people were dying from close contact with contaminated water. However, they were moved to a *reparto* just two kilometers away, when international law states that citizens should live twenty to thirty kilometers from such a site, Carmen says. Indeed, it is not just the water but the entire ecosystem that is damaged from this industry; for example, ISA burns two to three hundred *manzanas* of cane every day—'smoke we breathe.'

This is just one of the associations in town for people with CRI. In addition, they join forces with banana workers affected by the pesticide Nemagon (while the latter receive more recognition and press, they say more deaths are caused by CRI). This Thursday five hundred *afectados* will march in Managua. The goal is that the government recognize their illness as work-related so that they can receive the corollary benefits (the money we paid into social security, one ex-worker interjects). As blind Justice has her eyes covered, the government thinks it can do whatever it wants with the laws that it itself makes, protests Carmen; we are considered "las chatarras humanas," human trash.

'We're burning up inside,' one man describes. Numerous people mention feeling as if they are suffocating. That their head feels like it will explode. Nausea. Cramps. You can't walk. You feel so thirsty that you drink too much water and lose your appetite, you retain water, die bloated. This is a progressive sickness—you do not recover (at least not here). 'We're all going to die, every last one of us in this town.'

Most have one nonfunctional kidney with the other only partially functional. The functioning kidney of the man lying in bed dying is at 30 percent. Others chime in that theirs are at around 60 percent. The more prevalent indicator is creatinine level. Although it is common for patients to receive different readings from different doctors, Carmen describes this ladder: 0.9–1.2 is normal; 1.3 means you are contaminated; the intermediary levels indicate the second stage of failure; and above 2.5 you are on the downhill to death.

In hiring for the current season, ISA turned away three hundred people because their level was too high, says Carmen. One worker decries being denied employment due to creatinine after working for the *ingenio* for sixteen years. They contend that there are four thousand sick in Chichigalpa, and those are the ones who have been tracked. What of the workers who come from elsewhere in Central America, asks Carmen? She herself has *creatinina* although she lived but did not work at ISA. Her husband died of it.

Lester Alexander García Obán (twenty-three)

Alexander's face is scarred, so he looks like a sick person. Once I grow accustomed to his visage, I realize that he doesn't seem sick at all (the disfigurement is from a bicycle accident). He does not lie in bed nor feel weak. Only if he exerts himself physically, in the sun, does he get feverish and is reminded that he has chronic renal insufficiency. Since in this town manual labor is his only option, he does nothing. When I asked if I could come to his home and photograph, he responded that he just sits around. And that is exactly what we do. He and the elderly ladies and the children—everyone else has places to be. After witnessing the intense work of the cutting of the sugarcane, the loss of that work suddenly seems worse yet. 'The work is hard, but redeeming; here one feels useless,' he explains.

As I approach, the kids are dunking rolls in their morning coffee. There are many family members around—children mostly, but Alexander's siblings and cousins constantly pass through. It's Sunday for one thing, and Christmas–summer break has recently begun. Alexander is the ninth of twelve siblings, five of whom live at home with their mother and grandmother. He has a daughter in town whom he does not see. Alexander attended first grade and two months of second grade before his mother could no longer afford to send him to school. He can read but admits he never learned how to write properly. When he was twelve years old, he started working in the cane fields, helping one of his brothers. When he was fifteen, he began to work for ISA in his own right, doing three *zafras* before his creatinine level became too high for him to be hired back.

One day at work he had a high fever. He finished out the day so as not to leave his partner in the lurch. He spent the next twenty-four hours in the hospital and the next three months on paid sick leave. But his creatinine did not go back down, so he could not go back to work. With a good diet and the right medicine, you can get your level down, he says. But his has risen from 1.5 to 2.2. Two of his brothers, two of his cousins, and three of

*Alexander, who suffers from chronic renal insufficiency,
in front of his family's home in Chichigalpa.*

his uncles have CRI. His father never got tested but did work at ISA, and
when he died four years ago, the hospital said it was kidney problems. Yes,
Alexander says, everyone knows the risk involved with this work, but we
do it anyway.

Alexander worked on a relative's ranch for over a year and then got
a job at the *licorería* assisting a welder. He was hired only after procuring
false test results from the clinic; there are so many people with this sickness, he explains, and they are so desperate for work, that a health facility
would rather they work sick than die hungry. That job was one that he
could do comfortably. Then he had his bicycle accident.

Alexander surrounded by his family on their front porch. Seated next to him is his grandmother; his handicapped younger brother sits behind her.

Like the facial reconstruction he would undergo if he only had the resources, he thinks his brother could have been healed if they could have afforded physical therapy. His brother fell out of a tree and now half of his body hangs limp. His mother says it is a miracle that he is alive, and that he was "sanito y gordito" (healthy and chubby) before the accident. He was in a coma for a month, during which time Alexander's sister stayed with him in a hospital in Managua, and Alexander slept on a park bench outside. That is when Alexander became a Christian. Now he does not drink and he attends services every evening from six to eight and on Sunday afternoons. Throughout the morning, we listen alternately to the TV and evangelical music on the radio.

When I arrive a little after eight in the morning, Alexander has already gone to buy the ears of corn that his mom will spend the morning preparing, to sell in the street later that day. His mother looks old—she is missing her top teeth, her veins bulge from her calves—but she is not old; her own mother sits with us. To prepare the corn, all you do is boil it; but she's been tending the fire all morning. The smoke burns our eyes; the wood takes constant attention. The family eats "gracias a mi diosito," Alexander's mother says, because she goes out to vend the corn as well as tamales. She is afraid of the day that her younger sons marry and leave her alone. Alexander's grandmother combs her long black hair and laughs. She laughs a lot, and talks, and no one pays any attention. She is a very elegant woman, yet she can split wood forcefully with a machete. As we talk, various family members take turns in the shower—a square constructed of flat bricks with a piece of scrap metal and a shower curtain doubled over a wire for a door. Across the fence, the neighbor also enters his shower. We can see the top of his head as he scrubs it. One of Alexander's nephews, just seven years old, twists a handkerchief, *pailero*-style, around his wrist.

Juan Carlos (twenty-six)
MONDAY, NOVEMBER 21

"Siento con ánimo para hacer las cosas"—I am motivated to do things, but who's going to give me work where I just sit inside? Juan Carlos asks rhetorically. He could only do a job that did not require physical exertion, and especially not in the sun. If he exerts himself, he suffers a sensation of heat and suffocation. So instead he rotates throughout the day from where we are now on the front stoop, watching a constant stream of people amble past who in turn stare at us, to listening to the stereo, to shut in watching TV. At the same time, it is uncomfortable for him to sit for very long. It is uncomfortable for him to stand for very long. Lying down is the worst, he adds, because a bed under a tin roof gets hot. The physical discomfort; the burning up inside, and then the heat of the sugar region. Later in my visit, he punctuates one of many long silences with, "Es aburridito aquí"—'It's kind of boring here, even for me, who was born here.'

Juan Carlos's creatinine level is 11. When he started working at ISA, in 1998, it was 1.1. He was tested again in 2001 and it was found to be 3.2. He lost his job then. It's the sun that does it, he says. He can't eat anything but beans and rice with no salt, and no fat or sugar. He stopped drinking alcohol; he never drank until he found out he was ill. Some say it will cure you, some drink to forget. Now it's been a year since he tasted the stuff. Yet his level continues to rise. He cannot afford the diet and medications

Juan Carlos, who suffers from chronic renal insufficiency, sits on his front stoop with his six-year-old son, Luis Fernando, on his lap.

required to get his levels down, he says, although he does receive pills from the Ministry of Health. Given that it was city hall that supplied mortality statistics to the association, and it is there that the bereaved turn for the coffin or the pension papers, why does it seem that the magnitude of this epidemic is escaping the officials? Do the young men taking the jobs know it's dangerous? Yes, Juan Carlos answers, but there is no work if not with the *ingenio*. The only other option is to travel to 'the other side' [the United States] he believes, but if you do that, you come back in a coffin. He explains: 'We are disliked by those on the other side.'

The *ingenio* beckons you. María Lourdes—who gave me a tour of ISA's grounds—had divulged that the people think the *ingenio* has a pact with the devil, and that this marks the *ingenio* as special; there they appreciate the story as local color. But when Juan Carlos says it, he is talking about the fact that though you may not want to work there, you go anyway. He tells me about a man dressed all in white who went out into the fields but never got dirty. He tells me one or two workers always die at the beginning of every *zafra*, and three or four more at the finish.

Juan Carlos believes that it was the water that made him sick, the water he would drink when he worked in the factory (he held positions both there and in the fields). Now when he sleeps he is afflicted with terrible leg cramps, which are getting worse. Every day he experiences unbearable headaches. He has no appetite. His older brother Rodrigo, who is presently on his twelfth *zafra*, working nights loading the sugar onto trucks, adds that if you keep working after being diagnosed with CRI, you die sooner still. Which is why their mother, Cristina, beats the streets, selling food— "para que me dilate un poquito más" (so he lasts a little longer). There are oldsters walking around with this illness, affirms Juan Carlos, but if you have a wife and kids, you want to work. The *ingenio* won't hire you, and one despairs. So he has taken various jobs since leaving: a year at a mill that subsequently shut down; a position as a stock boy, which wasn't worth it at C$10 (US$0.59) a day; and a short-term roofing job for the same money and at too great a risk. "Tenemos necesidad pero todavía no tenemos hambre" (We suffer hardship, but we are not yet hungry.). Now he can't even get a job as street sweeper, his mom complains, because the mayor is a Sandinista and we're not, though we voted for him because he's a friend of the family.

Ten years ago, Juan Carlos was dating the woman who is now his wife. She was a young teenager then and he 'stole' her; she was being mistreated by her family and wanted to be with him anyway, he recounts, so they left together. After two months in Granada living under his aunt's roof, they returned. He took whatever job came along: street cleaning, building assistant. Four years later Luis Fernando, their only child, was born. This Saturday he will graduate from kindergarten (graduations are important here, but are yet another economic pressure on school attendance). Today Juan Carlos's wife is not at work; at his insistence she went to the clinic after spending the weekend ill. Cristina says that when Juan Carlos's wife gets home from work they cook together and play, and he is different. He relates how his wife used to sell food out of the front of the house, which was successful due to their location, but stopped because everyone buys

*Juan Carlos's older brother, Rodrigo, thirty-two, works
nights loading sugar onto trucks. This is his twelfth zafra.
Their mother Cristina stands to his left, partially shown.*

on credit, and your friends turn into enemies. Now she comes home at
seven every night after packing shrimp in Chinandega for C$200 (US$12)
per week, not enough to cover household expenses and transportation.

Juan Carlos laments that if he could just receive disability he could
get out of debt. He at least wants the money back that he paid in; one can
collect social security after five *zafras*, and he only worked three. This is
the system that the Asociación de afectados por IRC should help him to
navigate, he adds. He did receive C$16,000 (US$941) in compensation from
the *ingenio*, but in four six-month installments, which he feels kept him

from investing in anything significant. He bought some land, which he recently had to sell for the cash, and his stereo, which now provides one of the three activities available to him. Currently he has his hopes pinned on doña Carmen's securing a house for him. Apparently the government will be giving away three thousand prefabricated houses. He doesn't know where they will be located, but he paid his C$20 (US$1.18) to get on the list, and he is to be among the first three hundred people to receive one. All of the sick people will, he says. Going along with my apparent skepticism, he adds, 'Maybe they're just going to give us a piece of paper with a drawing of a house on it.'

When Juan Carlos introduces me to his mother he says, 'Thanks to this lady, we eat.' She lifts a huge metal tub to the top of her head and steps into the street. She will return only when all of the meats and cheeses that she has loaded into it are sold. Besides this, she does odd jobs: cleaning, or tying *nacatamales* that another woman makes to sell. She comes home late and the neighbors talk. Once a man offered her a good job on his ranch, because he knew that she was a widow and he would not have to contend with a suspicious husband, but she declined. 'Before, I didn't leave my kids because they were little; now I don't leave them because they are big. Only God can take me away from them. I'm mom and dad and grandma. Without me they are nothing, just as without them I am nothing.' Cristina proudly proclaims that none of her kids have gotten involved with gangs. One can recognize gang members by the bandanas they wear low over their foreheads; she would threaten them with a hot iron before they would go out like that. They were not allowed to hang around the town square (less than three blocks from their house). If they were to get put in jail, who knows when they'd get out, she says.

Cristina gave birth to eleven children, five of whom have survived; the others did not live past infanthood, save one who died at thirty-one in a swimming accident that his mother believes was not an accident and that has her nervous any time any of her children go to the lake or sea. Juan Carlos was born in 1979, during the war. His father worked at the *ingenio* from age thirteen to forty and died of cirrhosis at forty-seven, leaving this house to his family. In the fifth grade, Juan Carlos had to quit school and work. Eight months ago one of his sisters left for Costa Rica for the same reason, and they haven't heard from her since; her four children live here with their grandmother, who sends them to school in the knowledge that it is the only inheritance she can give them. Juan Carlos and his family sleep at his mother-in-law's (she is scared to spend nights alone). And so for now, eight live in this house. Behind a wall of black plastic off the entryway, a nephew of Juan Carlos's and his wife with their new baby have made their home. His brother Rodrigo lives separately with his wife and three kids, and Cristina says that before he moved out, 'We were happy: the more people the better.'

Juan Carlos uses the word *aflijirse* a number of times. He uses it to describe the anguish he feels being an unemployed head of a family. And he uses it to excuse his humble home as we drag our plastic chairs from the dirt stoop to just inside the front door when it starts raining. The house looks solid from the street, but it is not. We sit in the hall between a pile of stuff and the black plastic, and it's dark and smells of urine as it does out front. The floor is dirt, and raindrops fall through the metal roof. Someone had mentioned to me that the *ingenio* threatened to shut down if CAFTA passed; cheaper sugar could be imported from the United States. Maybe augmenting this industry, increasing work in this sector, is a bad idea, if this is what it does to people.

Juan Acuña
TUESDAY, NOVEMBER 22

In a comfortable house in the Reparto Candelaria—just around the proverbial corner from Alexander García—live Juan Acuña and his wife and two of his grown children. Juan's father was ten years old when he came to work at ISA. Juan was born on the *ingenio* and has worked there for thirty-six years, not counting a three-year hiatus in Los Angeles in the late 1980s, where he also sent his oldest son, to avoid military service. (His brother did the same but remained in the United States.) Juan has a university degree. All six of his children are professionals, thanks to the *ingenio*, he says. The children of workers can be educated at the *ingenio* through secondary school and then may apply for college scholarships.

Juan is another employee that ISA has set me up with in response to my request to be introduced to workers. He dedicates a day to showing me around, inviting me into his house, introducing me to his wife. I meet his grown son, who has worked as an overseer and is now hoping to obtain his master's degree in irrigation in Israel. We visit his twenty-eight-year-old daughter, Greggui (her name is a combination of Juan's mother's name and his grandmother's), at work; for the last seven years—this being her first job out of high school—she has been a secretary and receptionist in the sales department at ISA. The family moved into their current home five years ago; the children grew up on the grounds of the *ingenio*.

Juan says the *ingenio* moved the nine hundred families off-site to Candelaria so that workers could own their own homes, and because of environmental health concerns related to noise. He explains that the countryside is becoming more mechanized as a result of scarcity of labor; people are migrating in search of better salaries and better working conditions, to Costa Rica for example. Juan and I set out in a pickup truck to see ISA's shrimp farm, which he explains is another way the *ingenio* takes advantage of its resources.

When I bring up CAFTA, Juan has a ready answer: In order to be competitive, the mill has initiated an improvement program of its installations and worker training. The thing about CAFTA, he explains, is that a poor country with inferior equipment and unskilled labor can't compete. We arrive at the *ingenio*; two small airplanes are parked near the entrance. They are used to spread an agent that causes the plants to coincide in maturation, Juan explains. He then speaks of ways in which the *ingenio* tries to be environmentally conscious, informing me that they use a fungus to avoid blight, and that they can produce it here. We pass the Río Zepeda, which belongs to ISA and which they have dammed to use the water for irrigation and for cooling machine parts.

People talk a lot about the contaminated water at ISA, I suggest. They talk a lot, yes, he responds, but we do analyses that come out clean. He admits that *creatinina* is found more in the field workers than in others, but he maintains that this is because they are not interested in taking care of themselves: they often subsist on a diet excessive in fat and carbohydrates, they do not have the custom of drinking water, they drink *guaro* (liquor), and they don't eat breakfast, which is why ISA feeds them soy milk and crackers at the start of the work day.

The shrimp farm was contaminated during Hurricane Mitch, but it is up and running again. We are just one kilometer from the sea here and it feels like the end of the world; sugarcane from forever abuts the parking lot. Later Juan observes that the workers are all from coastal areas because no one else could tolerate the lifestyle: they live in barracks for two weeks, then go home for four days. We tour the five human-dug shrimp pools and then head back to the inhabited area of the *ingenio,* where I eat the free lunch provided for the technicians and professionals at the gorgeous, and usually empty, Casa Hacienda.

Conclusion

The sugar mills in Nicaragua are run by Nicaraguans, and they market most of their product domestically. At the same time, the industry is deeply intertwined with the global economy: pricing, tariffs, competition, even alternative labor opportunities for agricultural workers, together determine the livelihood of those involved. The prospect of CAFTA

When they finish their allotment for the day, the paileros *mark their row; they will be paid based on how much they cut.*

instigated worries that the United States could "dump" its surplus sugar in the region—thereby undermining internal production—as well as optimism that increased access to the U.S. market would mean a windfall for Nicaraguan producers. In fact, in my attempt to photograph at the mills, management seemed anxious that I might report labor abuses or sanitation violations back to the U.S. sugar industry, itself looking for ways to protect its territory.

Globalization is present in the politics surrounding chronic renal insufficiency. Advocates use international regulations to determine which chemicals are poisonous. Workers turn to international reporters and nongovernmental organizations for defense, support, exposure, and to bring pressure upon those who might protect them at home.

As has been true throughout the history of Latin America, the majority of land remains in the hands of a few. At the top here is the sugar baron Pellas family, who have become owners of a globalized, diversified conglomerate of businesses. The rural proletariat depicted in this chapter is a sector of the economy that struggles mightily. It is born of monoculture, of crops large enough to impact the Nicaraguan economy. On both a familial and a national level, income becomes dependent on a global marketplace, as does sustenance—exporting one foodstuff to import others.

*Cayos Miskitos. I am told that the Cayos
are nearly deserted compared with the open season,
when there would be many more boats around.*

Lobster

Puerto Cabezas
SATURDAY, NOVEMBER 26

Stepping off the airplane there is an intense silence, not only in terms of sound, but movement. It's not the lack of activity of a small town, because the stillness resounds. By the time I drop off my bags and make my way to a café for lunch, I am in a trancelike state. Any movement that breaks the slow rhythm, that runs counter to the molasses drip of the day, seems notable.

Most of the houses are on stilts. Some short, some one story up; all made of planks, all painted blues and pinks now fading. Not only is it unbearably picturesque, it hides the poverty. Lying between these structures are red roads; the red dust swirls behind infrequent vehicles and after the noise of the motor is gone, the dust still twists in the air, but slow now, and silent, falling back to the way it should be. At times it is impossible to determine if passersby are speaking Miskito, Creole English, or Spanish.

Arriving downtown, Puerto Cabezas suddenly loses its charm; dirty now, honking taxis, sidewalks crowded with pedestrians. Shaken from the reverie of the back streets, I realize what's different about this place: people look me in the eye. And smile. My instinct is to meet the eyes of people I pass on the street, but in Managua this is an invitation for negative interactions. The women in Puerto don't stare at me with curiosity, but rather make themselves as vulnerable to me as I am to them.

I double back after walking right past the parque central *and cut across it. Now there are the sizing-up stares. Clustered everywhere groups of young men. Gaunt, dark faces searching for the deep shade—and disappearing into it—of the gigantic trees with hanging down vines. Police frisk a group, apparently a routine check. This is the other side of Puerto Cabezas.*

Introduction

Connecting Puerto Cabezas and Managua is a 360-mile highway, opened in 1977, which, during the rainy season, waylays buses in axle-deep mud. Although the eastern lowlands of Nicaragua account for about half of its territory, most of the country's population is located in Managua and the west. Columbus did arrive here, but it was the English that dominated the Atlantic Coast during the colonial era. Today, Creole English is as commonly heard as Miskito, which is as common as Spanish. In the northern coastal region, the Miskito people, Nicaragua's largest indigenous group, make up the majority of the population,[1] followed by Afro-Nicaraguans, who in large part are descended from African slaves brought by the English, and of freed slaves who migrated here to work from other areas in the Caribbean.

About fifty thousand people live in the municipality of Puerto Cabezas, more than half of them in the city itself. Thirty-seven percent of urban residents have potable water, while 25 percent do in the rural towns. Eight percent have electricity.[2] The integration of the Atlantic Coast into the national telephone system was announced in 1965 but not completed until twenty years later.[3] The cost of living is 15–20 percent higher here, as many staples are flown in;[4] many products are not regionally manufactured, but even locally grown foods are often imported, as intraregional transit is so difficult.[5] Most homes in Puerto are elevated, not for the lovely breeze, but to avoid flooding. I visit in December, when many houses are given a fresh coat of paint in honor of the upcoming Christmas season, and spherical, many-pointed stars are hung on the porches, a tradition brought by the Moravian missionaries from Bethlehem, Pennsylvania, according to local journalist Shirlene Green. (The Moravian Church in Nicaragua comprises nearly two hundred congregations, the vast majority of which are on the Atlantic Coast.)

The municipality of Puerto Cabezas includes the region's capital, which was originally, and since 1996 is again, named Bilwi. For many years, however, it was also called Puerto Cabezas, and that is the name I use in this text, as that is the name that people use in speech. The changes in name are significant however; in both instances they signified a realignment of identity, first strengthening ties to the rest of Nicaragua and more recently insisting on recognition of indigenous presence.[6] The Atlantic Coast is divided into two autonomous regional governments, north and south, which are referred to as the RAAN and the RAAS in Spanish. These were approved in their present form in 1987 and the first elected authorities were installed in 1990. The autonomous regions were created to counterbalance the weight of the central Nicaraguan government in this area that is so distant and different; to assure regional representation in national policymaking. A recent report by the United Nations Development Program notes that

La desterritorialización de las relaciones sociales que conlleva la globalización puede fragmentar el territorio nacional y también el espacio y tejido social comunitario en el que hoy operan los gobiernos autonómicos. Esto se hace más evidente si consideramos que, por la fragilidad y empobrecimiento de la Costa Caribe, las materializaciones concretas de la globalización, en estas regiones del país, con frecuencia son las más dañinas.[7]

The material manifestations of globalization—as opposed to ethnic identity or national sovereignty—referred to above include *narcotráfico*, migration (the Afro-Nicaraguan population in Bluefields has an especially high rate of emigration, including by "shipping out," or taking work on a cruise ship, as they speak English, which is a requirement for the job), and overexploitation of resources by and for foreign interests. Precious wood, small amounts of gold and silver from inland, and more recently lobster are some examples. Divers on the Atlantic Coast risk life and limb for a catch that nets them a fraction of the dollar amount lobster brings when ultimately sold in the United States.

The 1920s saw the boom of Puerto upon the establishment of Bragman's Bluff Lumber Company (under the same ownership as Standard Fruit) with a concession of eighty thousand acres of timber and the duty-free import of machinery. The company invested five million dollars in infrastructure, including the port.[8] Bragman's retained more salaried employees than any other venture in the nation.[9] And in 1929, the Atlantic Coast enjoyed the lion's share of foreign investment in Nicaragua.[10] While the banana business would see its climax in 1931 (with the export of six million bunches, low in comparison with other Central American countries),[11] lumber continued to be a primary export, not reaching its pinnacle until 1960 with 28,419,710 surface feet.[12] These companies evolved over the years, but what did not change was their importance in local economy and services.

Cuando se afirma que a mediados de los años veinte la Costa Atlántica era más norteamericana que nicaragüense, no se exagera. Las compañías bananeras, madereras y mineras eran las principales empresas existentes en Nicaragua.[13]

The spiny lobster is one of the most important traditional exports in the country (in addition to coffee, beef, shrimp, gold, and sugar), and for the indigenous people on the Atlantic Coast, it is *the* most important. Dennis

Williamson of UCA in Managua explained the recent history of the industry in an interview at the Centro de Investigaciones y Documentación de la Costa Atlántica, where he is director.[14] The spiny lobster is most abundantly found north of Puerto Cabezas and around the Corn Islands. Originally, processing plants were located near the latter, onshore in Bluefields, but after the 1970s oil crisis, when transportation costs became an issue, the Sandinista government relocated them to Puerto. The lobster are frozen and exported by air or by sea, meaning that ice and refrigeration are concomitant industries. The principal economy of the Puerto Cabezas region has always been export, and the principal activity has always been fishing. At first, encouraging the commercialization of fishing was a way to diversify as other resources began to expire. After the end of the civil war it began to be industrialized, until in the year 2000 exports of frozen lobster tails were worth sixty-two million dollars.[15] By 2003, however, the amount earned had been cut nearly in half, as they became scarce. According to the *Utne Reader*, "U.S. corporations such as Darden Restaurants, owners of the Red Lobster chain, and Sysco, a wholesale food distributor, are the primary customers."[16]

"Choose to ignore it or not, we—the vast consumer we—have forged a highly nuanced social contract with [the lobster divers]."[17] Learning to fish, learning to dive, is a legacy passed from one generation to the next, and it always has been. And as it always has been, on the Miskito Coast the most important source of food is the sea. Thirty years ago the scuba tank was introduced; this, in addition to increased market demand, caused a shift from free diving to semi-industrial diving.[18] Commercialization resulted in the proletarianization of those who practice the activity. Another result, due to corporate and institutional negligence—there are protective laws on the books, but they are not enforced—has been an increase in the health risks involved, most notably decompression illness, common due to lack of training, proper equipment, and regulation.[19] Local sociologist Edda Moreno asserts that the shift was a traumatic one for the community because of the common belief that all death occurs for a divine reason, thus, when divers use equipment that they have not been trained on—which is the rule and not the exception—and suffer an accident, the aggrieved do not seek legal action against the employer. This situation, she posits, is one that the companies take advantage of.[20]

Scuba tanks are necessary because the divers, or *buzos*, are diving deeper; they are diving deeper because the shallows are overfished. The more that tanks are used, the greater the need for them becomes. In response to increasing scarcity, international laws have been put into place declaring illegal all lobster tails under 5 ounces or 14 centimeters, which are

Cayos Miskitos. A buzo *between dives,* barilla *in hand.*
His cayuquero *is in the boat with the tanks of air.*

from animals too young to have reproduced. These are now trafficked on a global black market. There is constant fear industry-wide of international sanctions due to the environmental irresponsibility of catching young lobster, as well as the labor rights violations involved with catching all lobster. The majority of the Miskito population relies on natural resources for their subsistence; they are vulnerable to environmental conditions, but also to commercial ones, such as access to the international market.[21]

In August 2005 the regional autonomous governments issued a memo outlining their position with respect to CAFTA. In it they demand that if the treaty were to come into effect, it should be accompanied by a legally binding transitional agenda to insure the implementation of policies and institutional reforms which would strengthen the competitiveness of those sectors sensitive to commercial liberalization and take into account the ethnocultural specifics of the Nicaraguan Caribbean. The memo calls for policies that foster local and organic production, the certification of environmentally sustainable products, and the invigoration of the local economy through loans and jobs. It outlines minimum conditions required for the ratification of CAFTA and the imminent competition with U.S. markets associated with it, including a call for infrastructure development and criminalization of the misuse of natural resources.[22]

The *veda* is closed season on the sea. The lobster are spawning and for a few months the government disallows harvesting them (since the inception of the *veda* seven years ago, its length has shifted under pressure from all directions). There are pirates from Honduras and Colombia who do so anyway. There are Nicaraguans who cannot last from April until June without income, and so although they may support the protection of the species (and therefore the industry), they violate the prohibition. For the second time, in June 2007, the federal government of Nicaragua distributed a subsidy of C$1,000 (US$59) each to those in the industry who were desperately, seasonally, unemployed.[23] Dennis Williamson identifies four themes that must be addressed when discussing the work of the *buzo*: occupational health, remuneration (improving incomes), the drug trade, and the need to find alternative employment in the face of pressure to phase out the business.

He cites anecdotal evidence published in a magazine he oversees, in which a local businessman states that there are 22,035 people that directly and indirectly depend on the fishing industry in Puerto, counting the workers in *buceo industrial* (commercial diving), 2,210; *pesca artesanal* (divers who work for themselves), 1,350; and *las plantas* (processing plants), 847, and estimating that each worker supports a family of five.[24] The count differs depending on the source, but there are somewhere between 1,600 and 4,000 *buzos* on the northern Nicaraguan Atlantic Coast. The amount of their income is an equally uncertain number. In the mid-1990s, when commercialization was incipient, *buzos* brought in high salaries (around twelve thousand dollars per year).[25] What has not changed over many years, however, is the pay per pound of lobster tail. *Buzos* earn but do not take home US$3.50 per pound that they catch; the company first subtracts the *buzo*'s advance, any medical expenses, and fees for use of certain equipment and necessities (including food) consumed during the standard twelve days at sea. Also, each *buzo* has an assistant (*cayuquero*) to whom he pays up to 20 percent of what he earns.[26] Income thus also varies by individual catch, with around 30 percent of *buzos* bringing home upwards of C$5,000 (US$294) per trip, 40 percent around C$3,000 (US$176), and the remainder less.[27] After passing through the hands of the broker, the processor, and the exporter, the lobster reaches Miami, where the price paid per pound is US$14–US$18.

> *Ratty bedrolls slung across their backs, many half-drunk or stoned, the* buzos *pushed ahead in the late afternoon sunlight, hoisting yard-long metal lobster-hunting spears called* barillas *over their heads like the weapons of an attacking medieval force. The descendants of indigenous tribes and escaped African slaves, and now attired in soiled T-shirts of global celebrity . . . the Miskitos were looking for a boat. They wanted to sign on with one of the dozen or so lobster-fishing vessels tied up to the rickety quarter-mile-long pier.*[28]

The fishing companies directly contract one person, a middleman called the *sacabuzo*. He hires the *buzos*, who in turn employ *cayuqueros*. The *sacabuzo* earns a fee per diver that he recruits and is responsible for dispensing the *buzos'* pay. It is from him that they buy food on board the boat, which can result in a cycle of debt. *Cayuqueros* are usually *buzos*-in-training and according to some critics, child labor. Starting at age twelve and into their teens, they are responsible for the boat, equipment, and product of their *buzo*. While his diver dives, the *cayuquero* sits in a small canoe on the open sea, following the surfacing bubbles. At night on the main boat there is hardly room enough to lie down; the *buzos* share hammocks, if they are lucky. Up to seventy-five people cram onto most boats: captain and second captain, five machinists, two seamen to handle the air compressors for the *buzos'* tanks, one to weigh the lobster and one to ice them, a cook and his assistant, the *sacabuzo* and a pastor, plus thirty *buzos* and thirty *cayuqueros* (and their canoes, or *cayucos*).[29]

This is a description of semi-industrial diving. It requires a steel boat of perhaps 80 feet with inboard engines and a permanent crew. It requires the ability to ice the catch for twelve days. The two *buzos* interviewed for this chapter work on commercial boats, which also means that they have migrated for work opportunities to Puerto Cabezas from outlying communities and are away from the safety net of their extended family. Artisanal *buzos*, alternatively, work for themselves. Instead of diving where the captain anchors his boat, they stick to shallower waters, such as at the Cayos Miskitos, and use their own equipment. They too however set out in a *cayuco* with their *cayuquero*, and they too use the scuba tank. One might catch a glimpse of a free diver as well, using only a mask and a harpoon

Nina Yari, Sandy Bay. Lester Salomon has been a buzo *for seven years.*

and no tank. The other way to catch lobsters, in the semi-industrial as well as the artisanal mode, is with traps. Trapping, while eliminating health issues for divers, has its own problems. One is that the *buzos* are three times more effective at catching lobster than are the traps (too effective, actually, for species replenishment).[30] Another is that in order to make a living, an average fisherman would require more traps than he could afford.[31] And a boat collecting lobster traps requires a crew of eight, leaving scores of men unemployed in a single trip.[32]

Half of the *buzos* are in their twenties. Almost all of them are Miskito Indians. Two-thirds practice the Moravian religion. Sixty percent are bilingual Miskito and Spanish, while 20 percent are trilingual, also speaking Creole English. Thirty-six percent have five or more children.[33] Fermín 'Jimy' López, a stringer in Puerto Cabezas for the national newspaper *El*

Nuevo Diario, explains their culture: the *buzo* is paid well, but the money means nothing to him because he faces death every day at sea. What he wants is to feel alive and to have fun. When he lands, he might hire a taxi to be his private chauffeur, to drive him around for five days, play the music he wants, and party. Shirlene Green adds that when he lands, his woman might be waiting for him on shore, not necessarily because she missed him but to collect his pay or some lobster for the family before he goes drinking. "Easy come, easy go," is how Dennis Williamson describes the lifestyle of the *buzos*. "They earn well, and then they go party, so despite a high income, the family does not improve its situation." In response to this problem, the *buzo* does not collect his own advance, but rather signs on with a boat and is already out on the dock when the advance, perhaps the equivalent of US$50, is passed to his wife. It used to be paid a day early, but the temptation to spend it on alcohol before leaving, thus possibly not showing up to the dock at all, was too great.

Every day during the two weeks that the Miskito *buzos* are at sea they make three or four trips out from the main boat. For each trip they load up the four scuba tanks that will fit in the *cayuco*. This means that they are diving twelve to sixteen times a day, for just under thirty minutes each time. Generally, the recommended limit is three dives per twenty-four hour period. The *buzos* don't come away unscathed; they may come away with varying degrees of paralysis or they may come away with an embolism. They are diving with vastly insufficient equipment that they have never been trained to use. The Center for Disease Control states that the risk of decompression illness (DCI)—or the bends—is increased at depths greater than 60 feet. The *buzos* are commonly spearing lobsters at 120 feet. As a diver goes down, the toxicity of the compressed air he is breathing goes up; his body is using the oxygen but can't expel the nitrogen accumulating in his respiratory system, except through the bloodstream and subsequently the body tissue. The *buzos* experience a greater buildup of nitrogen due to repetitive dives, making injury all the more likely. It is also not uncommon for them to be diving under the influence of illegal drugs—crack cocaine or marijuana—and therefore to not realize their depth.

A well-trained diver, using standard decompression tables calculated for specific dive depths and bottom times, will ascend slowly, making periodic stops to allow the nitrogen to escape his body. A *buzo*, having no pressure gauge, is ignorant of how much air he has left in his tank and can find himself at the bottom of the ocean, empty. He rockets to the surface, and the nitrogen, which expands as the pressure lessens, forms bubbles that can supersaturate his tissues, disrupt circulation or affix themselves to the nervous system. One symptom of DCI is pain in the joints or bones, which will force the *buzo* up even faster. Lasting neurological damage, partial or complete paralysis, and possibly death can result. The treatment for DCI is recompression within minutes in a hyperbaric oxygen chamber that simulates the underwater pressure of the sea, allowing the diver to reemerge correctly. On the entire Atlantic Coast of Nicaragua there is sometimes one, sometimes functioning, hyperbaric chamber, which can take days for a *buzo* to reach.

The water spirit *liwa mairin* protects all creatures born in the sea. Any man who takes more than he needs runs the risk of angering her and receiving her punishment. She is like a siren, harvesting the *buzos* who harvest the lobster; "Ahí está y nos espera seductora para llevarnos al paraíso" says Alex, a *buzo* interviewed in a Nicaraguan news magazine.[34] The Miskitos' belief system dictates that if they have an accident or become ill while diving, it is repayment for their depletion of a divine resource. Thus ethnic, cultural, and linguistic characteristics compounded with ignorance of the risks involved, absence of professional training, inadequate equipment, and lack of other employment options, endanger the Miskito *buzos*.[35]

Twenty percent of *buzos* suffer paralysis,[36] and half live with work-related injuries.[37] Very few receive compensation from the company that hired them. As the *buzos* most often enter into a verbal contract—recognized by Nicaraguan law but easier to negate—with the *sacabuzo*, the companies evade financial responsibility for disabled workers by claiming that their only employee is the *sacabuzo*.[38] Still, when the hyperbaric chamber is functioning, it is most often the company that pays for the *buzos*' treatment. And the two *buzos* that I interviewed, Simón and Milton, both felt that their employers took direct responsibility for them. Some argue that it is the government that is not doing its part in recognizing the *buzos*' employment status and related illnesses, in order for them to receive disability payments. Miskito *buzos* used to be heroes for their feats at sea but now are more likely to become burdens upon their families.[39]

The Atlantic Coast of Nicaragua is infamous for existing outside the law. Functioning under the RAAN government and far from the central government, workers' rights and the regulation of conditions—for example diving licenses, certificates of health or insurance—are unknown or unenforced. But the industry faces a crisis. Nicaragua is the only remaining Caribbean country to allow lobster diving—elsewhere only traps are used.[40] So when workers strike, owners protest: Why invest in boats that will be obsolete as soon as the law changes? Or, as lobster becomes scarce and companies' bottom lines drop, they simply can't afford to pay more per pound. The debate continues, however, in fear of the unemployment explosion that would result if diving were to be banned.

Puerto Cabezas. Ana combing her hair in the living room.

It makes perfect sense. We've had ten years of war which tried to crush an alternative economic model and now no reconstruction program. What else are the thousands of demobilized troops and their families to do? They've been told to "insert" themselves into the world economy so they export cocaine to you in the USA.[41]

This was the view of Miskito leader Dr. Mirna Cunningham in the early 1990s. Most people concur, however, that the Miskito just happen to be in the stream of the drug trade—positioned between Colombia and the United States—from which they have both benefited and suffered. A report by the United Nations on the region explains, "Drug traffickers transporting cocaine north would apparently throw it overboard upon being pursued by authorities." The people who live and work along the coast find it. Some communities have capitalized on this latter-day bounty of the sea, constructing houses, churches, and schools. Other communities have experienced increased drug abuse, something to which the *buzos* are particularly vulnerable, as they have easy access (trading one product for the other at sea); they use drugs to bear the cold, deep water every day.[42] Edda Moreno points out another factor: The *buzos* spend extended periods of time in the exclusive company of other men, their evenings long and empty. She goes on to show that by stereotyping the *buzos* as druggies and drunks, and thereby rejecting them from society, people feel free of the obligation to right the wrongs that the *buzos* face on the job.[43] She cites a *buzo* explaining why, upon reaching terra firma, the first thing they do is hit the bottle: "[W]e're young and don't have a lot of responsibilities, plus in 12 days we'll earn the same amount of money again. We also drink because after 12 days in the water, the body is cold and drinking keeps us from getting sick."[44] Edda quotes another *buzo*, describing asking the captain to stop where soda and cigarettes, and illicitly, narcotics, are sold: "We take the opportunity to buy courage and strength."[45]

The drug and lobster businesses are intertwined. *Buzos* buy from *narcos*. Women, looking to provide for their households and posing as buyers for the local fish market, exchange crack for lobster. The *narcos* buy back what they had to throw into the sea from the communities that collected it on the beach, or trade them drugs for gasoline, supplies, or a place to hide. Communities sell what has washed ashore to dealers who take the product to Managua or Honduras. In 2004, the Nicaraguan navy confiscated nearly six thousand kilos of cocaine. In November of 2005 a navy commander told the newspaper *La Prensa* that on average a boat headed north, loaded with cocaine, passes by every two days.[46] Most people here believe that the U.S. Drug Enforcement Agency (DEA) investigates on shore. Whether or not this is true, they do seem to pursue the *narcotraficantes* in the water. Journalist Jimy López opines that the U.S. agents should take responsibility for the drugs that come into the hands of the locals; if the authorities do not recover the cargo, they are therefore giving the drugs to the people. But the drugs are not the root of the problem, Jimy explains. Poverty propels the Miskitos to deal in the first place, and it is racism that causes them as a group to be labeled *narcos*. As a result, he continues, the police can raid, arrest, and sometimes kill them with impunity.

Sandy Bay

What I will remember of Sandy Bay is corporal punishment, *narcotrafi-cantes*, and death by gunshot, although I see none of these.

I get up at four in the morning to be at Gilly Landing by five, when I will embark for Sandy Bay with Edda Moreno, who has invited me along. Gilly Landing is the secondary harbor in Puerto Cabezas, used for private motorboats, and Sandy Bay is a conglomeration of ten indigenous communities, a couple thousand inhabitants, a couple of hours north of Puerto Cabezas by sea. There are no streetlights in Puerto, so I admire the moon as I have not in years; the silver crescent against a full, black circle.

The massive, rolling ocean defies our brittle boat; from every wave we cross we slam down with violent force, compressing my spine from tailbone to jaw. The physical experience consumes my body, freeing my mind to focus on the environs; the wind, the white sky white water white sun and air misty and damp. To the left are trees and to the right the sea. In some corners of the world, one finds out that nature still works; despite extinction, contamination, and global warming, she's still doing her thing. And there are still people who live by it. We pass dugout canoes with black sails like pirate or death ships, but small and modest, the sails crumpled

Nina Yari, Sandy Bay.

and torn. This sight provokes Edda to comment on the dire need for a water ambulance to quickly transport injured *buzos* to Puerto Cabezas. Currently the indigenous people apply their own healing methods on the spot, like resubmerging the *buzo* into the water three times over. We pass groups of men on shore catching shrimp. The sea is bounteous; in contrast to *campesinos* and wageworkers, people on the coast need only gather. The lobster is dwindling now, and cocaine comes to replace it; perhaps it seems a natural way to make a living.

Encroaching mangroves shape the bay's entrance like a river. We wend our way confusedly until reaching Nina Yari—the central community in Sandy Bay, where we will spend the day—and hop off the boat to wade ashore. There is no way to enter town without getting your feet wet; the path is a continuation of the sea. Horses graze ankle-deep. Children trudge along, appearing to walk on water. Eventually it dries out and I put my shoes back on. Heading through town toward the school where Edda will give the workshop that brought us here, we pass a group of people gathering, gesturing. Edda grumbles that she doesn't come to Sandy Bay by choice; she prefers the communities further in, where they are waiting for you when you arrive. Those towns are similar to this one, but poorer. They do not drive motorcycles. One passes and she explains that they are a result of drug money. Bicycles, horses, or on foot are the only other ways to get around; I don't see one car all day.

No one is at the school yet and I busy myself, then realize that Edda and her assistant are gone. They have walked toward where the tangle of people has settled. People are yelling and I don't want to get too close. "Son of a bitch" is the phrase I hear over and over, growled and panted and spit. There are men thrashing around. One of them has his hands tied to a branch above him. Then I notice another one has his hands tied behind his back, with a rope also leading to a tree. I wonder if this is how they force people to work out their differences. A shrill woman talks over the crowd, then another voice, then the men. I inch closer but not enough to see more than the men's poses, reminiscent of a lynching. There is a third one, also tied. Edda finally explains that they have been accused of robbery, and that before our eyes invaded, the three boys had been being hit. The boys are addicts, she says, and steal for money to buy drugs. Children circle in close and hang from the tree to which the boys are tethered. The authorities were here but yielded the matter to the people to solve, Edda adds. Eventually a parade heads off, led by a single, very tall man. The boys are left to their families, who do not take them down immediately. Their mothers seem to be berating them now, and the boys are pissed. Edda comments that if everyone were disciplined this way, we would all walk a straight line; discipline in the communities is hard, and public. Even though it is a disturbing sight that has the potential to get out of control, it doesn't, and it doesn't really feel like it is going to. It seems more like an emotional release and a grassroots way of dealing with problems. Edda complains that they were only hitting one of the boys; the other is a brother-in-law of the man who was robbed. Some other people watch from afar, some smile hello as if this were an everyday occurrence, some continue on their way with stern faces.

This is a Miskito town, so everyone speaks Miskito. Some people speak Spanish. They greet you, however, with "morning" in Creole English. Fishing is the primary industry and provides the staple diet. There is no hospital. The church is Moravian. The houses are striking, pastel colors, elevated an entire story. In Nicaragua they don't use glass in windows, and these have heavy wood shutters with a Z brace, perhaps because the region is highly susceptible to hurricanes. There are big trees, flat land, trash, and roaming horses and cows.

While Edda is working, I ask to spend some time with *buzos* in their twenties. I land in the home of Bernard Padilla, thirty-seven years old, and his wife, Edith Cattus Gómez, thirty-three years old. We talk for a while and I photograph the family. Bernard tries to convince me that there are no *buzos* in their twenties in town right now—they are all out at the Cayos Miskitos—but that later we can go out looking. I inquire about injured *buzos* in this town, and he responds that there is one man with decompression illness, but he lives too far away. Everyone Bernard introduces me to works on the same boat. The same men always work the same boat together. First we meet Lester Salomon, who claims he is twenty-five. He and Bernard both have six children (Lester's oldest is fifteen years old). He is from Sandy Bay and has been diving for seven years. Bernard and Lester explain their jobs.

The *buzos* kill the lobster with a *barilla*, a long metal rod that they swim with; it sports a hook at one end and a spike at the other. One scuba tank gives them fifteen to twenty minutes underwater. They pull each lobster from its home with the hook, turn it over in their hand and stab it. They maintain that they bring up forty or so animals (about 20 pounds), grasping them by their antennas. Repeat twelve times per day. Five ounces is the legal limit on how small, and therefore young, a lobster can be. But because they are killed first and weighed later, the small ones also bring a price (C$20 per pound, or US$1.18). Of every 30 pounds of lobster caught, about 5 pounds will be under the limit. Or a *buzo* might come home with nothing. When he can't dive, he will work in the fields harvesting yuca, rice, and banana. From November through

March or June the catch will be too small to bother with, while August and September are high season.

The *sacabuzo* has three days after landing to pay the *buzos*. Sometimes he drinks the money away and says there is none. Six days of rest and again the boat comes up from Puerto—only one company, Maricasa, sends a boat to Sandy Bay to pick up divers. They sign a one-year contract, and, as Bernard puts it, then the company thinks it owns them. 'The company doesn't know what it means to get the product, they just want it.' They don't know how cold it is, how you have to swim slowly anyway because of the pressure. Whether or not a man likes this work is irrelevant; there is no other employment. Twenty-four to thirty men go out on these boats. It is dirty and they all crowd into a few beds to sleep. There is a cook on board, but their diet does not vary from rice, some beans, and fish. There is no drinking out at sea. The boat will come again today or tomorrow or the next day, and when it does, they will go out.

We come upon a knot of young men playing cards. When I make my request to spend time with them and photograph, they do not understand me. Abraham Salvinias (twenty-eight), who speaks Spanish in addition to Miskito—although he comments that he has not spoken Spanish for a number of years and has trouble finding the right words—translates. Everyone but him declines to participate. Abraham and I stroll to the porch of a *ventecita* where we can sit (the proprietress of this little store is a teacher and the men have suggested that I speak with her). It has been explained that the reason people are afraid of the camera is that the DEA has sent plainclothes officers here in the past, and that Nicaraguan federal law enforcement enter people's homes 'at night, like robbers,' photograph any expensive belongings, any nice house that might have been built with drug money. The authorities treat us as if we were Colombians, Abraham complains, as if we exported from here. There is a drug problem in the community, he affirms, when I ask about the incident that morning under the trees; since around 1990, crack is the drug of choice. He confirms that the boys being punished are users, and had stolen some gasoline and some barbed wire to sell.

When Abraham was twenty he spent a year in Managua. He attended the university, until he got sick and the doctors told him that if he kept studying he'd go crazy or else blind, so he came home and started diving, as there was no other work to speak of in Sandy Bay. No, he doesn't like it especially, and after these nine years, he says he's tired; but that's life, one has to work, and one has to make a living by the sweat of one's brow. Like the other *buzos*, Abraham is well aware that diving for lobster may be made illegal in the near future, but he does not exhibit alarm. Still, he has

CHAPTER FOUR

188

*Nina Yari, Sandy Bay. The traditional wood houses of
the region—as opposed to cement. These were in all probability
destroyed by Hurricane Felix in the fall of 2007.*

considered trying to get to the United States, and figures that he should leave before a ban is enacted, as the only way to earn a living here is by the sea, and if all lobster is going to be caught by trap, there won't be enough room for everyone. You should see Puerto during the closed season, he comments, "La gente camina desesperada" (People are without hope).

Often all of the men are out at sea and the women, children, and old people are left alone for two weeks. The navy has a station in the Cayos, but there is no way to communicate between Sandy Bay and Puerto. Right now, all of the *buzos* are home due to bad weather, Abraham says, contradicting Bernard. It is a calm and sunny day, but he explains that it has been raining, and the water remains stirred up for four or five days. Abraham used to work on the bigger boats, but now he prefers to hire a motorboat out to the Cayos and dive on his own. On the commercial boats, you earn less because the company earns more, he explains. They kill you, he blurts, then restates, 'They squeeze the juice out of a diver.'

This is a description of *buceo artesanal*. Up to eight men, *buzos* and *cayuqueros*, will hire a motorboat (for a percentage of their catch) to take them and a cook out to the Cayos. After paying for the gasoline—which they travel to Puerto to buy because it's that much more economical than buying it in Sandy Bay—and the use of the boat and the cook and the *cayuqueros'* salaries and food and C$12 (US$0.71) to fill each scuba tank, a *buzo* might finish work in debt. Some men free dive out there, but a *buzo* must have the tanks; contractors at the Cayos have compression equipment. You go down one time per tank (or a few times if you are not finding any lobster), seven to ten times per day, depending on how many tanks you own. Abraham at first estimates that he brings up about 20 pounds of lobster per tank, but later says that he might gross 10 pounds on a great day, for an average of 100 pounds in a two-week trip.

There are a profusion of houses under construction in Sandy Bay— many of cement instead of the more common wood slats. When I point my camera at one that is particularly gaudy to my eye, the workers yell at me not to take pictures; so I ask Abraham about other jobs in the community—carpenter, construction worker? But those jobs require special skills, he rejoins. Later I meet a *cayuquero* just back from the fields where he was pulling yuca; most of the plantations are not far. Or you can fish, you can catch turtles; everyone knows how, 'We grow up learning.' You can catch sharks and sell the fins; they are exported, but Abraham doesn't know what people do with them. Here, they throw the body away, or maybe salt and dry it in the sun, also for export. And there are odd jobs to be done around the *comunidad*, so you get by. Abraham says in their down time they take walks, talk, play cards and if there are dominoes, play dominoes. We meet up with his brother who adds that they play basketball from two to five o'clock each day.

Abraham announces that he's single and free, although he is wearing a ring on his ring finger. I get the sense that this is a new arrangement. He has three children but lives apart from them, with his mom. It turns out his sister is the teacher who owns the store where we're sitting, and that the surrounding houses belong to his mother, his aunt, and his grandmother. But when I ask how to find him if I return someday, he says to inquire under his father's name. It is mid-afternoon now and I am to rejoin Edda.

Nina Yari, Sandy Bay.

A local family has been contracted to make lunch for those participating in her workshop and we walk to their house and climb the stairs. In a big metal bowl under the open window (on the outside of which is a sill where the dirty dishes go—the kitchen sink is a wooden crate hanging off the side of the house) is a gigantic turtle head, still noble though the eyes are dull and staring above the bloody mass of its neck. The indigenous peoples in this area have the right to hunt turtles, although populations are dangerously low.

On the way home I overhear Edda mention that a Sandy Bay boy was killed. Halfway through our boat ride, another motorboat flags us down. It is filled with people, and it is drifting. Although shore is near and many boats pass, it looks like a desperate situation, just because boats are small compared to the sea and people even smaller. As we get close, we see that they are all women in the boat. They don't look especially scared, but then I can't understand what's being said. They watch us and we watch them, us in our boat with three extra tanks of gas and a running motor, us with only five passengers in the boat, and their outboard motor silent, their vessel crowded. Our driver pours some gasoline into their tank and we leave. As we travel on our way, we see two more motorboats, also floating. The guy next to me explains that the second boat is carrying the dead boy. One of their engines is not functioning—the other boat is flagging us down but we ignore it; I guess the first boat can take care of them now. Back at my hostel, the neighbor lady says a boy was killed in town last night. He was from Sandy Bay. He was out celebrating the end of school. There was a robbery and the police shot him, but he was just an innocent bystander.

Simón Benito (twenty-six), *buzo*
THURSDAY, DECEMBER 1

Simón has been diving for nine years. He is twenty-six years old. Being a *buzo* is the only job he's ever known (though he studied three years to be an electrician). He is reticent to the point of rude, until the union representative who has brought me here is gone. Then he is polite and responsive, though as Miskito is his first language, his Spanish is labored.

Simón lives in Puerto Cabezas, as do his two siblings. He lives with his wife and their three children in this house and he says he is the only *buzo* in the neighborhood. His dad is visiting for the day; his parents live in the *comunidad* Sisín, where he is from. Today, our first meeting, he expounds on his work. While we are talking, his wife comes home with a bag of fish and lobster.

When Simón is out at sea, he can bring up 3 pounds of lobster a day or 70, with 7 to 20 pounds being typical. It's like when you plant in good soil he analogizes, and your plants grow good roots; sometimes you are in good lobster territory. Usually he works two weeks on and one week off. However, as of today he has not worked in five weeks because of the winds. And his company doesn't offer advances.

Even when you're way down under, he says, you can see clearly; there is light and you are wearing a mask. It looks like what you see on the Discovery Channel, he explains. It is difficult to maneuver with the weight of your equipment (*barrilla*, tank, regulator, mask . . .), especially coming up when you are carrying the lobster. New divers get sick because they do not know to surface slowly. Many divers use drugs and then dive too deep;

Puerto Cabezas. Simón on his front porch. His wife's aunt,
Elsa Blucha, sits for the picture. Standing behind Simón is another
buzo from his boat, and his cousin, who stopped by to visit.

the freezing water, the current, not eating, and being high, and they get sick, paralyzed, Simón describes.

Simón says that he has a contract with the company that employs him, so if he were to become disabled, it would pay the related expenses. Even though I made contact with him through his union, he opines that the C$50 (US$2.94) that each *buzo* must pay the union for each trip out he makes (plus the C$25 (US$1.47) that each *cayuquero* pays) is money lost. And he says that it is to the *sacabuzo*'s house that a *buzo*'s wife goes, two days after her man has headed out to sea, for a loan to get the family by.

I arrive at Simón's house a little after two o'clock. He is sitting with his wife and kid under the house, smoking a cigarette. Everyone around here hangs out in the deep shade under the houses, but they receive me on the porch, where we pass the afternoon.

Simón's wife, Lisette, is trilingual and has an easier time chatting with me than he does, volunteering family history. Her parents are originally from the surrounding communities, but she was born in Honduras and grew up in Bluefields. Her family was visiting there when her mother passed away, and so there they remained, and there her sister raised her. As a teenager, she went on an outing to the Corn Islands. Simón was living there, diving, and she caught his eye. He asked her to be his, she remembers, but she wasn't interested. She returned on another vacation, however, and that time she stayed. They have been together for seven years now. Before the first child came, she would go with Simón everywhere he went. She relates accompanying him in his *cayuco*, and how she too put on a mask and stuck her head underwater and saw him swimming down, down, below, moving like a fish. She's scared to bathe in the sea, but not him. Now, with three kids, she doesn't get as far as the corner, she says, and she asks friends to go to the market for her.

Lisette doesn't go to church much either. Simón attends the Moravian church every Sunday. Plus, a pastor accompanies the *buzos* at sea, where they hear mass every morning. I imagine Lisette must feel alone when Simón is gone for two weeks at a time—scared to sleep alone, scared he might not come back. Yes, of course, she responds. Simón adds that sometimes he spends Christmas on the high seas. He is to leave again on Sunday and says it is a shame I won't still be here when he debarks, because he would bring me one of each thing the sea has to offer, listing them off: conch, shark fin. . . . While the company forbids them to take lobster home, if they are lucky enough to get a shark they can take the fin ashore, selling the less valuable body to the company. Sometimes a diver might get four sharks, sometimes none. Simón doesn't know what the shark fins are used for, just that they make something from it in other countries. The divers all sneak lobster out—not only their own women wait for them on shore, but also women who buy lobster directly. Sometimes these women will supply the *buzos* with cash when they need it—like these last weeks when Simón hasn't been able to work—and get paid back with lobster when the *buzos* have it.

If I retrace my steps through Nicaragua five years from now, will they still be living in the same location, I ask? As long as a hurricane doesn't hit, and God grants me life, we will be, Simón answers. They bought this

Puerto Cabezas. Simón's wife, Lisette, braids her oldest daughter Keyshel's (six years old) hair on the front porch.

house one year ago—previously they had been renting in another *barrio*—so they don't plan on going anywhere. Because it is on a large plot (roughly 500 by 460 by 165 feet), it is worth C$60,000 (US$3,529), while Simón estimates that the house being constructed across the way might cost C$10,000 (US$588). Behind the house but not belonging to them is a large green stretch of land. That used to be a lagoon, Simón comments.

One would think that more people live here than Simón's immediate family; various friends come by, and Lisette's uncle is visiting with his family. Throughout the day numerous people request, through Lisette, that I take their picture. Over and over; they sit very straight, I click. A longhaired teenager named Johnny (a friend of the family from Río Coco who will accompany Simón out to sea to determine if that is the life for him) puts his adolescent nonchalance aside to ask for a photo, and then again with his hair down. The neighbor calls up from the yard below, 'Take my picture from there!' Lisette's aunt, Elsa Blucha, arranges herself formally, folding her hands in her lap. But her uncle, standing very close to me, a crucifix dangling over a muscled bare chest built from working in the mines, declines when I ask him if I can photograph him. He extends his hand though, and upon explaining that *las minas* were owned by Americans before the Sandinista era, he asks if I can please do something, because the miners do not receive their pensions. These days he does odd jobs in different communities.

I ask if Simón or Lisette has traveled to other areas of Nicaragua; they have both been to the capital. Two years ago, when she moved to Puerto, around the same time that she gave birth to her youngest child, Lisette slipped off the stairs of the house onto some glass and had to spend a month in the hospital in Managua, she says. She was supposed to return to the doctor for facial reconstruction but did not have the money. Her eye remains disfigured from the scar. The stories that make up people's lives, the problems and the tremendous forbearance they require, are recounted with an element of expectation to the foreigners who come to hear them, but in the end, they must be borne by the teller, and it is the teller who retains the power to interpret them.

Whenever there is a lapse in our conversation, Simón asks me questions about life in the United States, "Allá en su lugar . . . ." He asks me a question that many others have asked: Is life happier in the United States? People expect me to confirm that it is prettier there, and happier, *más alegre*.

SATURDAY, DECEMBER 3

This time when I arrive I begin photographing immediately. The sun shines on the women taking turns scrubbing laundry; the clotheslines are already full, there are piles of colored fabric on the ground. The rest of the day we sit on the porch, and I take few pictures. As on my previous visit, Simón asks a lot of questions about the United States, but unlike most Nicaraguans who ask because they want to get there, live there, work there, Simón asks out of curiosity, to compare that faraway life to the life he knows. The way he speaks makes him appear slow, but it seems apparent that he understands what I am trying to accomplish; he describes his own work in detail and invites me to accompany him tomorrow to the pier and to church in the morning.

Puerto Cabezas. The view from Simón's porch on laundry day.

We talk about the packages of cocaine that the *buzos* come upon float-ing on the water. You can try to sneak them ashore, Simón confides, but if the police find it on you, you pay the price. The ones who get away with it, take it to Honduras to sell. We talk about the bad habit that men and women have in Nicaragua of being overly possessive of their partner. And that men have of keeping multiple women, Simón adds. His friend will not let him off so easy: You're one to talk, he ribs, with four kids, one of them with another woman! Simón inquires if I know what it looks like under the sea, if I know what creatures live down there, and again references the Discovery Channel as the most likely educational source. He wonders if I have ever gone on a cruise ship. From a distance, he sees Americans going by on the big ships. He adds that the community where he is from got twenty-four-hour-a-day electricity a week ago.

Simón brings out a worn, spiral-bound notebook—his daily log. He reads off his catches, line by line—how many kilos per dive, June through October. He slowly counts the numbers out, jumbling them with the dates. He describes an incident when, come time for his bonus, the com-pany for which he had made various trips claimed he had not worked for them at all. When he brought out his record book, though, they found his name on the rolls. He was told to come back on a certain day to collect, but it was a day when he was out at sea; upon his return they said he was out of luck, but he stood up for himself and in the end received a C$200 (US$12) food voucher.

Before I leave, Simón's cousin stops by. He was paralyzed for two years from DCI but now he is better and diving again; a not uncommon occurrence. He explains that it is the only work to be found.

MONDAY, DECEMBER 5

I lived for ten days in this port town before I saw the sea; from the center of town, you would never know it lies just three blocks away. Commerce, in its myriad forms, is the only reason to descend to the water's edge through

Puerto Cabezas. Looking through the screen door
at Lisette's cousin, Ana Blucha, sixteen years old.

the surrounding neighborhood's muddy paths and industrial detritus. I finally walk the pier, along with fishermen, strolling couples, young girls in groups of three, and a few military men, but only after passing through two sets of chain-link fences posted No Entry, Authorized Personnel Only. The final section of the pier no longer exists: only rotting posts and broken planks, realm of the pelicans. The rest of the pier is headed in that direction. I peer nervously into the choppy sea, not only on either side of me, but directly below, cold and gray. One of the three boats moored today is *Aljhon*, the vessel that Simón works. I try to visualize seventy-five people aboard this boat, the deck of which is already crammed with the *cayucos*, stacked at least ten high. I try to visualize where they sleep. I try to visualize being out at sea for two weeks in this rusty, beat-up old boat that to my eyes doesn't even know how to spell its own name.

Simón was going to head out to sea today, but he didn't. Yesterday, he was going to attend church, but he didn't. Or did he? The little girls were all dressed up, and Simón led the way, but he sped off quickly in order to lose them, looking over his shoulder nervously until we arrived not at a Moravian church, but the Catholic one, where he greeted no one and during the service didn't seem familiar with when to stand or when to sit, and where he did not pray or sing along with the rest of the congregation. I did not question him and he did not explain, and when he made it clear that it was not a good day for me to stick around, and then this morning that he would not be setting sail after all, our relationship disconcertingly, abruptly ended.

Carlos Alemán

SUNDAY, NOVEMBER 27

'The primary market for this area has always been and will continue to be the United States,' says Carlos Alemán, president of the Comisión de recursos naturales del consejo regional. '[CAFTA] is going to increase the amount of resources available for the market. . . . What we have is raw materials, so the most important thing for us is the balance between using them and protecting them.' Regarding the decreasing lobster population, he sees three options: create value-added products and products derived from the lobster, identify types of fish that have not previously been commercialized, or begin farming shrimp or other seafood.

As Alemán understands it, the international pressure to stop lobster diving has to do with declining numbers in the Caribbean Basin, not the health of the *buzos*. Diving for lobster has historically been an individual undertaking; there is no training, no medical exam. His solution to the health problems is to implement licensing to ensure that divers have previous experience and are in good physical condition. But federal regulators are less optimistic about this prospect. According to Alemán, the Ministry of Health (MINSA from the Spanish) maintains that it will take three years for them to perform the necessary examinations to license every *buzo*. The Nicaraguan Social Security Institute (INSS) reports they can only offer about 10 percent of the services that would be required of them if the fishing companies were to comply with INSS's own suggested regulations. No one party holds all the blame, Alemán emphasizes: The companies can't enforce physicals because the government does not provide the necessary facilities, and the *buzos* cannot be held responsible for their own unsafe practices, as this is one of only a few employment options.

There are a number of progressive laws and policies already in effect, according to Alemán. No new licenses are being issued to fishing boats, the quantity of lobster being caught is going down every year (the current amount, worldwide, is 2.8 million pounds per year), the number of traps allowed is fewer every year, and the local government will take charge of licenses for *buzos artesanales*. A new law is to become operative in January, under which for every pound of lobster exported, a few cents will be dedicated to meeting health needs such as those mentioned above, as well as securing a water ambulance and retaining a doctor for the area who specializes in diving-related medicine.

Alemán claims that 50 percent of lobster fishing on the Atlantic Coast is *artesanal*, and its being disallowed would provoke political and social upheaval; the government must invest in a transition. He mentions the Ley de Pesca, which he says currently requires the industry to shut down in one year, and opines that five years would be more practical. Nicaragua needs to investigate its alternatives, as some of the other countries in the Caribbean have. One example being the *casa cubana*, a cage for lobster farming that not only avoids the safety issues associated with diving but allows the lobster to be exported live, and therefore more profitably than lobster that have already been frozen for days.

Edda Moreno

WEDNESDAY, NOVEMBER 30

Sitting on the beach at Gilly Landing as dawn broke, waiting to get in a boat and ride up the coast to Sandy Bay, I had had my first conversation with Edda Moreno. She is a sociologist at URACCAN, the regional university.[47] She articulated her point of view on globalization as an educated Miskito woman from a developing country. She compared Nicaragua's relationship to the International Monetary Fund (IMF) to that of a child and a parent who does not let the child make any of their own decisions. She lamented that people in the community don't take it upon themselves to work together, by setting their own limits on how much lobster can be caught, for example.

Rich countries have money and poor countries have natural resources, she said. The rich countries create a situation in which the poor countries have to give up those resources for money. One result of this is debt; the national debt is addictive, like cocaine. The transnationals aren't going to solve this problem for us, Edda continued, we need an internal strategy; they may provide certain opportunities, but beyond that it's up to us. She believes that one form of activism is education: leaving one's community, preparing oneself and then returning to share what one has garnered. She is working to bring Miskito professionals back to their *comunidades*.

Today I stop by Edda's office to ask her more questions. She estimates that one hundred families in Sandy Bay depend on semi-industrial diving. The advantage to this work over *buceo artesanal* is that if you fall ill, theoretically you have an employer and therefore a safety net, but, she points out, contract or no, any compensation is at the discretion of the company. Edda details the hierarchy: company, boat owner, boat captain, *sacabuzo*, *buzo*, *cayuquero*. It is the boat owner who pays for the food and the fuel, and who loses money if the catch is meager. The *cayuquero* depends on the *buzo*. If the *buzo* earns nothing, he pays him nothing. The captain will pay the *buzo* for his catch, and the owner sells it to the company at US$9 per pound of lobster. The company processes, packs, and refrigerates the product and sells it in the United States for considerably more. Since the most recent hurricane, a number of companies have not been able to get to the United States to sell the product, so they don't have the money to pay the workers, and the boats have not gone out.

During the *veda* one can fish, and it's also the season for working the communal lands. I ask if *buzos* typically stash money for this time off and she says, 'Yes, the majority do, but we do not have a culture of savings; there is no tomorrow. If today you have, today you consume.' Edda outlines three pressures on the industry. First, in order to avoid the high incidence of debilitating illness (the alternative being professionalization, which would drive wages too high), diving for lobster must be stopped. Second, the lobsters being caught are too small and the population is shrinking; the industry must diversify and fish other species. And third, low lobster production due to other environmental causes, specifically deforestation on land that is causing sediment to flow into the ocean, destroying the ocean floor ecology.

Edda describes how in the early mornings, beachcombers come out looking for drugs that may have washed ashore. The people do not have to move from their community to sell the drugs; buyers come to them. When residents find some, they treat it as communal property, Edda maintains, and give a little bit to everyone. Or they sell it and divide the money between the families. Edda denies that the DEA was in Sandy Bay; the people are referring to the *policia nacional*. And I was not allowed to photograph because of a story that Univision [the Spanish-language media company] did—filming without permission—in which the people that live in Sandy Bay were portrayed as *narcos*.

Emilio Hammer
THURSDAY, DECEMBER 1

Emilio Hammer of the *buzos'* union, Sindicatos de Buzos de la RAAN (SIBURAAN), and inspector for the Ministry of Labor, is the one who introduced me to Simón and Milton, both divers in Puerto Cabezas. He explains the practical and cultural basics of their work.

He says the divers go to a depth of 120–140 feet, although their equipment is not made to go below 100. Because the captain of the boat gets paid by how much the *buzos* find, and these days the lobster are few in the shallows, it is in his interest to take the boat to deeper waters. While the diver is down, he will keep collecting lobster as long as he sees them; as Emilio puts it, leaving a lobster is like leaving cash. Thus compounding the extremity of his depth is the rapidity with which he ascends. A diver should always be below his bubbles, says Emilio, but the *buzos* come up ahead of their bubbles. They are also supposed to stop 15 feet below the surface for four to five minutes to liberate the nitrogen from their bodies, but they don't have a watch. The union has recommended that each diver be outfitted with the following: scuba tank, snorkel, breathing regulator, dive watch, depth and pressure gauges, and a tank that has been properly inspected. The tanks should be filled to 2,500 pounds, but the *buzos* do not fill them over 2,000, as they are old and can explode. If they were diving at 40–50 feet, they could come up quickly without worrying about the pressure change, but at 100 feet and over, Emilio says, 'Just by being there, their lives are already in danger.'

If equipment is one area of need, then training is another. Divers do not know how much air to take in. And they do not realize how much they are exerting themselves (another reason they keep hunting until their air is gone); Emilio makes a comparison of being underwater to running in the rain—you don't realize how hard you're working. Without flippers, the current would be too strong for the *buzos*. Divers should also rest between dives. In his capacity as inspector, Emilio has offered to train divers at cost. His interpretation of the ministry's disinterest is that the companies don't want the divers to know their labor rights. Drugs are another issue. The naval officers check the divers for drugs before they set out. Emilio gives a parable, which perhaps was truer in the past, of the Miskitos' place in the drug trade. When Columbus landed at Cabo Gracias a Dios, he and his men saw gold just lying on the ground. One could describe the cocaine that washes ashore today in the same way; the indigenous people here find it, and although it may be as valueless to them as gold was then, if they sell it, they profit.

Ninety-eight percent of divers are Miskito (and those that aren't are in Bluefields), quotes Emilio. The owners of the boats are mestizos, and he believes that because the divers are not 'their people,' they don't care what happens to them, making workers' compensation difficult to obtain. Companies will use tricks such as saying a diver worked for them less time than he actually did, to avoid paying. When they do pay, it's negligible. The *buzos* work for eleven days (including Sundays) and rest for three, explains Emilio, which means that they only work twenty-two days per month. Labor laws dictate at least two and a half days off a month, so companies use the *buzos'* more extensive days off as leverage. Emilio feels that *buzos* need legislation specific to them. He points out that Nicaragua's labor laws were written by businessmen in Managua and do not address maritime issues. If there is an accident, the company is obligated to pay for the hospital stay and medications, but the family must make the claim within one year. If a worker dies, his family is to receive 620 days' wages and they must make the claim within two years. Emilio recognizes that many times people do not follow these regulations, making it difficult for companies to comply. Additionally, *buzos* often change employers frequently (if they don't get along with the captain or don't like the food on a certain boat) as well as change names (in order to be rehired if it is known that they have been ill), making it hard to track them down.

Milton Perrera (twenty-two), *buzo*
THURSDAY, DECEMBER 1

Milton receives me with eyes engaged and sparkling. He is twenty-two years old, four years younger than Simón, and the difference between them is that between a kid and a man. The reason Emilio has brought me here is that Milton is in a wheelchair; ten months ago he was struck with decompression illness and became paralyzed from the neck down, after working for six years as a *buzo*.

Puerto Cabezas. Milton in his wheelchair, looking out the kitchen window.

Milton's goal is that within one year of his accident he will walk again, albeit with a cane. For the previous three years he worked for the same company—Nafcosa, or National Fishing Company of South America— and now they cover his physical therapy and medication (the union rep says he's lucky, as usually the physical therapy only lasts five or six months). And every Monday he can stop by their office to collect C$350 (US$21) for food and C$150 (US$8.82) for taxi expenses that the company pays him weekly, along with C$400 (US$24) toward rent that they pay per month. Milton rooms with three cousins, a sister, and an aunt, all of whom are young teenagers.

Milton is from the outlying community of Pahra, where his parents still live. In his community there are seven other affected *buzos*, two of whom have gotten better and are diving again. Milton started out as a *cayuquero*, but the older men would give him a hard time, and to prove himself, he had to dive. Milton's father is a teacher, and when Milton is walking again, he will become one too (before diving, he completed two-thirds of the necessary schooling). He wants to study in another country, maybe the United States if he could get a scholarship. He will not return to the life of a *buzo*; it involves too much suffering. Advice for a rookie? Try to stop diving. And if you can't, then don't drink your money away, because you don't know if the company will pay your expenses when you fall ill.

The stairs to the house are, like most, open, consisting of a collection of mismatched planks for treads. If I am nervous as I descend, how does Milton get up and down?

FRIDAY, DECEMBER 2

In his wheelchair, shoulders bowed, Milton sits with an air of despondence. But he seems pleased to have a visitor, and we pass the entire morning talking in the kitchen. Certain topics bring a light to his eyes, transforming his demeanor.

Both of Milton's parents regularly come to stay a few days. In between their visits, his primary caretaker is his fourteen-year-old sister, Tania. The cooking and cleaning fall to all three girls. He depends on the two boys, both cousins, to watch out for him. It is they who take him to his physical therapy appointments or to the doctor, or move him from chair to wheelchair and back. Milton speaks to the girls in an authoritarian manner. When they come in to start cooking lunch, he and the other guys move into the entranceway to play cards. They must take care that the cards do not fall through the floor; now and then a shadow catches my eye, through the gaps: people walking under the house. As the boys play, I hear them counting in English. Later, Milton explains that these are Miskito words: "one, two, three . . . ."[48]

Nacira, Milton's mother's sister, is sixteen. She has just graduated from *secundaria* and wants to continue studying. The kids are all being supported by their families—none of them work—as they have come to the city from their *comunidades* in order to attend high school. Milton is the eldest of the six. Besides the kitchen, off the entryway there is a bedroom for the girls and one for the boys, though Milton says the boys tend to sleep in the kitchen, where it's cooler. The four walls, the floors, ceiling, and furniture are all of the same bare planks. After Milton got sick, he spent a month in the hospital, then moved into this house. At one point in our conversation, Milton's leg begins to shake uncontrollably, rocking the bench beneath me. Sometimes his toes twitch involuntarily. Today, and every fifteen days, he has to go to the hospital to have his catheter changed. He would do it himself if they would allow him. It used to be that he couldn't feel it, but now it hurts. Milton sees this philosophically: "Cuando uno tiene dolor, tiene vida" (Where there is pain, there is life).

When I mention the proposed ban on current diving practices, Milton says divers need wetsuits; the *buzos* go down in just shorts, insufficient protection. He pulls down a snapshot jammed into the crack between the window frame and the wall; it shows him sitting in a green plastic chair. He asks when I think it was taken. A while ago, I guess. Last week, he grins. It looks like I'm healthy, like I'm a normal man, he proudly explains. A cloud passes over the sun; 'I was sad when that photo was taken.' Milton is quiet; he seems terribly sad now too. Then he looks up and the cloud is gone.

Milton says the houses in Sandy Bay are even nicer than these that I find so agreeable in Puerto Cabezas. It's because of the cocaine, he says; you sell one kilo to the *narcotraficantes*, you have C$75,000 (US$4,412). In a tone of neither scandal nor tragedy, Milton observes that drugs take many lives here, and he describes how an addict can get skinny and then swell up and then die. Although it's a constant in his world, he pronounces that he has never done drugs.

Milton is most animated by the optimistic questions. What does he like to do? Play cards? His eyes immediately go to a deck that sits on a high shelf in the kitchen. And before? "Pasear"—go out, walk around, see and be seen. Listen to music? He lists the nightclubs. And last night? The girls went to watch a movie (all of the neighbors have a TV), the boys to *pasear*, and Milton stayed home alone. I ask if he has a radio. Yes, but the plug is broken. Although around here you can always hear somebody else's music, perhaps this only serves to accentuate the distance of the near neighbors for Milton, in his wheelchair in this tower in the dark of night.

But Milton is content. He is obviously aching to walk again, but he is not unhappy now, he is not bitter toward anyone. He talks about his physical therapist, and it is apparent that he considers her a close friend. He is to travel to Pahra for one month and he will miss her, as well as his sessions on the equipment she has at her office, but he is counting the days—ten more—until he leaves. It has been ten months since he was there last—too long. Not that he dislikes Puerto Cabezas, but here it's only fun if

Puerto Cabezas. Milton's sister, Tania,
fourteen years old, prepares fish for lunch.

you have money, he has discovered. In the city, all you do is spend money. In the *comunidad*, you don't have to buy anything. There is fish and yuca and rice and corn; each family has land where they can plant. Milton has three children, by three different women, in three different communities of Sandy Bay (he's single now, though, and interested in meeting someone new). His kids are three, two, and one and a half years old, which he communicates matter-of-factly, with neither bravado nor chagrin.

Frequently, Milton tells his cousins to run an errand. He sends one of the boys for a bar of soap, which he immediately rips open to expose the pink, and inhales appreciatively. Later one of them comes in to use it, and he too puts it right to his nose and breathes in. Milton sends a cousin to buy soda; he offers me the bottle but I suggest we share. There are no clean glasses and the girls are not to be found. In the commotion of another cousin coming in to help the first cousin wash one, a light bulb rolls off a shelf and breaks. They ignore it and escape. The girls eventually come back and tidy up, in a fashion appropriate to the no-frills interior, sweeping the broken glass into a corner, pushing a plastic bag out through a crack in the wooden "sink" to the ground below. They too move around the kitchen awkwardly, adolescents that they are, completing their tasks with halting movements, dropping pans and knocking pitchers off shelves.

As I prepare to go, Milton asks me how much it costs to travel to the United States. How much I'm paying at the place where I'm staying (and that if I don't like it I can come stay at the house—whether for the company or the ludicrous notion of paying so much for a place to sleep, I don't know). He stares at my camera; how much did it cost? He comments that last week two foreigners were here, researching the *buzos*, and that they too took many photos of him.

SATURDAY, DECEMBER 3

Visiting Milton today was thoroughly depressing, even though I enjoy his company; it is, in fact, his searing sweetness and good faith in spite of his illness and all that it entails that makes it hard to be around him. There is nothing else but to believe that he will be walking by March. Two months ago he regained the use of his arms. Now he can bend his legs by grasping each knee and pulling up. I met a *buzo* today who was paralyzed for two years and is now walking again. And diving. Milton swears that he will not. He won't even work as a *cayuquero*. He will fish, yes, but he will not hunt lobster.

We are sitting in one of the bedrooms. It is dark but for a shaft of light from the window. I only stay two hours and take few pictures, leaving Milton in the same position I found him, slumped against the wall, hands palm up and listless on the mattress. The teenagers giggle when I, a foreign white woman, disappear into the dark bedroom to sit on the floor across from Milton. They come in to ask for C$10 (US$0.59) for this or that, and Milton, like a father, slowly pulls the money from his pocket. When Milton looks up, he is young. His desire to walk, his exertion in physical therapy, is that of a young man. But when he is thinking something over, he drops his head, shaking it back and forth, reminding me of my grandfather.

Through the cracks in the floor Milton observes the kids in the neighborhood. Underneath us his housemates swing in their hammocks and talk and joke. We hear girls next door giggling over cell-phone calls. Two boys scuffle to the entertainment of all, until someone's older sister puts an end to it. All of this Milton spies through slits centimeters wide. He will know if a thief approaches, he envisions, and he will spear him with his *barilla*. The boys come in and out and in again; they are getting dressed to go to the *parque central*; it is Saturday afternoon, and they have to wear just the right thing. On open shelves above the mattress, their clothes are stacked and folded with perfect corners. Milton has not gone to the park once these ten months; he is ashamed of the wheelchair. This morning he did sit below the house with the others, though. His cousins carry him down; they will always help him, never leave him, he declares. In January he plans to move to a cheaper place, and they will move with him. His sister will not be living with him anymore, so he'll have to hire a woman to wash his clothes. But the boys know how to cook, he affirms.

'I am not going to marry my wife,' Milton explains. Marriage is held in high esteem here, and couples often live together and form families without being officially married. When Milton can walk again, he will return to his *comunidad* and he will support his children, but only the mother of his first child would he marry. She is willing, once he is healthy. Milton helps provide for his kids with the support that he is receiving from the company. And his mother helps take care of all her grandchildren.

Milton is Moravian. He sometimes goes to church, but not tomorrow. I ask him about Christmas in his *comunidad*, as speaking of that always cheers him. People attend services, he says. And some drink and fight. In Sandy Bay it's dangerous because everyone has a gun, so any disagreement can be deadly, but in his *comunidad* it's safe. I hand Milton my pen and notebook to spell the name of his community: Pahra—the name of a fruit in Miskito, he translates. He is still shaky with the use of his hands, and can barely write. He has sores on his legs; divers die from this, he says, it eats you from the inside, eats your flesh. It is the nitrogen bubbles finding their way out of the body, he understands. I ask Milton what he thinks about as he sits alone. 'Oh, I think a lot,' he says, smiling at the remembrance of all of the thoughts for him to think. 'I think about walking. I think about dying. I've had this illness a long time now.'

The day Milton became paralyzed was a good day for lobster, a phenomenal day. There were so many lobster, he dove down and dove again; he used six tanks of air in three hours, amassing 45 pounds of lobster. Back in the *cayuco* he began twisting off their heads. He had finished four when a pain seized the top half of his body. 'I'm not alright' he told his *cayuquero*. 'I'm dying.' They returned to the main boat, where, with a diver holding each arm, they lowered him to 135 feet below, where he had been, in order to reemerge slowly. When he came up, he felt better. On deck, the *sacabuzo* gave him a massage and he regained feeling in his arms. They took him down again, and this time, upon resurfacing, his whole body was dead to him. It was not a good idea to keep diving, Milton says now, but 'I did it out of need.'

Milton has had no problems with his employer, Nafcosa, in terms of receiving money and support, and so when I ask what the union does for him, he cannot say exactly. But the *sacabuzo* takes C$50 (US$2.94) from each *buzo* per eleven-day voyage.[49] Later, when we discuss all of the outsiders who research the situation of the *buzos*, Milton explains that they come in response to discussions with the union regarding alternative employment for the day when this mode of diving is prohibited.

MONDAY, DECEMBER 5

Milton is waiting for his mom to arrive, but once midmorning comes and goes, he knows that she'll not get here before tomorrow. She will be en route to Managua, where she buys clothing and other products to sell in the *comunidad*. This visit I am not overcome by sadness, perhaps because we are sitting by the kitchen window, in the light and bustle of the lane below, with the girls working around us. I notice toothbrushes blooming from the walls, where they are conveniently wedged. I notice Milton's catheter tube hanging from his chair to the floor; he explains that when he pees, he can just put the tube through the gaps between floorboards. I notice his tattoo, which, he clarifies, is not a cross but a star, done two months ago with a needle and shoe polish.

I ask Milton why he stopped attending school and he replies that he didn't like it; it's hard to study, but easy to dive. And you make a lot of money. He says a *buzo* earns around C$5,000 (US$294) per trip, but could make up to C$30,000 (US$1,765); according to Milton, when he was diving he would catch 50 pounds of lobster on a bad day, and 140 on a good one. This in addition to the Class B lobster and fish. Some *buzos* build nice houses for themselves with their pay, Milton observes, but you can find others soliciting the *sacabuzo* for an advance the very next day, because they went drinking. Milton would give his earnings to his wife and his mom.

I drop by the house again in the afternoon, hoping to accompany Milton to his physical therapy session. He is sitting under the house with the group; as I approach, it breaks up, and Milton wheels over to me alone to say that he's not going today.

SATURDAY, DECEMBER 10

I stop by Milton's to say goodbye and explain why I missed our previous date. 'The *miriki* (light-skinned person, in Miskito) is here,' the kids yell up to him from below the house. As I enter, his cousin again announces my arrival and motions for me to go into his room. It is pitch-black. It's always dark in here, but today is overcast, and as the window is just a few feet from the next house, almost no light enters. I can't really see. Milton is lying down, and a girl sits on the bed next to him. He and I shake hands, as we always do. He says he waited and waited for me on Tuesday. I explain that I've been in the Cayos and that tomorrow I'm leaving Puerto. Milton says he'll come to the airport to say goodbye, and that he'll be sad that I'm gone. Milton and the girl are holding hands, and he has only a towel draped over his midsection. Since I can't see his face, I have trouble understanding what he's saying. He asks when I'll be back, and we shake hands again. On the steps outside, his cousin is surprised to see me leave so soon.

Cayos Miskitos
TUESDAY, DECEMBER 6–FRIDAY, DECEMBER 9

The boat ride out is five hours that leave me physically exhausted and hurting for the next forty-eight. Lost at sea (or so it feels), slamming hard against every wave, crowded among strangers, all hunched under a plastic tarp when the rain comes, in a diminutive motorboat that may not belong beyond sight of land, and under the care of people who bold-facedly over-charged me. It is with great relief that I receive the comment, 'When you see a *zopilotero* (a kettle of vultures) you'll know we're approaching.' Which means that we are now 22 miles from the eastern coast of Nicaragua, 45 miles from Puerto Cabezas, in the Cayos Miskitos. The boat drops me at the house of Eddie "Miriki," which seems to be the center of this par-ticular community; a pastor and a biologist have also found comfort here. Although I arrive unexpected, I am received without hesitation, the biolo-gist handing me his only towel to dry off with. For three days they feed and host me with no remuneration and with unwavering friendliness and courtesy.

This intermittent community began in the 1960s for subsistence pur-poses, but after the war (referred to obliquely as "the eighties") there was no employment, and because this is a lucrative business, a larger-scale community has grown. The Cayos Miskitos includes at least five clusters of mostly three-sided shanties on stilts in the middle of the ocean. The houses rock only gently, though one is at sea. Eddie's is one of around 120 structures in the principal group of dwellings, also named Cayos Miskitos—the others comprise three to sixty houses each. He estimates that there are between two and four hundred "permanent" residents, but if one includes the pastors, the women who buy the reject lobster, visitors,

*Cayos Miskitos. Buzos from Sandy Bay relax on the back deck
of the lobster broker they work for in Diamond Spot.*

and vendors, up to one thousand people might pass through here. There
are stands of mangroves that make it seem like there is land nearby, but it
is mostly underwater sandbanks. Around us are reefs where men dive for
or trap lobster. The zone where we are staying is too shallow for *buzos*;
some people free dive (going to a depth of about 7 *brazados*, or 40 feet) but
mostly they use traps. Eddie is collaborating with URACCAN to test traps
that allow the undersized lobster to exit.

The first evening they pass around the bottle of rum (which is prohibited in the Cayos and so is sold for US$8 instead of US$2) and as I lie
awake later, feeling myself to be at the mercy of the middle of nowhere,

I imagine that they drink in order to be able to fall asleep in spite of the absence of everything but wind and water. I don't see alcohol again for the remainder of my stay, although I gather from conversation that drinking binges are an important part of life out here. I lie on a piece of foam on the floor, wrapped in a threadbare fitted sheet that does not block the cold air pushing through the open door and window of my room. I am a few boat-lengths away from Eddie's, in a half-finished structure that is to be the start of the tourism industry in the Cayos; Eddie's brother is building a hostel. In the pre-dawn, I awake to what sounds like mass in the nearby church; clapping and singing skim over the surface of the water. Not until the next morning do I witness Pastor Iván Díaz leading morning prayers over Eddie's breakfast table. The pastor is a calming force throughout the days, as he sits tranquilly for hours between visits to other outposts, though his unflappable smile and his interjections of "Gloria a Dios" are sometimes incongruous if not inopportune.

My first full day in the Cayos I go looking for *buzos*. Unfortunately for me, most have gone home until January. I have hired a boat for the day, and the captain, Oldemar "Bogus" Broocks Flores, takes me to two lobster brokers in the areas where *buzos* work, the Cayos Maras and Diamond Spot. We are accompanied by one of Eddie's workers, Alberto "Cucu"

Cayos Miskitos. Visiting pastor Iván Díaz at Eddie's greets a passerby in a boat.

Cayos Miskitos. Diamond Spot. Noemi, twenty-two, from Puerto Cabezas, and buzo *Gozman Brooks, twenty-three, from Sandy Bay.*

Kroshman, who with much compassion explains everything that is new and strange to me. Bogus, with his pockmarked skin, gold rings and chains, and sunglasses, looks like a *narco* but is a reliable captain and patient escort. Our first stop is a little store where we buy gasoline. The proprietress tells me that she is putting her five kids through college with this business, and that she stays here by herself. Although she buys lobster from the *buzos*, she finds them difficult sometimes, 'strange,' from diving so deep, she believes. In Cayos Maras, they are sorting lobster bought yesterday from a *buzo* into Classes A, B, and C. At the broker in Diamond Spot I meet seven young men, all from Sandy Bay, and a woman named Noemi (twenty-two) from Puerto. Upon the death of Noemi's father nine months ago, she dropped out of the university to support her two-year-old child, by keeping the *buzos* company, I presume.

The next day it becomes apparent that although I am not on a desert island, I am indeed stranded at sea. I can't afford to hire Bogus again, and there is little activity to be found anyway. Plus, I wouldn't want to miss a return ride to Puerto, if one were to materialize. So I sit at Eddie's watching boats cruise by, none of them heading back. What was to be one night here turns into three. The lack of freedom weighs heavy after a few days; to move from house to house, or to go to one of the tiny stores or the church or the navy outpost, one would need a boat. Every morning I get a ride from the hostel site to Eddie's. They feed me fish and rice—the kindness of strangers—and then I wait. At any given time ten other people are at the house; a woman who comes by to clean, the many women who buy lobster too small for export, guys who work the traps (in their teens and early twenties), and the biologist, named Eddy. He is my most constant companion, as he too gets stuck at the house with no boat. He is living the life of the fishermen, though he is also cognizant of the need to educate people to stop diving for lobster, to collect dead wood instead of cutting down the mangroves, to stop throwing trash in the water.

I am told that there are banana trees and iguanas among the mangroves, and a lagoon. At the edge of the mangroves the trash collects.

Cayos Miskitos. At a lobster broker in Cayos Maras, lobster tails, flesh exposed, wait to be measured and categorized.

Cayos Miskitos. Alberto "Cucu" Kroshman playing dominos at Eddie's.

While preparing dinner, one takes the spaghetti from the box and the tomato sauce from the can, and tosses the can, the box, and the plastic bag into the water below. I throw in my banana peel and think of the Spanish poem: *A la mar fui por naranjas / cosa que la mar no tiene* (I went to the sea for oranges / something the sea does not have).[50] One drops a bucket down in the same spot, draws water as if from a well and washes the dishes. On the other side of the house, one goes to the bathroom in a latrine suspended 10 feet above the Caribbean. If overfishing threatens the lobster population here, contamination does as well. Salt water is used for bathing and washing, though clothes are given a rinse with fresh water, which is utilized freely—dip a cup into the barrel of drinking water, take a sip, and toss the rest to the sea. Every afternoon the rain comes, ominous, then sweeping quickly through and gone. The water runs from the roof into a gutter into the top half of an upside-down plastic jug into a tube that directs it to a barrel. The day after a big rain, a boat full of people sidles up to our deck to ask for fresh water, which they are given without question.

Eddie works three days on, twelve days off (setting traps, waiting for them to fill with lobster, then pulling them). In "tiempos buenos," which he identifies as July—when there are boats everywhere instead of it being nearly deserted like now—he might pull traps once a week. Today he has brought in C$5,000 (US$294) worth, and in high season he will gather 600 pounds a month, pulling hundreds of traps in three days. In the middle of the house is a gray covered tub that looks like a Jacuzzi; it is an ice chest where the lobster (and fish and chicken for meals) is stored until sold. Eddie and Eddy are conducting an experiment comparing the catch of thirty new traps and thirty traditional ones. Tonight they measure each lobster with what they term a "langostímetro" (lobster meter). Eddie explains that in the year 2000 the government implemented a closed season of one month per year, which was to increase by an additional month annually until reaching a four-month *veda*. In 2005 it was up to three months.

Cayos Miskitos. Lobster heads.

Cayos Miskitos. One of Eddie's workers bathing on the deck.
The mangroves can be seen in the background.

The night that Eddie returns with the bottom of his boat thick with lobster, the women gather. First the boys rip the animals' heads off and throw them into the sea. Then the bidding for the undersized ones begins. "Miriki, Miriki!" the crowd of women clamors from the darkness. They will buy a pound for C$10 (US$0.59)—C$25 (US$1.47) and sell it to another middleman in town at C$30 (US$1.76)—C$40 (US$2.35), who will sell it to hotels and restaurants in Managua or Costa Rica. Eddie initially insists that he participates in this illegal business out of sympathy and obligation to the women who make their living at it. He later admits that he too needs the cash it provides him today to keep working tomorrow, and acknowledges his responsibility in the cycle. But he places the blame of depletion of resources on the large fishing boats; they bring in a higher quantity of lobster, and more than their share of undersized ones, than do traps or *buzos*.

In the morning I am offered *atol* (a traditionally corn-based drink) made from algae. Flies land on the food, the rim of my cup, constantly swarming. At least we have a breeze; there is a season when the sea is still and smooth as a mirror, I am told, and the mosquitoes that live in the trees drift toward the houses. The radio is on for the duration of the day, alternating between static and a selection of stations that seem to randomly ride that frequency. The boys experiment with a makeshift boat, their oar a shovel. The first day they proffer lollipops, which they all suck starting first thing in the morning, but the offers taper off as the days pass, and the boys begin to ignore me, although they always serve me food unasked and always watch out for me at night, always polite. They seem different, mature for their age, cooking in shifts and seeing to their laundry and hygiene. When they have the day off, they run and boat all over, swim and play dominos, but when it is time to work, they work, taking initiative and personal responsibility to make the whole production run. At one point I notice a telling absence: The boys that work for Eddie, in contrast to everyone else I have met in Nicaragua, do not ask me with desperation how to leave their country for a new life.

Cayos Miskitos. Diamond Spot.

What I saw no longer exists. Before Hurricane Felix hit Sandy Bay on September 4, 2007, as the most deadly category of storm, with 160-mile-per-hour winds, it hit the Cayos Miskitos. Hundreds had been evacuated from the keys, but hundreds chose to stay, while others were out to sea when the warnings came. The official death toll was over one hundred, much of which is represented by *buzos* said to be missing at sea. This is particularly devastating to Sandy Bay, as so many of the men were heads of families. Nearly 100 percent of homes in Sandy Bay lost their roofs or were destroyed. In the Cayos, only the pillars of the buildings remain. The mangroves and reefs will take years to restore themselves.

I return to Puerto on a company boat, 200 horsepower now instead of 60, that is bringing back 'product': lobster tails that shift color and lose value if they experience a temperature change. The trip takes just three hours. I have been reassured that the direction of the current on the way back makes for a smoother ride, but, perhaps because of the high speed, hitting each swell is a kick in the stomach, and coming down a slamming to the floor. I feel that my innards must rupture. The Miskito passengers next to me sit calmly, as if floating down a river.

Conclusion

CAFTA may open new markets for seafood, but the continuation of the spiny lobster industry depends on various factors. Lobster is a desired product that many countries cannot supply domestically. Like so many raw materials in Latin America—such as timber, minerals, and bananas in this region—it has been sought after at an unsustainable rate and is now a depleted resource. As on the Pacific Coast, where sugarcane is grown, this part of Nicaragua has long subsisted on an export economy, hosting foreign companies or selling to them; the sea as their highway.

The drug trade is the new bounty of the sea in these parts, as *narcotraficantes* travel this Caribbean waterway en route from the growers in South America to their market. The insatiable appetite for cocaine in the United States makes it possible to find globalization in the showy new homes of Sandy Bay, a community otherwise incommunicado from the nearest city, let alone the rest of the world.

The endangerment of a species does not obey national boundaries, and it is often international organizations that campaign on its behalf. Bans enacted to that end—such as prohibiting the buying or selling of undersized lobster tails—are first felt by the people who make their living in that industry. This same global consciousness can aid in ending unsafe labor practices, if consumers worldwide refuse to buy a product available only through hazard or damage to humans, as occurred with international protests against sweatshops. Health regulations for divers also cross borders.

Lobster tails provide pay that is lucrative by local standards, though skewed in comparison both to the risk undertaken in obtaining them and to the profit they bring the companies that sell them overseas. When the market is good, divers are more likely to endanger themselves to obtain the product. If demand falters, they may turn to illegal sources of income. For the last half-century the Miskito *buzos'* livelihood and culture have been shaped by a product firmly fixed in the global marketplace, leaving the divers, those who make it all possible, precariously vulnerable to shifts in demand in that same market.

Epilogue

WHILE I WAS IN NICARAGUA, I OFTEN WONDERED WHETHER A photographer from that country would be welcomed into North Americans' homes the way I was there. Documentary work engages many of the different kinds of power in play between societies, but it also allows people from different worlds to forge real connections. The potential for exploitation is serious, but in practice it was difficult to feel that I might be endangering those I was photographing: people who fed me, kissed me when I left, and above all invited me back.

Globalization means that we as citizens and as consumers have increasing impact on the lives of others as remote as the dairy farmers in the mountains of Central America. While that in itself need not be negative, when it is transnational corporations that effect it, and sometimes inaccessible governmental policy that allows them to do so, it is difficult to conceive of one's individual responsibility when shopping or eating. In explaining that neoliberalism and globalization are not equivalents, John Rapley contends that "there seem to be more fruitful possibilities in globalizing to resist neoliberalism, than in resisting neoliberalism by rejecting globalization."[1]

Nicaragua experienced a significant increase in exports in the first few years of CAFTA, though growth statistics for the region are more complex. Exports to the United States (not including those from *zonas francas*) grew 19 percent in the first year after the agreement's implementation (April 2006–March 2007) compared to the same period in 2005; a higher number of goods were exported than anytime in the previous three decades. Imports from the United States, meanwhile, grew by 14 percent.[2] In April of 2008—CAFTA's two-year anniversary—a large new *maquila* opened in Nicaragua, to produce denim. It was expected to provide around 850 jobs directly and up to 20,000 indirectly. Simultaneously, three companies moved from Nicaragua to Vietnam and Cambodia, where wages are lower, and 8,000 people were left jobless.[3] Wage competition, infrastructure, and investor confidence remain issues for attracting capital.

223

"Total annual trade with the region is less than that traded with China in just three weeks," according to the *Houston Chronicle*. Between 2005 and 2006, clothing imports to the United States from the four Central American countries where CAFTA was in effect decreased about 7 percent, while imports of the same from China to the United States were up 22 percent.[4] (Nicaragua fares better than others in the region as it has preference under CAFTA that allows it to import fabric for assembly rather than manufacture it.) The Americas Program Center for International Policy reports that besides the reasons mentioned above, competition from China threatens the region in part because of the recent expiration of an agreement that "granted ample quotas to several small countries like Nicaragua, while restricting access to the U.S. market for behemoths like China." This change, combined with lower wages in China, resulted in more *maquila* jobs lost than gained in the first half of 2007 in Nicaragua.[5]

What has not increased is production of food for local consumption. Small and medium-sized producers in rural, agricultural areas are not thriving.[6] Following the worldwide trend of rising energy and food prices, and subsequent high inflation, in April 2008 the economist Néstor Avendaño announced in the newspaper *Nuevo Diario* that food prices had risen 45 percent in one year.[7] There is fear that deeper recession in the United States would mean fewer remittances as well as less demand for imported goods. The International Monetary Fund points out that those countries that have free trade agreements with the United States would feel this change most strongly.[8]

Another important aspect of the stories presented in this book is one that I did not set out looking for: health problems. In three of the four industries portrayed, serious threats to worker wellness became a focus. *Maquila* employees suffer from respiratory illnesses as well as negative effects of repetitive motion. Sugarcane cutters and their families are dying from kidney disease. And lobster divers risk paralysis from decompression illness. The physical danger that people undertake in order to work, and the lack of institutional protection this reveals, highlights the precariousness of their existence. They have little recourse and, oftentimes, little opportunity for treatment.

The remuneration wageworkers receive for jobs that often require great sacrifice is a fraction of the eventual retail or wholesale price of products that may wind up in the closets or on the dinner plates of ordinary U.S. citizens. CAFTA is a small part—whether salve or bane—of a great, global imbalance in life, liberty, and the pursuit of happiness. Earning so little means that most of the people portrayed in this book live in extreme poverty. But despite the frustration, pain, drudgery, and fear this can generate, their lives are rich. The growth CAFTA brings to different industries is following a tortuous path, different for each one. But the Nicaraguans I met conveyed dignified strength and inveterate humor in the face of these larger forces and the living conditions they have yet to rectify.

NOTES

Overview

1. In 2006, the median age in Nicaragua was twenty-one years, according to the *World Fact Book* of the CIA. http://www.cia.gov/cia/publications/factbook/geos/nu.html#People.

2. All from *La Prensa* 2005: "Pro-CAFTA" (23 Sept., sec. A); "Costa Rica" (23 Sept., sec. A), (11 Oct., sec. A), and (18 Nov., sec. A), among many others; "Blows" (21 Sept., sec. A).

3. *Economist*, 28 July 2005.

4. *Economist*, 16 June 2005. Tom Ricker puts it another way: "[T]he combined GDP of countries in Central America was $58 billion in 2000—smaller than the total income of just two U.S.-based agriculture companies that will benefit from the accord: Cargill and Archer Daniels Midlands. The smallest economy, Nicaragua, produces just $3 billion a year in goods and services" (2004).

5. *Washington Post*, 13 May 2005, sec. E.

6. *Economist*, 28 July 2005.

7. Starmer 2003.

8. Partido Liberal Constitucionalista.

9. All from *La Prensa* 2005: "Ortega" (opinion, 11 Oct., sec. A); "Calm" (11 Oct., sec. A); "Costa Rica" (18 Nov., sec. A).

10. Stokes 2004.

11. *La Prensa*, 25 Aug. 2005, *Guía Comercial*.

12. *La Prensa*, 23 Sept. 2005, sec. A.

13. "Per capita income is only half the Central American average" (Stokes 2004).

14. Stokes 2004.

15. Robinson 2003, 19.

16. *La Prensa*, 11 Oct. 2005, sec. A.

17. Carlson 2005.

18. Carlson 2005.

19. James 2005.

20. *Washington Post*, 13 May 2005, sec. E.

21. Robinson 2003, 78.

22. One of the IMF's six stated Purposes is: "To give confidence to members by making the general resources of the Fund temporarily available to them under adequate safeguards, thus providing them with opportunity to correct

maladjustments in their balance of payments without resorting to measures destructive of national or international prosperity" (IMF 1992).

23. Teresa, one of the *maquila* workers I photographed, gave me a simile for Nicaragua's situation: If you own the house I live in and I owe you money, I can't deny you the use of some of the rooms.

24. Robinson 2003, 79.

25. For a discussion of foreign aid and debt, see both Spence 2004, 94, and Robinson 2003, 79. The former notes that because of international debt and Hurricane Mitch in 1998, Nicaragua has received a lot of aid; in the year 2000, it was US$111 per capita.

26. James 2005.

27. One specific example: "North Carolina has more than 50,000 recipients of federal benefits for workers who can prove they lost their job as a result of NAFTA" (White 2005).

28. James 2005.

29. Global Exchange n.d.

30. Starmer 2003. This segment of the population generates 30 percent of Nicaragua's GDP, according to the World Bank Development Index, cited by Starmer, or 21 percent of the GNP cited in *La Prensa*, 13 Oct. 2005, sec. A.

31. (Unión Nacional de Agricultores y Ganaderos) *La Prensa*, 26 Sept. 2005, sec. B. (We know that that treaty will finish us off when it throws us into competition with subsidized producers from the U.S., meanwhile we don't have roads, nor financing, [we have] problems with property [titles], a destroyed environment, lack of water, hunger and poverty.)

32. *La Prensa*, 26 Sept. 2005, sec. A. (If Nicaragua enters this free trade agreement in the current conditions in which it finds its local economy and the position of the government, what awaits national products is to be easily displaced by other products of the region and condemn ourselves to the consumption of foreign products that are offered at a better price, as a consequence the extermination of local producers.)

33. *Economist*, 28 July 2005.

34. *Economist*, 28 July 2005.

35. Federación Nacional de Cooperativas Agropecuarias y Agroindustriales.

36. Cáceres 2005.

37. "The only real potential beneficiary of expanded quotas for dairy import into the United States under CAFTA, Parmalat is currently squeezing dairy farmers in Nicaragua." It controls the only processing plant in the country that can meet the pasteurizing requirements for import into the United States (Ricker 2004).

38. Marvin Taylor, head economist at the Banco Centroamericano de Integración Económica, which has allotted monies to help the region in the implementation of CAFTA, states that while his institution has determined that textiles, electronics, forests, and tourism are the best areas to support, attention must be paid to agriculture workers, as that sector shelters the highest concentration of poor people. "Hay que ver cómo se mueve esta población a sectores más avanzados y con mayor productividad y que al mismo tiempo generen mayores ingresos para salir de la pobreza." (We'll have to see how this

population shifts to more advanced sectors with higher productivity and that at the same time generate higher income to get out of poverty.) *La Prensa*, 18 Oct. 2005, sec. A.

39. White 2005.
40. Cáceres 2005.
41. Cardenal Óscar Rodríguez Maradiaga (*Nuevo Diario*, 20 Nov. 2005, sec. A).
42. The U.S. secretary of commerce cites the World Bank, saying that those countries that sign free-trade agreements usually experience 0.6 percent growth per year for the first five years after the treaty goes into affect. CAFTA would therefore purportedly lift half a million Central Americans out of poverty by 2010 (*La Prensa*, 18 Oct. 2005, sec. A).
43. Dye 2004, 6.
44. Dye 2004, 5.
45. Nicaragua's population is currently over five million, in a country just smaller than the state of New York.
46. Walker 2003, 2.
47. Walker 2003, 20.
48. Walker 2003, 6.
49. Unless otherwise noted, the information on the revolution in this paragraph is from Thomas Walker 2003, 31–32.
50. Walker 2003, 25.
51. Spence 2004, 8.
52. Walker 2003, 6.
53. Pérez-Brignoli 1989: 167–71.
54. Robinson 2003, 73.
55. Jack Spence, personal communication, November 2007.
56. Spence 2004, 9.
57. Robinson 2003, 83–84.
58. Bickham 2002, 11. Lisa Haugaard adds that under Bush I, the United States sent US$440 million in aid to Nicaragua in the first two years of Chamorro's administration, "tied directly to meeting the conditions of an unusually strict structural adjustment plan." This aid was "ideologically driven" rather than economically sound (1997).
59. This drop in consumption was accompanied by an increased infant mortality rate as well as lower wages. William Robinson explains that although much aid was earmarked for Nicaragua during this period, most of it never actually entered the country, but instead was used to pay off foreign lenders (Robinson 2003, 80, 85, and 78).
60. Dye 2004, 9.
61. Spence 2004, 20.
62. Dye 2004, 17.
63. Dye 2004, 11.
64. This, along with "an effective political machine, and a divided opposition" were the three elements which led to his win, according to a Report for Congress. Taft-Morales 2007, 1.
65. Vulliamy 2001.
66. *Economist*, 2007.

67. Speech given at the University of New Mexico by Ambassador Arturo Cruz Jr., 17 October 2007.
68. St. Bernard 2003, 13.
69. St. Bernard 2003, 13.
70. Robinson 2003, 19.
71. Rapley 2004, 6, 40.
72. Rapley 2004, 42.

Chapter One

1. While they are referred to as *maquiladoras* in Mexico, the meaning is the same—companies that ship in raw materials and ship out value-added finished products, taking advantage of cheap labor to assemble anything from televisions to T-shirts. Traditionally, it has been women's work, and in Juarez, at least three hundred women have been killed in the last decade (this was before the more recent increase in *narco*-related violence). The murders have not been solved and are not directly related to the *maquilas*, but are associated with them because it is often from the shantytowns where the workers live—indeed, migrate to in large numbers—that women disappear, and where bodies are found.
2. Bilbao, Rocha, and Mayorga 2004, 20.
3. Movimiento Mujeres María Elena Cuadra (MEC).
4. Ramos and Vargas 2002, 18, 20.
5. Published MEC interviews show that around 70 percent of women working in the *maquilas* are mothers (Ramos and Vargas 2002, 18).
6. A *zona franca* is an industrial park where factories of numerous separate companies are gathered. The usually foreign-owned companies are granted special tax status; for example, they are not taxed twice upon importing raw materials and exporting saleable products. The park itself—and sometimes the installations within it—is often built by the host country to attract corporations.
7. Unless otherwise noted, information in this paragraph is afforded by CNZF 2005 and CNZF n.d.
8. Bilbao 2003, 13.
9. Bilbao 2003, 13.
10. Jon Ander Bilbao, anthropologist at Universidad Centroamericana (UCA), gives a slightly different history. He says that the maquilas began under Somoza in 1965 with twelve factories and eight thousand workers through 1979. He agrees that under the Sandinistas there were five state-run factories, but employing three thousand workers (Bilbao 2003, 11). Jennifer Bickham Mendez of the College of William and Mary writes that the Chamorro government's privatization of the Sandinista factories put ten thousand workers out of a job (soon reinstated in the transnational corporations' *maquilas*, without unions) (Bickham 2002, 12).
11. Decree 46–91.
12. Figured at nine hours per day, Monday–Friday, and five hours on Saturday.

13. According to the Banco Central de Nicaragua, in September of 2005 the average cost of basic food, clothing, and household items in the city of Managua was C$2,709 (US$159).

14. Two examples of salaries are: primary school teacher, US$75 per month; "recently graduated medical doctor working in a public hospital," US$100 per month (Dye 2004, 8).

15. "Nuestro país tiene el índice más bajo de la region en ausentismo y rotación de personal" (CNZF n.d.).

16. Bilbao 2003.

17. Bickham Mendez 2002, 20.

18. Thomas Walker shows this to be *dependency*. When the elites in a society are externally oriented (export being their primary goal), the citizen is seen only as labor, not as a potential consumer. One result is concentrated ownership of resources. "Though impressive growth in the GNP often occurs, significant benefits almost never 'trickle down' to the people, no matter how long the process goes on and no matter how much development takes place" (Walker 2003, 3).

19. During the fall of 2005, when these interviews took place, the currency exchange rate of Nicaraguan cordobas to U.S. dollars was around 17:1, which I have preserved throughout the text. Dollar amounts over US$10 are rounded to the nearest dollar.

20. This interview took place on 10 October 2005. I returned to Las Mercedes on November 24 of the same year to photograph.

21. "La Corporación Zona Franca es una empresa pública del estado que administra techo."

22. Centro de Trabajadores Nicaragüenses.

23. Interview with Orlando Valverde of FENACOOP in its Managua office on 11 October 2005.

24. Bilbao, Rocha, and Mayorga 2004, 26.

25. *La Prensa*, 25 Nov. 2005, sec. A.

26. *Envio* magazine published in 2003 that three-fourths of "cargos de dirección y control en las fábricas maquileras" are foreign (Bilbao 2003, 13).

27. The land had belonged to the Somozas but the *ley de la piñata* protected Carolina's family from having it taken away, she explained, putting a new twist on the old scandal.

28. This was the understanding of the term I at first developed talking with people in the city. According to a magazine for women published by Puntos de Encuentro, it is often a euphemism—especially in a rural setting—for what is essentially kidnapping and rape of younger girls by older men (Dixon 2005, 5).

29. Jennifer Bickham Mendez refers to this as the "triple shift" for women who work outside the home and are also responsible for housework, which constitutes the "second shift" (2002, 13).

Chapter Two

1. Fifty percent of Central America's population is rural (Replogle 2004).

2. While IICA puts it at nearly 38 percent (see note 3), the *Multinational Monitor* puts it at 47 percent, "unlike the United States, where perhaps 2 percent of the workforce is in agriculture. . . ." (Ricker 2004).

3. IICA 2004, 15, 16.

4. Despite the major social upheaval that it caused, just over 10 percent of *finca* land was affected by Sandinista land reform policy. Of that amount, less than 10 percent was given to individual *campesinos*, while 30 percent went to cooperatives, and over 50 percent became state land, which was later given to party cadres or spontaneously taken by people displaced by war (Levard, Marín, and Navarro n.d., 54–55).

5. Enríquez 1997, 1.

6. "Para el sector agropecuario del Municipio de Matiguás, los años 90s han sido una década de lenta y desigual reactivación económica, después de cerca de diez años de situación conflictiva" (Levard, Marín, and Navarro n.d., 76).

7. In an interview with the author at UCA on 23 September 2005.

8. Specifically, in 2002–3, increase in beef production was 9.1 percent and beef exports grew 10.7 percent, while the increase in cheese exports was 10.2 percent (IICA 2004. 17). According to *La Prensa*, in CAFTA's first year, beef exports to the U.S. were expected to generate US$21 million and milk US$3.9 million. Each year thereafter, the quotas will increase by 5 percent, measured in metric tons of the product (*La Prensa* 11 October 2005, sec. A).

9. The clients of the FDL in Matiguás are: 19 percent subsistence *campesinos*; 44 percent *campesinos-finqueros*; 37 percent *finqueros*. Accounting for all credit-granting institutions in the municipality, one thousand of the five thousand producers have access to credit (Levard, Marín, and Navarro n.d., 57, 61).

10. Unless otherwise noted, the following two paragraphs summarize the history given in section 1.2, "Breve Historia Agraria del Municipio," of *Cuadernos de investigación #11* (Levard, Marín, and Navarro n.d., 14–18).

11. Overall consumption boomed during these decades: by 1970, U.S. citizens ate an average of 117 pounds each of red meat a year (Williams 1986, 84).

12. Williams 1986, 77.

13. "Los sectores campesinos más acomodados y ubicados en las principales vías de acopio lechero, se ven favorecidos y logran consolidarse" (Levard, Marín, and Navarro n.d., 15).

14. Williams 1986, 77.

15. Williams 1986, 78.

16. Williams 1986, 92.

17. Williams 1986, 131.

18. Land grant beneficiaries included both those who benefited from agrarian reform under the Sandinistas and some members of the "ex-resistencia nicaragüense" (*contras*)—*campesinos* all—who received land in 1990. (Mayorga Rocha 2004, 34–35). By the mid-1990s, 80 percent of all land in Matiguás given to individuals by the state had been sold by them back to the landowners from whom it had been confiscated. Reasons for this were: (1) insufficient government programs to help them insert themselves into civil society, (2) land title insecurity (and the dangerous environment created by it) and, most

of all, (3) inadequate availability of long-term loans. These people returned to wageworker status (Levard, Marín and Navarro n.d., 54–55).

19. Spence 2004, 84.

20. Levard, Marín, and Navarro n.d., 13.

21. Prolacsa was an *acopiador* and processor of pasteurized milk. When Orlando commented that the dairy industry had an unfair advantage through government subsidies, he was probably referring to the period when Prolacsa instigated the building of roads and the availability of loans and technical assistance, creating patches of intensive dairy farming (Ruíz García 1994, 12).

22. Enríquez 1997, 6.

23. "'En Estados Unidos existe para este queso (nicaragüense) un mercado étnico potencial cercano a los tres millones de centroamericanos, pero también unos 25 millones de mexicanos que consumen una variedad de queso morolique,' dijo [Arnulfo Pérez, experto mexicano en temas lacteos] refiriendose al queso que tiene una especial salinidad que gusta tanto a mexicanos, salvadoreños y guatemaltecos" (*El Observador Economico* 2004).

24. Levard, Marín, and Navarro n.d., 12–13.

25. In the interior region I often heard the term *cachar* used in place of *robar* (see endnote 28 from p. 231), with the literal meaning of to seize, to obtain, to rob.

26. Four of every ten children show signs of malnutrition (Levard, Marín, and Navarro n.d., 13).

27. Deforestation is an issue in this area due to unchecked agricultural expansion, lack of control over the cutting of precious woods, and the traditional slash-and-burn method of planting, which can lead to accidental fires (Mayorga Rocha 2004, 17, 46).

28. Oscar explains that compared to San Lucas, which sits higher in the mountains, San Rafael is arid. Here, the three summer months are dry and the calves do not fatten. For this reason, Pablo Damian waits to sell his bulls later than the usual maximum age of two years.

29. He transports them to whichever of the three large slaughterhouses—in Managua, Nandaime, or Chontales—is currently offering the best price.

30. *El Nuevo Herald* reports that in 2005 the minimum wage for a *campesino* without land was US$46 per month (7 May 2007).

31. Fifty-four percent of inhabitants in the municipality of Matiguás are illiterate (Levard, Marín, and Navarro n.d., 13).

32. "El precio de la carne está muy ligada a la evolución del precio mundial." 'The price of beef is closely pegged to shifts in the international price.' (Levard, Marín, and Navarro n.d., 66).

33. They pay at least C$5,000 (US$294) per head for cattle, while to a producer a dairy cow is worth at least C$8,000 (US$471) and a bull around C$10,000 (US$588). They are priced by the kilo: A 400-kilo animal will go for C$7,000 (US$412).

34. The Sandinista government claimed to have lowered the rate of illiteracy in people over the age of ten from more than 50 percent to under 13 percent in just five months during 1980 (Walker 2003, 124).

35. In 2004, David Dye wrote that one-third of Nicaragua's GDP was from remittances (Dye 2004, 6). And Oscar of FDL tells me: 'Remember how

important emigration is in this town; most families have someone in the United States or Costa Rica, whether because of the war or the economy. When peace came, some of them returned and set up businesses, but not all of them readjusted well, and they went back to the U.S. Now they send money: remittances are the primary and most stable source of income in Nicaragua.' Migrants might send C$2,000 (US$118) per month, to be divided among different family members; even kids get their remittances, Oscar maintains.

Chapter Three

1. The following historical outline is informed by the *Documento base Chinandega*. Nitlapan 1990.
2. Murray 1994, 38–40.
3. Paige 1997, 93.
4. Murray 1994, 38–40.
5. Grigsby 2007.
6. Walker 2003, 2.
7. López 2003, 10–11.
8. American Sugar Alliance.
9. Nitlapan 1993, 36.
10. Nitlapan 1993, 14 and 36.
11. Sánchez 2004, 17.
12. Everingham 2001, 71–72.
13. Walker 2003, 49.
14. De Franco 1994, 11 and 22.
15. Trucchi, "El drama y la lucha," 2006.
16. Trucchi, "Cosechas amargas," 2006
17. López 2003, 58 and 60.
18. Nicaragua Sugar Estates Limited 2004–5, 16.
19. Ethical-Sugar 2007.
20. 10 November 2005, 1A–10A and see note 54.
21. *El Nuevo Herald*, 7 May 2007.
22. *El Nuevo Herald*, 6 May 2007.
23. *NotiCen*, 12 July 2007.
24. *El Nuevo Diario*, 9 March 2001.
25. *Miami Herald*, 30 April 2007.
26. *El Nuevo Herald*, 7 May 2007.
27. Paraphrase from Medline Plus, an on-line service of the U.S. National Library of Medicine and the National Institutes of Health.
28. The CIA World Factbook.
29. *La Prensa*, 7 April 2001.
30. *Miami Herald*, 30 April 2007.
31. *Nuevo Diario*, 9 March 2001.
32. "Victims of Nemagon" 2005.
33. Asociación nicaragüense, *Nota de Prensa* 2005.
34. De Franco 1994, 2.
35. López 2003, 31.

36. Ministerio de Agricultura y Ganadería 1997, 9.

37. Nitlapan 1993, 16.

38. De Franco 1994, 2 and 37.

39. López 2003, 60.

40. López 2003, 24.

41. Roney 2004, 321.

42. López 2003, 28.

43. López 2003, 9.

44. *Miami Herald*, 30 April 2007.

45. López 2003, 15.

46. [Galián] 2004, 22.

47. Roney 2004, 322.

48. Suppan 2004.

49. Office of the United States Trade Representative 2005.

50. Suppan 2004.

51. Cáceres 2005.

52. Whisnant 1995, 44.

53. Trucchi, "Cosechas amargas," 2006. "[E]l principal atentado histórico contra la soberanía alimentaria ha sido el monocultivo."

54. Different sources varied regarding the amount paid per *tonelada* of sugarcane cut and the average quantity cut in a day. Antonio Vargas said C$12 (US$0.71)/ton and between five and ten tons in one day (eight to nine tons being usual); one *pailero* put it at C$12.94 (US$0.76), commonly cutting fifteen tons in a day; and an article in *La Prensa* stated that the salary was C$20 (US$1.18)/ton with six being the average number cut in a day (10 November 2005, 1A–10A).

Chapter Four

1. Dennis and Herlihy 2003, and *Wani* 36 (2004): 11.

2. Programa de Naciones Unidas Para el Desarrollo (PUND) 2005, 36.

3. *Wani* 36 (2004): 57.

4. PUND 2005, 158.

5. PUND 2005, 161.

6. *Wani* 38 Suplemento 2 (2004): 5.

7. PUND 2005, 33. 'The separation of social relations from our physical space that accompanies globalization can fragment the national territory as well as the communal social fabric and space in which the autonomous governments operate today. This is made more evident if we consider that, because of the fragility and impoverishment of the Caribbean coast, the concrete materializations of globalization, in these regions of the country, are frequently the most damaging.'

8. Tucker 2000, ch. 7.

9. *Wani* 38 Suplemento 2 (2004): 5.

10. *Wani* 36 (2004): 50.

11. *Wani* 36 (2004): 78.

12. *Wani* 38 Suplemento 2 (2004): 6.

13. *Wani* 36 (2004): 75. Quote from Oscar-René Vargas, *Historia del Siglo XX,*
    Tomo III. Nicaragua 1926–1939 (Centro de Estudios de la Realidad Nacional de
    Nicaragua and Centro de Documentación de Honduras, 2001). 'To say that in
    the mid-1920s the Atlantic Coast was more North American than Nicaraguan
    is not an exaggeration. The banana, timber, and mining companies were the
    principal existing firms in Nicaragua.'

14. Interview with the author, 11 November 2005.

15. Wappani Productions 2002.

16. Demko 2005.

17. Jacobson 2004.

18. Jacobson 2004.

19. Paisano 2004, 6.

20. Moreno 2001, 4.

21. PUND 2005, 156–57.

22. "Documento de Posición" 2005.

23. *El Nuevo Diario*, 21 June 2007, by Fermín López.

24. *Wani* 38, Suplemento 1, 2004. Interview with William Chow 13–15.

25. Moreno 2001, 19.

26. Paisano 2004, 87.

27. Instituto de Medicina Tradicional y Desarrollo Comunitario 2005.

28. Jacobson 2004.

29. Paisano 2004, 78.

30. *Houston Chronicle*, "Nicaragua lobster divers risk life and limb," 8 July 2003.

31. Jacobson 2004.

32. Wapponi Productions 2004.

33. Instituto de Medicina Tradicional y Desarrollo Comunitario 2005.

34. Aragón Renuncio 2004, 26.

35. Instituto de Medicina Tradicional y Desarrollo Comunitario 2005.

36. "Comisionado Derechos Humanos" 2006.

37. Demko 2005.

38. *El Nuevo Diario*, "Mortandad de buzos, una crueldad que clama al cielo,"
    by Fermín López, 29 October 2006.

39. Wapponi Productions 2004.

40. Wapponi Productions 2004.

41. Parenti 1994.

42. PUND 2005, 147–48. Translation of a quote by Dennis: "El tráfico de drogas y
    sus efectos disociadores en el capital social comunitario," 2003. "Traficantes de
    drogas que transportaban cocaína hacia el norte, aparentemente la tiraban por
    la borda al ser perseguidos por las autoridades."

43. Moreno 2001, 29.

44. Moreno 2001, 28. "Harry expresa, 'Los Buzos [*sic*] cada vez que llegamos del
    mar lo primero que hacemos la mayoría es tomar, los jóvenes por que no
    tenemos tantas responsabilidades, a demás [*sic*] dentro de 12 día [*sic*] vamos a
    volver a obtener la misma cantidad de dinero. También tomamos porque al
    estar 12 días en el agua nuestro cuerpo se enfría y manteniendo alcohol en el
    cuerpo se evita el resfrío.'"

45. Moreno 2001, 28. " . . . aprovechamos el momento para comprar valor y poder (la droga)."

46. *La Prensa,* "Ofensiva contra narcos: La Fuerza Naval incautó 871 kilos de coca en el Caribe nicaragüense y detuvo a 10 hondureños," 25 November 2005, 5B.

47. Universidad de las Regiones Autónomas de la Costa Caribeña de Nicaragua.

48. Any number of English words have entered the Miskito lexicon: *paun* (pound), *gul* (gold), *arait* (alright), *bip* (beef), etc. *Tininiska* 2003 and 2004.

49. Alternatively, Edda Moreno estimates that the *sacabuzo* makes C$100 (US$5.88) per *buzo* per trip.

50. "A la mar fui por naranjas" is a poem by the Canary Islands poet Pedro García Cabrera based on popular song and published in his book *La esperanza me mantiene,* 1959.

Epilogue

1. Rapley 2004, 42.

2. *Nuevo Diario,* 21 November 2007, reporting on a study published by USAID.

3. *Nuevo Diario,* 23 April 2008.

4. *Houston Chronicle,* 27 February 2007.

5. Beachy 2007. The Multi-Fiber Agreement was in place from 1974 through 2004.

6. *Nuevo Diario,* 22 January 2008.

7. *Nuevo Diario,* 23 April 2008. Inflation in Nicaragua was at 19 percent in June 2008 (*The Economist,* 7 June 2008).

8. *Nuevo Diario,* 22 October 2007.

SOURCES

Alvarez, María José, and Claudia Gordillo. *Estampas del Caribe Nicaragüense*. Managua: Instituto de Historia de Nicaragua y Centroamerica (IHNCA) and the Universidad Centroamericana (UCA), 2000.

American Sugar Alliance. "'05 Retail Sugar Prices Flat Despite Hurricanes." Press Release (24 January 2006).

Aragón Renuncio, Antonio. "El triste canto de la sirena." *Reportaje Magazine* 20 (10 October 2004): 21–26.

Asociación nicaragüense de afectados por insuficiencia renal crónica "Domingo Téllez." *Nota de Prensa*, 17 November 2005.

Beachy, Ben. *Dead-End Trade Deal Nears Dead End*. Americas Program, Center for International Policy (25 July 2007). http://americas.irc-online.org/am/4425.

Belli, Giaconda. *La Mujer Habitada*. Barcelona: Publicaciones y Ediciones Salamandra, 1996.

———. *The Country Under My Skin: A Memoir of Love and War*. New York: Anchor Books, 2003.

Bickham Mendez, Jennifer. "Gender and Citizenship in a Global Context: The Struggle for Maquila Workers' Rights in Nicaragua." *Identities: Global Studies in Culture and Power* 9 (2002): 7–38.

Bilbao, Jon Ander. "La maquila es sólo una aspirina: Alivia, no cura y sus efectos duran poco." *Envio* 255 (June 2003): 11–16.

Bilbao, Jon Ander, Olga Rocha, and Magdalena Mayorga. "La maquila de Sébaco: Sueños, realidades y frustraciones." *Envio* 265 (April 2004): 20–26.

Cáceres, Sinforiano. "CAFTA Will Be Like a Brand-Name Hurricane Mitch." *Envio* 290 (Sept 2005): (electronic file).

Carlson, Laura. "CAFTA: Losing Proposition for the Hemisphere." *www.counterpunch.org*, 9–10 July 2005.

The Central Intelligence Agency. The World Factbook. https://www.cia.gov/library/publications/the-world-factbook/geos/nu.html.

Comisión Nacional de Zonas Francas (CNZF) informational CD. Managua, February 2005.

Comisión Nacional de Zonas Francas (CNZF) newsletter. *Zona Franca. Zona libre de desempleo* 1, no. 1. Managua, n.d.

"Comisionado Derechos Humanos denuncia muerte de más de 50 buzos." ACAN-EFE (23 July 2006). http://www.nicaraguahoy.info/dir_cgi/index.cgi.

D'Exelle, Ben, and Miguel Alemán. *Evaluación del impacto socio-económico del crédito del FDL en Wiwilí y Matiguás: Resultados de una encuesta de impacto.* Managua: Nitlapan/UCA, 2000.

De Franco, Mario A., Rolando Sevilla, and José Ma. Buitrago. *"La agroindustria del azúcar y su impacto en la economia nicaragüense."* Comité Nacional de Productores de Azúcar, Managua, March 1994. Photocopy. (Nitlapan reg # 2011).

Demko, Paul. "Dying for Lobster: Impoverished divers comb the Mosquito Coast for 'red gold' and pay the ultimate price." *Utne Reader* (January/February 2005): electronic.

Dennis, Philip A., and Laura Hobson Herlihy. "Higher Education on Nicaragua's Multicultural Atlantic Coast." *Cultural Survival Quarterly* 27, no. 4 (15 December 2003): http://www.uvm.edu/sistercity/URACCAN.html.

Dixon, Helen. "¡Se la llevó! El rapto de chavalas." *La Boletina* 61 (Sept. 2005): 5–10.

"Documento de Posición de las Regiones Autónomas respecto al Tratado de Libre Comercio de Centroamérica, Estados Unidos y República Dominicana (CAFTA-DR)" 3 August 2005.

Dye, David. *Patchwork Democracy: Nicaraguan Politics Ten Years After the Fall.* Cambridges, MA: Hemisphere Initiatives, 2000.

———. *Democracy Adrift.* Brookline, MA: Hemisphere Initiatives, 2004.

Economist. "The CAFTA Conundrum." 16 June 2005: (electronic file).

———. "America's Economy." 28 July 2005: (electronic file).

———. "Ortega's Crab Dance." 13 October 2007: (electronic file).

———. "Inglorious." 7 June 2008 v387:51.

Edwards, Beatrice. "Selling Free Trade in Central America." *NACLA Report on the Americas* 37, issue 5 (Mar/Apr 2004): 8.

Eiras, Ana Isabel. "Commentary & Analysis: The Democratic Benefits of a Free Trade Agreement with Central America." The Heritage Foundation: *www.unc.edu,* 2005.

El Observador Economico. "A Nicaragua le falta mucho en el tema de la calidad." Issue 153 (Nov/Dec 2004): 19–20.

Enríquez, Laura J. *Agrarian Reform and Class Consciousness in Nicaragua.* Gainesville: University Press of Florida, 1997.

Ethical-Sugar. "Memorandum International Justice Mission." http://www.sucre-ethique.org/?lang=en (23 May 2007).

Everingham, Mark. "Agricultural Property Rights and Political Change in Nicaragua." *Latin American Politics and Society* 43 (Fall 2001): 61–93.

Fundacion Ortiz-Gurdián. *III Bienal de Artes Visuales Nicaragüenses.* Managua: Fundacion Ortiz-Gurdián, 2001.

[Galián, Carlos.] "A Raw Deal for Rice Under DR-CAFTA: How the Free Trade Agreement threatens the livelihoods of Central American farmers." *Oxfam Briefing Paper 68.* Nov. 2004.

Global Exchange. "Top Ten Reasons to Oppose the Free Trade Area of the Americas" (flyer). San Francisco, n.d.

Gordillo, Claudia, ed. *Semblanza de Nicaragua en el Siglo XX.* Managua: IHNCA, UCA, and the Real Embajada de los Paises Bajos, 2003.

Grigsby, William. "Needed Reflections on the New Government's Communication Policy." *Envio* 308 (March 2007): digital edition.

Haugaard, Lisa. "Nicaragua." Latin America Working Group. Brief 2, no. 32 (March 1997).

Houston Chronicle. 8 July 2003 and 27 February 2007.

Instituto de Medicina Tradicional y Desarrollo Comunitario. *El síndrome de descompresión y los factores socioculturales que inciden en su causa, prevención y rehabilitación entre la población indígena de la región autónoma del atlántico norte*. Bilwi: Universidad de las Regiones Autónomas de la Costa Caribe Nicaragüense, September 2005.

Instituto Interamericano de Cooperación para la Agricultura (IICA). *Contribución del IICA a la Agricultura y al Desarrollo de las Comunidades Rurales en Nicaragua, Informe Annual 2004*. Managua: IICA, 2004.

International Monetary Fund (IMF). "Article I—Purposes" of *Articles of Agreement of the International Monetary Fund*. http://www.imf.org/external/pubs/ft/aa/aa01.htm (amended 1992).

Jacobson, Mark. "The Hunt for Red Gold." Natural Resources Defense Council: *OnEarth Magazine* (Fall 2004): electronic.

James, Deborah. "CAFTA: Democracy Sold Out." *www.alternet.org*, 29 July 2005.

La Jornada (Mexico City). 28 August 2005.

Leonardi, Richard. *Nicaragua*. Bath, United Kingdom: Footprint, 2005.

Levard, Laurent, Yuri Marín López, and Ivania Navarro. *Municipio de Matiguás: Potencialidades y limitantes del desarrollo agropecuario*. Cuadernos de Investigación #11. Managua: Nitlapan/UCA, n.d.

Levi Strauss, David. *Between the Eyes: Essays on Photography and Politics*. New York: Aperture, 2003.

López L., José Guillermo, consultant. "Comercialización de la caña de azúcar en Nicaragua, casos comparatives con Honduras y Costa Rica." Proyecto IICA/EPAD, Managua, July 2003. Photocopy.

Mayorga Rocha, Aida. *Diagnóstico Participativo Rural: Matiguás y Tola*. Cuadernos de Investigación #21. Managua: Nitlapan/UCA, 2004.

Medline Plus. http://www.nlm.nih.gov/medlineplus/.

Meiselas, Susan. *Nicaragua, June 1978–July 1979*. New York: Pantheon Books, 1981.

Miami Herald. http://www.miamiherald.com/.

Ministerio de Agricultura y Ganadería. "Crece producción de azúcar en Nicaragua." *Agricultura y desarollo* 32 (August 1997): 7–9.

Moreno, Edda B. "Tercer Informe: Análisis integral de la situación de vulnerabilidad de los buzos y sus familias, sus efectos en las comunidades de origen y el pueblo miskito." Proyecto "RLA/98/01M/UNF—Fortalecimiento de las capacidades de defensa legal de los Pueblos Indígenas en América Central." Bilwi: Organización Internacional del Trabajo (OIT), November 2001. Photocopy.

Murray, Douglas L. *Cultivating Crisis: The Human Cost of Pesticides in Latin America*. Austin: University of Texas Press, 1994.

Nicaragua Sugar Estates Limited. *Informe Annual 2004–2005*.

Nitlapan (Instituto de Investigación y Desarrollo, Universidad Centroamericana, Managua). Reg#0214. Documento Base Chinandega. *El doble rostro de la agroexportación: Burguesia y campesinado en el occidente*. October 1990.

Nitlapan (Instituto de Investigación y Desarrollo, Universidad Centroamericana, Managua). Reg #2908. *Estudio de mercado de la industria azucarera en Nicaragua*. July 1993.

El Nuevo Diario (Managua). November 2005; January and October 2006; June, October, and November 2007; and January and April 2008. http://archivo.elnuevodiario.com.ni/index.html.

El Nuevo Herald. http://www.elnuevoherald.com/.

Office of the United States Trade Representative. *CAFTA Facts. Sugar: A Spoonful a Week*. CAFTA Policy Brief. February 2005.

Paige, Jeffery M. *Coffee and Power: Revolution and the Rise of Democracy in Central America*. Cambridge, MA: Harvard University Press, 1997.

Paisano, Renfred. "El buzo, trabajador del mar: Régimen especial de contratación laboral en la Región Autonoma del Atlántico Norte de Nicaragua." JD thesis, Facultad de Ciencias Jurídicas y Sociales, Universidad Nacional Autonoma de Nicaragua, UNAN-LEON, June 2004.

Parenti, Christian. "King Cocaine in Nicaragua." *Z Magazine Online* (January 1994) http://zmagsite.zmag.org/curTOC.htm.

Pérez-Brignoli, Hector. *A Brief History of Central America*. Berkeley: University of California Press, 1989.

La Prensa (Mangua). August–November 2005.

Programa de Naciones Unidas Para el Desarollo (PUND). *¿Nicaragua assume su diversidad? Informe de desarrollo humano 2005, Las Regiones Autónomas de la Costa Caribe*. Managua: PUND, 2005.

Ramos, Sandra, and Julia Vargas. *Avances y Retrocesos: Mujeres en las maquilas de Nicaragua*. Managua: Movimiento de Mujeres Trabajadores y Desempleadas "María Elena Cuadra," 2002.

Rapley, John. *Globalization and Inequality: Neoliberalism's Downward Spiral*. Boulder, CO: Lynne Rienner Publishers, 2004.

Replogle, Jill. "Hunger on the Rise in Central America." *The Lancet* 363, issue 9426 (19 June 2004): (electronic file).

Ricker, Tom. "Competition or Massacre? Central American Farmers' Dismal Prospects Under CAFTA." *Mulitnational Monitor* 25, issue 4 (April 2004): (electronic file).

Robertson, Roland. *Globalization: Social Theory and Global Culture*. London: Sage Publications, 1992.

Robinson, William I. *Transnational Conflicts: Central America, Social Change, and Globalization*. London: Verso, 2003.

Roney, Jack. "The U.S. Sugar Industry: Large, efficient and challenged." *International Sugar Journal* 106, no. 1266 (2004): 315–23.

Ruíz García, Alfredo. *Tenencia y uso de la tierra en Matiguás-Matagalpa, Nicaragua*. Rome: United Nations, 1994.

Ruíz García, Alfredo, and Yuri Marín López. *Revisitando el Agro Nicaraguense: Tipología de los sistemas de producción y zonificación agro socioeconómica*. Gobierno de Nicaragua: Managua, 2005.

Rushdie, Salman. *The Jaguar Smile: A Nicaraguan Journey*. New York: Penguin Books, 1987.

Sánchez, Héctor. "El Ingenio San Antonio recibe Premio a la Investigación Técnica." *El Pailero, Revista informativa del Ingenio San Antonio* 26 (June 2004): 16–17.

Saxgren, Henrik. *Solomon's House: The Lost Children of Nicaragua*. New York: Aperture, 2000.

Solo, Teri. "Neo-Liberal Nicaragua is a Neo-Banana Republic: The U.S. is still punishing Nicaragua for attempting to gain independence." *Z Magazine Online* 16, no. 9 (Sept 2003).

Spence, Jack. *War and Peace in Central America: Comparing Transitions Toward Democracy and Social Equity in Guatemala, El Salvador and Nicaragua*. Brookline, MA: Hemisphere Initiatives, 2004.

St. Bernard, Godfrey. "Major Trends Affecting Families in Central America and the Caribbean." Prepared for the United Nations Division of Social Policy and Development, Department of Economic and Social Affairs, Program on the Family, May 2003.

Starmer, Elanor. "Re: Concerns over potential CAFTA impact on small farmers in Nicaragua." Washington Office on Latin America (memo), 8 April 2003.

Stokes, Bruce. "Will Free Trade Help Nicaragua?" *National Journal* 36, issue 23 (June 2004): (electronic file).

Stonich, Susan C. "The English-Speaking Bay Islanders." Chap. 5 in *Endangered Peoples of Latin America: Struggles to Survive and Thrive*, edited by Susan C. Stonich. Westport, CT: Greenwood Press, 2001.

Suppan, Steve. "Analysis of the Central American Free Trade Agreement (CAFTA) Concerning Agriculture." Institute for Agriculture and Trade Policy, 22 April 2004.

Taft-Morales, Maureen. "Nicaragua: The Election of Daniel Ortega and Issues in U.S. Relations." Congressional Research Service: Report for Congress, order code RL33983, 19 April 2007.

"Thousands Dying from Chronic Renal Insufficiency in Nicaragua; Agrochemicals Suspected but not Proven." *NotiCen: Central American & Caribbean Affairs* (12 July 2007). http://www.allbusiness.com/caribbean/4505302-4.html.

Tininiska: Revista de la cultura Indígena de la Región Atlántica de Nicaragua 5 (April–May 2003).

———. 6 (January–February 2004).

Towell, Larry. *Somoza's Last Stand: Testimonies from Nicaragua*. Trenton, NJ: The Red Sea Press, 1990.

Trucchi, Giorgio. "El drama y la lucha de los cañeros. La 'chatarra humana de Occidente.' Testimonios de ex trabajadores y viudas." http://www.rel-uita.org/ (7 February 2006).

———. "Cosechas amargas: Los monocultivos del hambre." http://www.solidaridad.net/ (17 October 2006).

Tucker, Richard P. *Insatiable Appetite: The United States and the Ecological Degradation of the Tropical World*. Berkeley: University of California Press, 2000.

Turok, Antonio. *Imágenes de Nicaragua*. Mexico City: Casa de las Imágenes, 1988.

Vulliamy, Ed. "Nicaragua's Daniel Ortega: In the Lions' Den Again." *Observer*, 2 September 2001 (electronic version).

"Victims of Nemagon Hit the Road." *Envio* 287 (June 2005): digital edition.

Walker, Thomas. *Nicaragua: Living in the Shadow of the Eagle*. Boulder, CO: Westview Press, 2003.

Wani: Revista del Caribe Nicaragüense 36 (January–March 2004).

———. 38, Suplemento 1. "Voces de Bilwi" (July–September 2004).

———. 38, Suplemento 2. "Breve compendio estadístico e informativo del Municipio de Puerto Cabezas" (July–September 2004).

Wapponi Productions. "Los buzos Miskitos." Managua. November 2002 (video aired on television program "Esta Semana," 24 November 2004).

Washington Post. May 2005.

Whisnant, David E. *Rascally Signs in Sacred Places: The Politics of Culture in Nicaragua.* Chapel Hill: University of North Carolina Press, 1995.

White, Stephanie. "First NAFTA, Now CAFTA?" *E Magazine: The Environmental Magazine* 16, issue 4 (Jul/Aug 2005): (electronic file).

Williams, Robert G. *Export Agriculture and the Crisis in Central America.* Chapel Hill: University of North Carolina Press, 1986.